MESSAGES AND TEACHINGS OF MARY AT MEDJUGORJE

THE RIEHLE FOUNDATION

MESSAGES AND TEACHINGS OF MARY AT MEDJUGORJE

Chronology of the Messages
The Urgency to Return to God

by

René Laurentin and René LeJeune

Translated by
Juan Gonzales, Jr., Ph.D.

Edited and Published by

THE RIEHLE FOUNDATION
P.O. BOX 7
MILFORD, OHIO 45150

The publisher recognizes and accepts that the final authority regarding the apparitions at Medjugorje rests with the Holy See of Rome, to whose judgment we willingly submit.

—The Publisher

Published by The Riehle Foundation

For additional copies write:

The Riehle Foundation
P.O. Box 7
Milford, Ohio 45150

This book originally published in French as "Message et Pedagogie de Marie a Medjugorje," March 1988, by O.E.I.L. Paris, France.

Copyright © 1988 The Riehle Foundation.

Library of Congress Catalog Card No.: 88-063120

ISBN: 0-9618840-7-X

Table of Contents

PUBLISHER'S PREFACE

René Laurentin and René Lejeune bring you seven years of messages, allegedly from the Blessed Virgin Mary; over 500 messages from the Madonna to the seers, the parish, the world.

What was said to whom, and on what date, is ultimately not at issue. The importance is the compilation of all these messages and their relationship to the Gospels, and to the Doctrines of the Catholic Church.

The authors have accomplished this. They bring the messages of Mary to us in accordance with accepted Catholic tradition, and in the light of many forgotten (or abandoned) practices of the faith. This book verifies what has been proclaimed in Medjugorje for the past several years: "Our Lady has been running a school for holiness, a holiness workshop."

In the end, we can sum up all these messages into one. It is exactly the same as the first public words of Jesus Christ: "The reign of God is at hand, reform your lives, and believe in the Gospel." (*Mk.* 1:15).

Over ten million people have responded to this call in the past seven years. Now, we have the opportunity to put it all together in the context of Catholic teaching, Mary's teaching.

We wish to express our sincere thanks to Dr. Juan Gonzales, Jr., Ph.D., who is Director of Bilingual Education at Texas Southern University, Houston, Texas, for his most arduous effort in translating this work from French to English. Our thanks also to Kim Schrieber, who assisted, and to Beverly, Norma, Bonnie and Juliann for their assistance with the transcript.

The Riehle Foundation

What Has Taken Place

On June 24, in the afternoon, Ivanka Ivankovic (age 15), a girl from the hamlet of Bijakovici at Medjugorje, returning from a walk, sees a brilliant silhouette on the hill of Crnica. She murmurs: "It is the Gospa!" (Our Lady).

Mirjana Dragicevic (age 16), her friend, does not look. She is embarrassed because they had been out smoking secretly. She is afraid, and both of them run away.

But in the evening at 6:00, they return with four others. They see her on the hill, from a distance of about 300 meters. That evening, people laugh at them.

The next day, June 25th, both of them are back at the same place, with four others:

Vicka Ivankovic (age 16) and Ivan Dragicevic (age 16), who were also present at the second apparition on June 24th.

Maria Pavlovic (age 16) and Jakov Colo who came for the first time.

These four, along with Ivanka and Mirjana, become the six seers.

The white figure is there, high on the hill. She beckons them to approach; they climb with surprising speed and see the apparition close at hand.

During the first four days (June 25 - 29), they receive, in response to their random questions, the essential words of the message: A return to God, faith, prayer, fasting, peace, reconciliation.

Thousands of people surround them on the 26th of June. The police question them (June 27 and 29), and forbid access

to the hill. From June 30 on, the apparitions take place somewhere else, where the police are not able to intervene.

They gradually move to the church, where (since July 2nd,
1981), the pastor decides to say a daily Mass, at the hour of
the apparition. Beginning in January - February 1982, the apparition regularly takes place in a room opposite the Sacristy
and adjacent to the Sanctuary, which will be called from then
on, "chapel of the apparitions."

During the summer of 1981, the signs continue to multiply:
cures, luminary phenomena of the sun and on the hills. The
movement of prayer and conversions become greater; pilgrimages continue to increase.

The seers progressively receive 10 secrets, destined to be
revealed at the end of the apparitions; the third being a visible
sign which will be given on the hill.

Christmas 1982, Mirjana receives the 10th and final secret,
with the announcement that the apparitions had ended for her.
The same for Ivanka on May 6th and 7th, 1985.

Nevertheless, the Virgin promises each one of them a yearly
apparition:

For Mirjana, the day of her birthday (March 18), and also
when circumstances require it, and which has come to pass
since August, 1984 in order to prepare the revelation of the
secrets by a priest of her choosing: Father Petar Ljubicic.

For Ivanka, her yearly apparition happens on the anniversary day of the first apparitions on the hill (June 25th).

The Bishop of the place, Msgr. P. Zanic, at first favorable
(July 1981), gradually took a position against the apparitions.
The main reason for his change of mind was the complex
interferences of an old conflict in the diocese with the Franciscans. He announced a negative judgment by May 1986. But
Rome refused this decision and transferred the responsibility
of judgment to the Yugoslavian Episcopal Conference. Cardinal Kuharic established a new commission, which began its
work in March 1987. At all levels, one distinguishes more
and more between the facts to be judged (among which some
contest the supernatural character) and the fruits, recognized
by everyone, and understood by Bishop Zanic, as well.

On March 25, 1985, Msgr. Zanic forbade the ecstasies of

the seers to take place in the church. Consequently they were transferred to the rectory. They have taken place there every day, or wherever each seer is individually. For reasons of health, Vicka has them ordinarily at her home at Bijakovici, the village of the seers.

At the time of this writing, no one knows when the apparitions will end. For more details and information see the list of material available, shown at the end of this text.

PART I
The Message

DECLARATION

The authors have acquired, through their trips to Medjugorje and through their methodical studies, a moral certainty on the authenticity of the fruits of the apparitions at Medjugorje. They submit their judgment on these undisputed fruits and on the facts (discussed), to the authorities of the Church, to which they have wanted to make this humble contribution.

CHAPTER 1

Why This Message?

"Of what use is a book on the message of Medjugorje?" one will ask.

"We have THE message: the Gospel."

"Of course!"

"Then why another book?"

"It is not another one!"

Then, what purpose is it serving?"

AND THE GOSPEL?

That is really the problem. We have the Gospel: the integral and precious word of God. But what have we done with it? God has come to share our life, and invites us to share His, but we remain in our closed and sometime perverted humanism. Our civilization has looked for happiness and truth in the omission of God. From the dawn of the 19th century to the middle of the 20th, it has proclaimed (or practiced) with growing vigor, the death of God. Civilization believed it had found its liberation. In that, we have gone beyond the sin of Adam, who wanted only to be equal and a rival to the Creator: *You will be like gods.* In this civilization, God is no longer the Creator. He is treated like a myth, or the cultural product of a language, even if it requires appreciation of an archaic, venerable and beneficial element of culture.

Philosophers no longer condescend to even consider proof of his existence. And yet, God exists. Some individuals find him irresistible, even today. In atheistic countries, secretly and dangerously, there is on the rise, to the point of the intellectual

3

elite themselves, a mystical, strong and courageous faith. It prefers physical or psychiatric death to denial, because Eastern doctors are forced to treat, with all their means, this "mental sickness" which is faith.

The free and liberal world is more effectively ridding itself of Faith.

The lure of God, the lure of Christ, is clouded by the impulses of a basic desire, which Freud made prevail on the moral order. He knew how to theorize brilliantly and practically the permissiveness which he looked for, for himself.

Freud is only the last of the masters of suspicion, thus named, because they have eliminated the priority of God and the true goodness of man, for the benefit of a concept where everything is done from below, or for the material world. Nietzsche exalted the will of power, which triumphed with Hitler, and Marx substituted matter in place of God, as a principle of intelligibility, realism and effectiveness. He made a "scientific postulate" and theoretical system of it.

But the agnostic and practical materialism of our Western civilizations is still more corrupt than this dogmatic materialism. Thus, one has substituted a civilization founded on God for a civilization founded on the lowest of society's moral values.

In this climate, man is reduced to his own subjectivity. Desire takes over good, the Gospel becomes a dead letter. Those who are still born in Christ, through the water of Baptism, often become children who are stillborn. They need to be resurrected, or at least awakened. The Gospel is for them a dead letter. What should one do so that these cold words once again find their warmth and their life force, so that the word and the sacraments of God again give life to the world?

God is infinitely loving, but infinitely discreet. Man is infinitely disarming with superficiality, and negligence. He moves about cheerfully, and often intelligently, in his shipwreck. Divine Providence, which is merciful, comes to the aid of our weakness in a thousand ways.

The Blessed Virgin, who perceived at Cana the sadness at the wedding caused by lack of wine, knew how to speak to Jesus and the servants. She knows even today how to find the words, the signs (humble, popular, childish—so to speak), which reminds us of a God Who has been forgotten, but Who is present, because God, who has created us out of love, has never retracted in His declarations of love. God, Who has redeemed us by His human death, has never lost the power of His Resurrection. At Medjugorje, the Blessed Virgin never ceases to repeat:

> *I love you...If you would know how much I love you, you would cry with joy.*

A MESSAGE OF CONVERSION

It is in this paradoxical situation that I was surprised, also. Before writing, "Is the Blessed Virgin Mary Appearing at Medjugorje?", I had published 80 books. Being a conscientious theologian, I had written them in faith and for the Lord. I had never heard that any one of them (even the "Life of Bernadette" with over 500,000 copies) had converted anyone. I hope that that will come about, but I do not know about it. It is true that theologians convert few people. Perhaps it is not their mission. They are rather moderators, verifiers of the faith, and God, like the world, needs today poets, prophets and witnesses.

When I wrote that first book on Medjugorje, during the winter of 1983-1984, I felt within the entire producing team, an unusual dialogue, from the editor to the machine operator. After appearing in bookstores on a Monday in February, the book was out of print before the end of the week. An abundance of daily mail revealed that the book was upsetting some lives. It caused people to rediscover God, to pray, to fast, and among people of all environments: from those who were 15 years of age to those who were 80 years old.

It is not me, then, who was converting them. If it were me, the preceding books should have done no less. I was only the relay of the current of grace which was going beyond me. It was worth the effort to contribute to it. At a time when so many clerical actions, well-intended, were drifting from God and marginalizing the faith, it was necessary to recognize this *sign of the time.*

The prophets were always despised. So too, the bursts of fervor, understood in the Church, certainly in good faith. The Catholic press, often ill-informed or influenced by the ideological propaganda or polemics of the extreme right or of the extreme left, had widely spread the false news that the pilgrimages to Medjugorje were forbidden, but it did not publish the denials of competent authorities. On the faith of this false information, some good priests were sometimes obliged to tell their faithful that "by going to Medjugorje, you will put yourself outside of the Church."

This dissuasion created some cases of conscience and useless inhibitions to the detriment of this movement of grace. The press which had spread the false and ambiguous information, was careful not to echo the letters of Cardinal Kuharic (president of the Episcopal Conference responsible for the judgment on the apparitions), which repeatedly stated that one could go to Medjugorje in all the security of one's conscience, the fruits of the pilgrimage not being contested by anyone, not even the principal opponent.

If then, propaganda and polemics turned away a large number of Christians from Medjugorje, an increasing number continues, however, to live its evangelical messages. They place great importance on them. It was the same with my first book, which was devoured by its readers; it was the very short chapter on the messages and the appendix (where Father Tomislav Vlasic summarized it according to the striking apocalyptic formulas of the visionary Mirjana).

In March 1984, when Maria began to transmit a message each Thursday in order to encourage the parish of Medjugorje in its prayer, fasting and reconciliation, these messages were warmly received throughout the world. Loose sheets, tapes, and telephones were used to transmit them. Transmitters were deluged with thousands of calls each Thursday evening.

The interest in Medjugorje then is not one of curiosity, but a search for a presence which guides our lives, lives which have often gone astray.

The messages continue in their fervor. They contribute to the formation of hundreds of lasting prayer groups. The pastoral of Medjugorje has made them bear fruit in a remarkable liturgy, in living together, in helping themselves, and in a beautiful hospitality. The meeting with the seers, their candidness, their radiance, often spoke beyond words.

Those who devoured the crumbs of this message wished a more substantial knowledge of it.

I was hesitant to undertake this heavy work, but Professor René Lejeune stressed the priority of it, and proposed to help me with it. I placed at his disposal many books and dossiers that I had in my possession (10 meters of shelves). I had drawn from them my chronology. They also permitted me to establish the "chronological body" of these messages. I proposed a system of work. He approached it with a scientific preparation as a professor at Alger, Strasbourg, Sao Paulo and Geneva. In March and August 1987, he brought life to his work through a long fast at a Swiss medical clinic, founded for the purpose of this therapy and spiritual experience. In April 1987, he made his first pilgrimage and trip of studies to Medjugorje, at the same time that I made my 14th visit.

LIMITS OF THE UNDERTAKING

I must confide here my difficulties over critical questions, on the threshold of such a realization.

She who appears at Medjugorje has spoken a lot: too much, say the ecclesiastic skeptics. She has spoken through various channels. Each receiver (each seer) has received it in his own way. Is that why the teaching of the messenger adapts itself to each one? Or rather, does each one channel it in his own way? The means of communication itself is very different—the six seers meet Mary as a being of flesh and bones, whom they can touch. Jelena, Marijana and the charismatics of the second generation perceive her through a very intimate way—through their heart, to the point of a profound prayer. Finally, these exchanges do not always have the same function, nor do they have an equal value. One is the fundamental message which recalls these essential words of the Gospel: God, faith, conversion, prayer, etc. Another are the words which guide or teach the visionaries and the parish. Other certain familiar exchanges cause one to think of the chatter of a mother with her children. To collect all of these communications would result in something rather confusing. The apparently unusual words do not carry the same weight. Some may have been revealed through confusion, interpretation of transmission, as it often happens among the great mystics, among which, the oracles of communication were not always infallible. Benedict XIV stressed this point; also historians of mysticism (Poulain, etc.)

Our "Corpus" consists of soft parts and hard parts. It is a mass, so to say, to characterize a biblical encyclopedia of diverse and unequal contributions. It is a rather well established organism. An organism is not homogeneous. It is made up of bones, flesh and blood. The message of Medjugorje is more organic, better vertebrate than it appears; but articulated with hard and soft parts, strong and weak, without excluding the marks of human weakness, or of sin. Therefore, the messages interfere with our local conflicts. The difficult part is the call to the message of the Gospel; the living and muscular part is the fruitful teaching of Our Lady.

The nature of these messages is that they consist less in words (the cortex) than in lives, where they show what they are capable of. It is at this level that they bear fruit, and that one must interpret them, as we shall see later on.

It is necessary to enter into it, beginning with the words of the messages. It was therefore important to establish a chronological base because these prophetic messages were given in a history, and it cannot be understood except within that history, according to its progression. After a critique of the texts, (not always easy in following the current stages of development), it would be necessary to evaluate the respective weight of so many words. First of all, one has to conduct some checking, a critical judgment, according to accustomed norms, facing the difficulty of our oral tradition, which to a large extent, makes allowances for estimates. And then, not all is "message" in these familiar daily exchanges, whose content is seldom related by the seers.

AN ECHO

Our judgment starts from a fundamental principal: the message of Medjugorje is not another gospel. If it were, it would be necessary to say with St. Paul, "Even if it comes from an angel from Heaven, it will be anathema." (*Gal.* 1:8; cf. *2 Cor.* 11:14). If this message is authentic, it is only a faithful echo of the Gospel; a reminder of that fundamental but forgotten message.

One must add: It is in reference to the Gospel that this fragmentary message reveals its meaning. It is comparable to those designs covering a transparency, which certain archeological works insert within the pages of illustrations in order to show the lines of force, numeration of facts, or details, which we would risk not perceiving on a picture. That is the principal which I drew in writing "Sens de Lourdes" (1954). It remains the fundamental conduit for every serious and productive work on the apparitions. The priests in Medjugorje have admirably put it into operation. They have channeled the life of these messages into community prayer, liturgy, Mass, and all the fruitful consequences of hospitality, fraternity, reconciliation.

JUDGMENT AND AUTHORITY

But, one may say on editing this message, you are canonizing it prematurely; you are anticipating the judgment of the Church.

This work, as the preceding ones, does not intend to speak with authority, nor to anticipate the authorities, but only to help them.

A judgment on the signs of the times has never been a monopoly of authority. The magisterium is the guide and the authorized guarantee. The Church is not a place where the light would be the exclusive property of some, where others would only obey blindly. The council spoke reactively against this false and dangerous idea.

On matters of apparitions, all believers permit themselves to be guided by Divine light. They try to read, as the Gospel invites us, the signs of the times—prophetic signs which God gives. The apparitions are a sign among others. This perception is not a private game preserve, as some repeat excessively. The people (the sensus fidelium) have their role to play, according to the very tradition of the Church. History tells us that it is often a pilot role.

The people are generally the first to believe in apparitions and to know about them. If their judgment is good, the authority will confirm it. If the people go astray, it will rectify it after mature reflection. If apparitions were the exclusive matter of authority, neither Guadalupe, nor Lourdes, nor Fatima, nor other apparitions would have been recognized. They would have died without an echo. The Church would have lost, undoubtedly. She has recognized them because she was alerted by popular movement.

It is normal that the impetus from the people anticipate the authority. But, it must be prudent—respectful of the magisterium, endowed with a more decisive charisma, in order to denounce the errors regarding faith or morals.

The Fifth Lateran Council, which established legislation on such matters, invites Bishops to surround themselves with experts in order to pass judgments. Experts are no longer forbidden to gather information and knowledge in an orderly manner, in order to facilitate the judgment of the Christian people, and of the authority itself, so that no one may go astray. One can easily go astray in many ways, through illuminism, or rationalism, or through credulity or criticism. An expert can provide service to people and to authority, if he informs and judges beyond the passions and tensions which abound in these affairs.

It is to this effect, that I increased my trips (17), works, documentations, and called out a medical team of a very high level. This scientifc work has eliminated a good number of untruths which come from excessive fervor or, very often, from opponents ready to unduly discredit their opposition. Thus, the Bishop of Mostar himself, who had published in an "unofficial" but responsible manner, indicated that the apparitions were collective hallucinations. At least he readily renounced this error, which our scientific works eliminated.

A notable and sometimes major portion of my work consists of dispelling the anticipated errors of naive fervor, and the tense opposition, being permanent sources of false information. After that, begins the judgment which I presented in an organic way in "Is The Blessed Virgin Mary Appearing at Medjugorje?" and in subsequent texts. This is not the place to start all these judgments again. Let us only recall the essential conclusions.

As always, there are certainly some ambiguities, objections, and difficulties, which we will not try to hide, and we will attempt to clarify. (pages 325 to 350). The transmission of heavenly communications is never one of absolute reliability. But for the essential, Medjugorje verifies the best criteria of authenticity, which have been received in the Church. It verifies at a level comparable to the apparitions at Lourdes; because the apparitions at Lourdes also lent themselves to some objections. The gravest of these was the epidemic of more than 50 visionaries which had taken the relay from Bernadette and even invaded the grotto itself, from April 11 to July 11, 1858. If such a phenomenon had produced itself at Medjugorje, a negative judgment would have been reported a long time ago. And I admire the wisdom of Bishop Laurence (Lourdes), who knew how to wait for, then stop immediately the epidemic of visionaries, some who seemed highly recommendable, in order to protect Bernadette—St. Bernadette, who withstood the test until the end.

At the time when Msgr. Zanic announced his negative judgment in May 1986, I had openly raised the question: What should one do in that case? ("Latest News" #4)

Obey authority, I would say, in order to avoid polemics and chaos. But, except for new arguments (and I had reasons to think that there would not be any), I would hold such a judgment as an error because even the successors of the apostles are not exempt from any risks of human weakness. History proves it. Obedience to established authority, and to the good order of the Church, does not necessarily extinguish an interior conviction, nor the responsibility to prepare discreetly, a historical revision. Thus it was for Joan of Arc, condemned and burned in 1431, through a mature decision of a tribunal of the Church, constituted by the bishop of the place, Msgr. Cauchon, highly qualified in principle as the former Chancelier of the Sorbonne. Condemned by the legitimate authority of the local Church, Joan of Arc was canonized by the supreme authority of the Church in 1920.

In the case of Medjugorje, the negative judgment did not

take place. When Msgr. Zanic took the transadriatic ship "Traghetto" in order to present to Cardinal Ratzinger, Prefect for the Congregation of the Faith, the negative judgment which he had announced publicly for months, he received an order to set aside his unfinished conclusions and to dissolve the commission. Their work had not been finished and certain members expressed the regret of having to abandon it before its term was up. The Congregation of the Faith transferred the jurisdiction of the local bishop, Msgr. Zanic, to an Episcopal Conference, whose president, Cardinal Kuharic, formed a new Commission.

A very important doctrinal principal clarifies the situation. When the Church teaches revelation (faith and morals), she teaches it with authority. She requires absolute obedience "under penalty of anathema," one would say formerly. If the Church does not excommunicate the heretic anymore today, he excommunicates himself, supposedly by teaching the faith in the name of God.

The assurance of the Church is something else when She judges the authenticity of an apparition—a fleeting historical event, a different fact in the life of the Church. Is the Virgin appearing or is she not appearing at Medjugorje, or elsewhere?

In attempting to answer this question, the authority of the Church is not transmitting the word of God; it is Revelation. She expresses only the difficult and conjectural judgment. She proposes it, but does not impose it. She does so in virtue of a probable analysis relevant to human faith, and not of Divine teaching. She never stopped reminding us of it.

For the authority of the Church to recognize apparitions, Pope Pius X teaches in his encyclical "Pascendi," she does not wait to express her opinion on the "reality" of apparitions. She simply confirms that nothing in the facts which have been analyzed is in opposition to faith or morals. She thus gives a "nihil obstat," a permission to believe by him who judges it to be appropriate. If the Christian has reason to doubt that Our Lady appeared at Lourdes, he would not be in error. This dissent would not be, in itself, a matter for confession; while to deny the incarnation of Christ, or other revealed dogmas, is a mortal sin, which the authority of the Church condemns with assurance and firmness.

Is it necessary to say, according to the lesson which we have seen, that the apparitions are only objects of human faith, not of Divine faith? Karl Rahner had clearly analyzed the excess and the uncertainty of this principal, stated by the future Benedict XIV and, in some manner, taken up by Pius X in his encyclical "Pascendi."

According to Rahner, this clear cut opposition (human faith, Divine faith) forgets too much the nature of faith, because faith is a gift from God, a light of God. The pilgrims at the Grotto at Lourdes in 1858, like those at Medjugorje today, believe in Christ and in Mary, out of Divine faith, in the brilliance of a particular light of God. The seers would be ready to defend this proof of God with their own lives. This evidence of faith seems a gift from God. Faith is not purely extrinsic obedience to formulas of the Church. It is also, and more profoundly so, obedience to the light of God. Certainly, this light clarifies the teaching transmitted by the Church, but without this free gift from God, we would not be able to believe.

An old story! Before the definition of the Immaculate Conception by Pope Pius IX, Muratori attacked as idolaters and fanatics, those who said they were ready to give their lives for their belief in the immaculate origin of Mary. To give their lives for a personal opinion is a suicide and a blasphemy, he said. Today this faith must be defended until martyrdom. Before Pius IX had the same responsibility in the knowledge which the believers had received, they had already perceived it all.

It is in the sense of this same extrinsic, judicial, hardening of attitude, that certain authorities dare to say, so easily, that there is "nothing supernatural" in the places of fervent and fruitful pilgrimages or (recently) that the pilgrimages to Medjugorje are disapproved if one undertakes them for "supernatural motives." But, according to the tradition of the Church, and the nature of things, it is for a supernatural motive that one goes on a pilgrimage.

It is in this sense that Rahner wrote:

> "According to the principals of regular theology, one cannot see why a private revelation would not impose itself on the faith of those who had knowledge

of it, with sufficient certainty that it came from God. We cannot demand a greater certainty for private revelation than that which is required to guarantee formal revelation. It is unjustified, illogical, and even dangerous to demand (as one does), in order to authenticate private revelations after Christ, a degree of certainty which one does not demand for formal revelation. Then, every reasonable foundation of faith and Christian revelation would be impossible. Consequently, one does not understand why the faithful would not be able to recognize the beginning of a number of private revelations." (*The Private Revelations,* Karl Rahner—1949, Pg. 508).

Whether it concerns an apparition or other domains, one cannot reduce faith to a blind obedience, nor make an abstraction of the light of faith given by God, without which no one can believe. We believe what the authority of the Church teaches, in the name of God. But why should a sincere and serious believer, who would have reasons to doubt an apparition (even a recognized one), be in error? He is only asked not to disturb the good order which already exists. On my part, I have had to review a (official) retraction of Jeanne-Marie LeBosse, one of the visionaries of Pontmain, documented in good and proper form by Msgr. Grellier. The retraction was the result of a scrupulous illusion, as we have established in Pontmain. ("Historie authentique Lethielleux," 1971.)

The freedom which the Church allows believers, in the case of recognized apparitions, also exists in the case of apparitions which are not recognized. He who has good reasons to believe in them, like all the pilgrims at Lourdes and Fatima prior to official recognition by the Church, does not sin and is correct in following his conscience, the light of God in his life. And it is a fact, that these lights of the faithful ordinarily anticipate the judgment of authority.

TOWARD AN OFFICIAL RECOGNITION?

Will the Church recognize the apparitions at Medjugorje? In human eyes, that seems improbable, maybe impossible.

The presuppositions which are predominant today in theology (like exegesies and universal culture) are contrary to all recognition of apparitions. If none of those which occurred in the past 50 years received official recognition, Medjugorje has very little chance of escaping the common rule.

However, the prognosis had been more somber, until May 1986, the date which Msgr. Zanic openly announced the negative judgment, which didn't take place. It seems probable that the Holy See would support the bishop of the place, according to the principle of being an auxiliary. The refusal of the negative judgment and its transfer to the Episcopal Conference were an extreme surprise.

Did this new fact authorize a positive prognostication? No, because the methods in use for the past half century normally lead to the same negative result.

The declared opposition of the bishop of the place (Mostar), which remains a privileged position in the Episcopal Conference, will aid just like the negative vote of nine members out of 11, which he says had been gathered before the dissolution of the first commission.

To that, one may add the fear that weighs in a Marxist country. One prefers there, any language, to a firm declaration of authenticity. It is for that reason Msgr. Franic (and others) desire an international commission. I did not support that opinion because the experts and native bishops have the advantage of speaking the language of the country, and are better situated for the understanding and the knowledge of the facts. But it is true that international experts benefit from greater independence of judgment. Since this solution was not endorsed, the road toward a positive judgment seems blocked.

The best prognostication which one can make as of this moment would be a doubtful judgment, which would not compromise anyone, and would permit a pastoral continuing of the movement of grace, just like at the Rue du Bac, where the apparitions were never recognized; like at Saint-Bauzille de la Sylve (where the experts were divided); at Pellevoisin, at Lle Bouchard, at Tre Fontane (Rome), where the Cardinal Vicar of the pope has recently celebrated a solemn Mass, in order to endorse the cult and the pilgrimage, but without saying a word on the apparitions. The L'Observatore Romano had narrated the ceremony, without being in a position to make any decision of any sort.

Everything orientates itself in this sense: accept and cultivate the fruits without recognizing the fact. Cardinal Ratzinger recently told an Italian priest who wondered about the legitimacy of founding a community at Medjugorje, an apparition which has not been recognized: "Cultivate the fruits. We will concern ourselves with the facts."

It would be useful to recall these experiences and truths in a good sense, before presenting and analyzing the message of the apparitions at Medjugorje.

Each one is free to judge for himself in total obedience to God and to the Church. This book wants to aid in this regard.

WHERE ARE WE HEADED?

Here we come to the beginning of the work. How shall we proceed to introduce organically, the "Corpus" gathered at the end of this book?

 1. We will situate the apparitions at Medjugorje in the place and the environment where they have occurred. Then:

 2. Their history, their progress, their evolution.

 3. The actual message—a clear echo of the Gospels.

 4. The signs, which have done much to accredit it—notably cures and luminary phenomenon.

 5. Finally, the teaching essential to this message.

 6. And, the pastoral resulting from it.

CHAPTER 2

The Place and the Environment

The scientific study of the Bible applies itself to a certain predilection of situating the facts and messages in a location along with the ethnic, historical, and cultural environment. *The Sitz in Leben* (vital milieu) according to the German expression, was successful in exegesis.

This operation is useful for our messages of the apparitions under two sections:

> 1. God adapts them to the places and the environments. The Virgin speaks a local "Patois" at Lourdes, Portugese at Fatima, Croatian at Medjugorje, and the communications are registered in a Mediterranean code of communication.
>
> 2. Each visionary receives the message in his own way. *Quidquid recipitur ad modum recipientis recipitur,* according to the adage of St. Thomas Acquinas. That is: "Everything received, is received in the manner of the recipient."

Where did the apparitions take place? Who were the recipients?

It is a rustic village consisting of scattered hamlets. There, grapes and tobacco are cultivated and the work alternates conveniently to the change of the seasons. It is a Croatian parish in Hercegovina where the Muslim domination (1478-1878) reinforced the faith of some, but added a minority to Islam. It is in this painful tension that one must situate the ecumenical message of Medjugorje: Love your Muslim brothers, etc.

17

The horror of the apostasies of the past made them despise their descendents of that faith, and the situation is all the more paradoxical in that the government gave these Croatians, converted to Islam, the "Muslim nationality." This establishment of a religion in nationality, decided by an atheistic government, is without precedent in any other country in the world. But at Medjugorje there are no mosques. The village, surrounded by a vast circle of hills as its name signifies, (Medjugorje means between hills) has been protected.

It is a traditional Catholic parish where the Marxists are rare and isolated.

The priests are Franciscans, which is still the case in 80 percent of the parishes of the diocese of Mostar.

Medjugorje is situated inland some 40 kilometers from the beautiful dalmatian coast in Bosnia Hercegovina. It is one of the states which is included in the Yugoslavian federation. This country, at the juncture between east and west, distinguishes itself as a result of a remarkable independence. It has opened up dialogue with the west and even with the Vatican. It is the only Marxist country which has diplomatic relations with the Holy See, an embassy in Rome, and a diplomatic agency in Belgrade.

It is, in addition, a Mediterranean country. The outstanding success of the Italian pilgrimage to Medjugorje is explained in part by the compatability of these two peoples living on opposite sides of the Adriatic. In spite of the differences in language, of government, of environment, and despite conflicts caused by the territorial ambitions of Mussolini, Italians and Croats see one another as alike. Today, Italian is the foreign language most spoken at Medjugorje, including some of the seers—Jelena, Maria and Vicka.

Yugoslavia is also the most open of the eastern countries, the most hospitable to international tourism, which allows the greatest latitude to its nationals to go to work in western countries by the hundreds. The families of some of the seers work in Germany. At Medjugorje many fathers of families follow the same austere itinerary: exile, absence from their families for several decades, vacations one month a year, and their return at the age of retirement, or a little before, with an automobile, which is a symbol of success and freedom, along with the building of a home with the help of neighbors and friends.

The absolute authority of the unique Communist Party, officially atheistic, creates a difficult situation for Catholics. Vicka, an enemy of false ideals, preferred to abandon her studies to compromises. But Yugoslavia is one of the eastern countries under Marxist law, where a freedom of worship and conscience is best practiced.

At first the apparitions were badly received there. The hill where they took place was off-limits. There were many intimidations, interrogations and sanctions. The pastor, Jozo Zovko, and some others, were imprisoned.

One suspected a clerical political plot. In 1984, I, myself, was taken from the airport at Zagreb, subjected to legal proceedings, fines, and prohibition from returning for a year (December 27, 1984). But these repressions were neither radical nor definitive in this "Balkan state" where there are more ethnic, cultural, linguistic, and religious tensions than in Lebanon. Measures of prevention and control necessary to maintain order are altered with flexibility in respect for a certain number of freedoms. The worsening of the economic crisis invited the government to make concessions so as not to drive the population to a critical point under pressure.

The repression of the apparitions was less rude at Medjugorje than at Lourdes in the officially Catholic France of the 19th Century, or at Fatima. A *modus vivendi* was found, thanks to the orderly behavior and the discretion of the parish and the pilgrims. The Yugoslav authorities were able to understand that it was something that concerned a phenomenon which was not subversive, but purely religious, therefore legal and authorized.

The Marxist press commented on this issue with humor in saying that the Virgin was beneficial to the Yugoslavian economy.

Before the apparitions, the parish was traditional but not fervent, and disintegrating there. Fr. Jozo Zovko, named pastor in October 1980, eight months before the apparitions, found it lukewarm and lethargic. He mobilized the prayers of the contemplative convents in order to revive it. The faith, tempered by the Muslim domination, then atheistic, had fallen asleep. Vocal prayers, which the apparitions had revived (seven Our Fathers and seven Hail Marys, Rosary of Jesus, etc.) had fallen into disuse. The efforts of the new pastor to restore the old practice of fasting on bread and water came up against an insurmountable inertia, understood by the tertiary Franciscans. The "awakened fervor" surprised him on his return from preaching, during which time the apparitions had begun.

These apparitions then were not the result of fervor. They literally fell on this village. Faith was suddenly inflamed with the staggering consequences of reconciliation, peace and love.

The awakening began impromptu on the 24th of June, 1981. Ivanka, the brunette, and Mirjana, the blond, two girls on vacation, 15 and 16 years old respectively, were taking a walk simply to pass time, and also an escapade. They had gone to smoke in secret. The tobacco, object of labor of the village and its families, aroused their curiosity. The thesis, according to which the apparitions would be the subjective product of fervor, or an ordinary consequence of the traditional faith, are untenable. Faith passed ostensibly to the state of sociological religion and lukewarmness. The before, and after, are incomparable. Neither for attendence at the liturgy, nor for prayer, nor for love, peace, or hospitality. Relationships between the villagers of Medjugorje were strained and even violent. There had been deaths by gunshots at the beginning of the '40s, and reconciliations seemed utopian.

In summary, the *Sitz im Leben* was a good rustic land with a winter vegetation. The apparitions triggered off a new spring.

CHAPTER 3

The History

The apparitions of Medjugorje take place in the continuation of a history, and they themselves have a history.

HISTORICAL ANTECEDENTS

There are nearly five million Croats in Croatia and Hercegovina, and three million of them economically depressed. They came down from the Carpathians to the Adriatic. They were evangelized in the seventh century. It is the first Slavic people that came to Christianity. They have maintained a beautiful vitality in the course of history, which has been animated with both independence and oppression.

The Muslim domination by the Turks caused apostasies and martyrs. It lasted from 1478 to 1878, as we have said.

When this people found independence and freedom again, Leo XIII established, according to custom, the secular clergy side by side with the Franciscans. The transfer of parishes was difficult because the Franciscans had acquired prestige and familiarity among the people. During the persecution, where they swayed between prudence and secrecy, they were designated as "the uncle," (le tonton), a Croatian word which means "the maternal uncle," not that of the father and cut short a problem raised at the time of identity control.

The first transfers were carried out by Franciscan bishops until 1942—not without difficulty, but without drama. When a secular bishop (Monsignor Petar Cule) was named on April 15th, 1942, the situation became very difficult. The negotiation were painstaking, authoritarian. The Franciscans had the feeling that every concession on their part was immediately seized, and that every compensation agreed upon in the exchange remained a dead issue. Some of them resisted. The new secular bishop, Monsignor Cule, curtailed them with numerous penalties of suspension (prohibition to administer the sacraments). The conflicts were carried out particularly in seven parishes, which represented beautiful ornaments for the Franciscans, and for the secular clergy. Rich and prestigious places. Medjugorje was not one of the seven, which were Caplijna, Crnac, Grude, Hostarski-Gradac, Jablanica, Ploce, Klobuc.

Monsignor Zanic, the current bishop, named coadjuter by Monsignor Cule in 1971, began in distinguished fashion. He built a cathedral next to the bishop's residence. On September 14th, 1980, the day on which he became bishop upon the departure of Monsignor Cule, he opened it and linked it to 80 percent of the episcopal city, the central stronghold of the Franciscans. This caused resentment among the laity, and the majority remained unfailingly loyal to the Franciscans with the tenacity which had made them keep their Catholic faith in the time of the Muslims. They refused to attend the new secular parish, and remained away from the sacraments. In order to avoid the worst, the concerned Franciscans administered to them in the chapels that they had kept.

In the framework of this conflict, two young Franciscans, pushed to the fore by the people, and by their brothers as well, in due course, became the scapegoats. The bishop obtained from the Franciscan Curia General, that they be excluded from the Order, and slapped with suspension. They frequented Medjugorje and received there, some consoling assurances.

"Since this apparition supports the rebels, she is not the Virgin," concluded the bishop.

Attempted mediation, notably that of Monsignor Franic, failed. The shining horizon of the apparitions was being darkened by the artificial interference of this conflict, as we shall see. (Annex 1, page 325 to 343).

PROGRESS OF THE APPARITIONS

The apparitions began then on June 24, 1981. We will consider here, only the progression and the evolution of the message.

1. During the first phase (June 24-29, 1981), the apparitions took place on the hill of Crnica, against which is built the village of Bijakovici. It represents the preliminary contact, at a distance, from the foot of the hill (June 24th); then the ascent (June 25th), which leads the seers up, very near the Gospa. The message begins then, and develops without order, in answer to questions from the seers. It is a recall of the simple and fundamental words of the gospel: God, conversion, faith, prayer, fasting, peace and reconciliation, as we shall see.

All of these words were given from the 26th to the 29th of June. The continuation presents itself as a long teaching in order to make the message penetrate and bear fruit in the hearts of people.

2. During a second phase (June 30th, 1981-February 1982), it is forbidden to gather on the hill. The apparitions take refuge in secrecy, nourished by signs on the hill and in the sun. They take place here and there at someone's house, at the rectory, in the fields, or at night on the hill, wherever the police are not. Little by little, they become established in the church, the authorized place of worship, during the liturgy of the evening.

3. Finally, in January-February 1982, gradually the daily apparition takes place in the little room across from the sacristy, and adjacent to the sanctuary, which we call today, "Chapel of the Apparitions," because the apparitions took place there for more than three years (1982 to March 1985).

4. On March 25th, 1985, the bishop forbade the apparitions in any place adjoining the church. They were obediently transferred to the presbytery in April

1985. It was a great sacrifice because this disassociation changed the coherence of the liturgy, going from the rosary, to the apparition, to the Mass. The Virgin leads to Christ, to the Eucharist as a peak. The crowd gathered at one in the same place; but then, it found itself disassociated into two groups, those who waited in the church, and those who gathered around the place of the apparitions. It was not easy to control this division, which put the pastoral to the test.

The test was more disturbing than it seemed because the priests at Medjugorje had brought about, more than ever in history, an admirable harmony between two movements which were not integrated in themselves: the exceptional grace of the apparitions, and the liturgical life of the Church.

The apparitions arrived unexpectedly on one of those hills which surrounds Medjugorje, among young people with no particular fervor. They broke out as a marginal fact during the absence of the pastor. They enflamed, without him, those whom he had not been able to awaken. This new marginal pole gave rise to his criticism and normal distrust. He tried the impossible.

> "Your apparitions; I don't know what they are," he said, in substance. "If you believe in the Lord, come to the church. The Eucharist will be celebrated there every day at 6:00."

The people came to Mass at the church, which competed with the apparition. The prohibition from the hill, and the secrecy of the visionaries was advantageous to the church, where daily fervor took roots with the rosary before and after Mass. Gradually the seers came themselves to the church, and had the apparitions there, which became integrated with the exemplary liturgy. The clergy of Medjugorje had thus avoided, during nearly four years, the tension between the institution and the charisms, liturgy and popular gatherings, parish church and places of apparitions, priests and seers.

The ruling of the bishop (March 25th, 1985), who advised that the apparitions take place elsewhere, tended to create a rupture which had been avoided. The choice of the rectory permitted, not without pain, limited damage.

5. A new phase begins in September 1987. On July 25th, on the patron feast of Medjugorje, the bishop, who came to give Confirmation to 130 young people, publically mentioned the negative conclusions of his commission dissolved by Rome, and vehemently criticized the apparitions. The parish, in a state of trauma, heroically maintained a respectful silence. From this silence, the bishop concluded that no one believed in them any longer. At the end of August, he forbade the apparitions to take place in the rectory.

Where should they go? Outside of the church? Every religious gathering was illegal. At the beginning of September, since the order came, Maria, and sometimes Jakov or Ivan, would slip quietly into the choir loft which was closed to the public, one of their places of refuge. It is there that the apparitions have been taking place since then, privately. This new fact satisfied the bishop who wanted to supress any crowd or publicity, which had been polarized by the apparitions themselves. He leads the apparitions back to the semi-secret situation of July and August 1981. His ruling has the advantage of ending the disassociation between the gathering of the crowd outside the rectory and the liturgical assembly at the church.

EVOLUTION OF FERVOR

The apparitions aroused an extraordinary force within the parish. The parishioners rushed en masse to daily Mass, which had begun since the beginning of July 1981. This crowd was swelled by visitors who were becoming more and more numerous, from more distant places, and who were overflowing the large church.

The people arrived long before and stayed long after the Mass. This ardent phase prolonged, thanks to a profound pastoral and to the maturation of people during approximately three or four years, without a well marked transition or force.

But this style of mystical honeymoon could not last indefinitely. The history of the Church teaches us that the bursts of fervor must be organized, harnassed, internalized in patience and moderation under pain of ending quickly as a straw fire. The weariness, the weight of the day, the human need to turn the page often times extinguishes the force of great spiritual adventures. Medjugorje avoids such extinction. If attendance at daily Mass, the hours of prayer and days of fasting have quantitatively diminished, it is in order to return to a normal life after a life of exception, which goes beyond the requirements of a monastery.

In the meantime, the duration of the daily ceremony increased. After the 15th of August 1985, at the request of the Virgin, the visionaries said the daily rosary of fifteen decades, two rosaries of five decades each before Mass, the last five decades after Mass. This is prolonged by ceremonies of fervor: adoration of the Blessed Sacrament on Thursday, celebration of the passion on Friday, and prayer for the sick every day. All together, three hours on an average. Such a pace is unbearable for a large number of people, and one can ask himself if this increased extension of time is pastorally desirable.

TEST OF THE DURATION OF TIME

The parishioners have had to look for a rhythm of prayer compatible with a normal life. They have established, little by little, a cruising speed where perseverance is no longer borne on the wings of sensible graces, but stays strong, tested, interiorized, rich in witnesses of charity and hospitality. Pilgrims are among the most edified, because it is not only the seers, it is the entire community which supports the radiance of the pilgrimage. In the majority of families, members take turns in attending the daily ceremony. One goes to Mass a given day, another, another day. Each one adapts fasting to himself, to his temperament. But people no longer tend to surrender in number, nor to rejections which often follow great fervor, like an airplane nose dives when it loses speed, after a too vertical ascent.

TEST FROM THE OPPOSITION

Another test came from the opposition: the police, then the bishop.

In the beginning (July-August 1981), Monsignor Zanic showed himself favorable to the apparitions. He defended them courageously against slander of the government press until September 1st, 1981, in spite of a meeting at Sarajevo, where the government authorities of Bosnia Hercegovina played a great game against him (before August 15th). There follows a period of discretion and silence. It is only in the first months of 1982 that the interference with the Franciscan quarrel turns the bishop against the apparitions, a surprising shift.

While the Bishop became adversary number one, the government recognized the peaceful order and the loyalty of this purely religious phenomenon, which was appreciated by official tourism. A *modus vivendi* of surveillance and peaceful tolerance was set up, and the police had never had to watch over a more docile crowd.

It survived opposition from the bishop, joined for the moment with that of the government. Because of false news having been published about it, we wish to stress that the parish of Medjugorje is the most normally operated in the world. It obeyed the orders from the bishop, even in that where the liturgy and the good order suffered. The parish, suffocated by its obedience to untenable orders, referred several solicitations to Rome. No one ever answered, but obedience remains without recrimination.

Monsignor Zanic, a sensible and spontaneous man, on whom this disagreement weighs, often says to his intermediaries that he is threatened by the fanaticism of the pilgrims. His very life would be in danger. But, for whoever listens to what is said at Medjugorje, it is clear that the bishop is regarded with respect and without malice. One gladly prays so that the absurd

misunderstandings and tensions so annoying to him may be
overcome for all, and for the Kingdom of God. Some of the
seers have offered their lives so that this conflict ceases, and
that the Light will make reconciliation. It is always with respect that pilgrims visit the bishop of Mostar and know how
to listen to the accusations, often unjust, which accuse those
who support the apparitions, of lies, irresponsibility, bad
morals, and a taste for profit.

PROGRESSIVE REVELATIONS OF THE TEN SECRETS

The seers have progressively received, beginning in 1981,
10 secrets related to the future, secrets which have been well
guarded. Mirjana, who proceeded the others, received the 10th
and final secret at Christmas 1982.

From now on, you will not see me any more, the Gospa
told her, *except on your birthday* (March 18th of each year),
and when circumstances will warrant it.

This was very difficult because the daily apparitions brought
joy to the seers in spite of their brevity. Privation is very hard.

"For a month," Mirjana told me, "I was drowning in
depression."

But she then found the thread of normal prayer more profound. For 20 months, she kept her distance from Medjugorje
for she no more had reason to return, except during vacation
to the house of her grandmother. The Franciscans feared that
her faith would weaken far from the parish, while the tests
pursued her vigorously at all levels: police, school, family.
But her faithfulness to prayer "held" in this absence. She
returned more frequently beginning August 25th, 1984, and
periodically received at the rate of about once a month, at
very irregular intervals, some locutions, or apparitions destined to prepare the revelation of the secrets and the end of
the event.

On May 6, 1985, Ivanka, her companion at the very first
apparition, received the 10th secret, and the notification that
the apparitions were finished for her. For both, Our Lady
kept an annual apparition. For Ivanka, it is not the day of
her birthday, but the anniversary day of the first apparition,
which is for Our Lady, June 25th, because the double apparition

of June 24th, 1981 was simply a preliminary contact at a distance and without a message. The group of six had not been formed yet. It was still a preliminary one. It was only the second day that the seers saw her near and that she began to speak to them.

Ever since then, the situation remains the same. Apart from Mirjana and Ivanka, all the seers have received nine secrets. For a long time Vicka had only eight, but she received the ninth secret on April 22nd, 1986.

That same year, she was subjected to a triple test. She feared the end of the apparitions, not daring even to ask herself how she would be able to get used to the void, because the short daily visit of Our Lady is her viaticum of each day. Now, three times, in the course of the year 1986, the Gospa asked her:

Vicka, if you agree, I will no longer appear to you until. . .

The three trials lasted respectively:
50 days from January 6 to February 25, 1986
40 days from April 23 to June 4
57 days from August 25 to October 20

Vicka accepted them in a joyful and stimulating manner, while hiding some tears, for the privation was a very severe one.

A LETTER WRITTEN IN THE HEART

According to the requests of theology, I have tried to put this message in order and in well organized formulas. But it escapes from this treatment. It is presented in scattered words surging here, there, at random, from questions, or on the initiative of the Virgin. It was also as little objective as possible, not at all made to be engraved in marble.

I got out of this difficulty by understanding little by little that such was not the form, nor the destiny, nor the function of this message. It was not made to be inscribed on walls, but in the hearts of the seers, of the parish, of the pilgrims. Such is its place. It is there that one ought to interpret it as *a letter of the Holy Spirit written in the hearts,* according to a formula of Paul, the Apostle, in his Second Letter to the Corinthians 3, 2-3.

The message of Medjugorje should be read in the vital growth of Medjugorje on three levels: the seers, the parish, the pilgrims.

1. With the seers, it is an admirable human and spiritual blossoming.

. In the parish, the vital point is the prayer groups who form discreetly, elite spiritual groups who are exceptional. Let us recall three main ones.

a) The first, formed in May 1983, gathers 60 people of all ages in the basement of the presbytery. The commitment of the participants is remarkable. They make an annual retreat.

b) The second group began in June 1982 around Ivan (and Maria). They often pray at night on the hill, Monday and Friday, at the invitation of the Gospa. The two seers then profit from a second apparition.

c) A third group has been formed around Jelena and Marijana. At age 10 (1982), these two girls awoke to locutions and visions of the heart, which extended the grace of the apparitions. The messages of Jelena were of primary importance on the life of the parish from the summer of 1983 to the beginning of 1984.

In May of 1983 a group of little girls, today, young girls, gathered around Jelena and Marijana. For them, Jelena received from Our Lady a rule of life (June 14th). This group has promised not to make a choice for their state in life (marriage, religious state, and even a profession), for four years and to pray at least three hours a day. Today, the adolescents are 15 years old. The messages from Our Lady continue to guide them. This remarkable but discreet branching out constitutes, for the future of the church, a promise which would be premature to evaluate.

3. Among the pilgrims there is a vast movement of conversions, of confessions (150 confessors during the day of June 25, 1987), and the creation of

numberless prayer groups which disseminate this grace and its deepening study—hundreds of groups in numberless countries.

THE MESSAGE OF OUR LADY AT MEDJUGORJE

We now come to dealing with the message:

1. First of all, THE ACTUAL MESSAGE: Some seed words, an echo of the Gospel, given as a reminder by the apparition which gives them life.

2. Then the SECRET PART of the message, the 10 secrets and other revelations not disclosed. It is the most delicate, the most ambiguous, the most problematic chapter. Prudence and reserve impose themselves to the rules and experience of mystical theology.

3. The SIGNS, destined to recall the presence and the familiarity of God, invisible and therefore so near to man's life: cures and luminary signs, which we will have to consider with circumspection, without overestimating that which has not been clarified.

4. Finally, the PEDAGOGY of Our Lady and the pastoral which supports or prolongs it. It is the part which belongs to Professor René Lejeune. We will try to finish together.

CHAPTER 4

The Actual Message

What is a message? It is not necessarily a new revelation, and if a private revelation pretended to bring a new Gospel, one would have to condemn it according to the principle of St. Paul. (*Gal.* 1:8—already previously noted).

A. STRUCTURE AND ASPECTS OF THE MESSAGE

Function and Limitations

The twelve Apostles delivered the revelation of Jesus Christ during the first Christian generation. Subsequent revelations can only be a recall of that first unique, fundamental, revelation. They are not, however, insignificant. In case of neglect, a "reminder" can be infinitely precious. This is true in daily life. I forget a telephone number, a name. I have it on the tip of my tongue. A recollection escapes me. I gather all the means at my disposal to try to remember. That which brings this recollection back to me is good news.

To see again, what has already been seen, can be a rediscovery. This Rembrandt is familiar to me, and I see there, that an artist can make me see a message more clearly than I would have thought. Previously, I had not understood much about it.

Private revelations are of this kind because the Revelation has been achieved in Jesus Christ. We no longer have to wait for a new truth, for Jesus Christ is inexhaustible. But, we know Him poorly. All our lives, we will have to rediscover the fullness and the incandescence, under the ashes, to which we have been reduced.

The message of Medjugorje has as its function to recall, discover, illuminate the inexhaustible Gospel.

Levels and Aspects

These reminders of the Gospel reach us through various channels and diverse ways, according to different functions. They are of unequal value.

It is in different ways, not always easy to discern, that the six seers on the one hand, Jelena and Marijana on the other hand, receive the messages of Christ or of Our Lady. The visionaries see and hear the Gospa. She appears to them as a three dimensional real being. Jelena and Marijana perceive her internally with the heart, at the point of profound prayer to which they are devoted, and for which they prepare with their entire soul. If their preparation is insufficient, the message does not come at all, whereas the apparition does not fail the visionaries, though they may not be well disposed. For Ivanka and Mirjana, the first apparition took place without preparation, as they returned from an insignificant escapade.

It is necessary to discern, in each message, the part of the speaker and the part of the listener. The speaker is the Virgin (and also Christ, often through Jelena). The recipients are the seers. The speaker adapts herself to the listeners, and the listeners put their trademarks on the reception. They receive, in their own way, according to their capacities, according to their interpretations, which are not without interferences. The dispute between the Fransiscans and the Bishop has annoyingly interfered with the messages of Medjugorje, as we will see on pages 325 to 343.

Message and Teaching

It is necessary to also distinguish the fundamental message of Medjugorje, and the teaching which makes it penetrate our being.

The first part relates to the message. Pages 32 to 76.

The second part will relate to the teaching. Pages 79 to 142.

At Medjugorje, the actual message, this subjective recalling of the Gospel, was given directly in a few words during the apparitions on the hill, which lasted only five days, from the

25th through the 29th of June, 1981.

The following explains and details this message and places it within the prophetic reality of our times. In particular, it is the function of the 10 secrets and messages given to Maria and Ivanka on the future of the world and the Church. These prophetic messages, mixed with predictions, warn us of the formidable impact of sin which drags our world toward shipwreck.

The present chapter then has, at its objective, the fundamental message. It reminds us of the forgotten basics of the Gospel: priority of God, of faith, of prayer, of conversion, fasting and joyful penance to this effect for a world in danger.

This message has not been given in an organic and concise form, but in scattered words, as we have said.

A synthesis of it is not made, and we will have to discover the cohesion, according to three criterion: Its internal logic, the Gospel to which the message refers, and the life which it arouses in hearts, prayer, human relations, peace, etc. Such is the letter written in the hearts, according to the Apostle Paul. It is in living the message ourselves that we can understand it, because it is only understood through its practice, like music. In the 19th Century, my grandmother, a musician at heart, would come across Debussy and Fauré. She had to acquire an ear for it. Sometimes it is necessary to acquire an ear, and a new heart, in order to know the inexhaustible sense of the Gospel in every new epic.

B. THE KEY WORDS OF THE MESSAGE

As much as possible, we shall present words of the message according to the chronological order when they were given, and how they figure within the *Corpus* at the end of the present volume, and also in regrouping the words and repeated themes. We shall try to recapture here the origin, the dynamics, the coherence and the series of events, in spite of the absence of any plan, through the chain of naive, thoughtful, or inspired questions of the seers.

Identity of the Messenger

Since the 24th of June, at the foot of the hill, Our Lady made herself recognized. It is a fact which Ivanka declared right away, at first sight.

"It is the Gospa." (That is to say, Our Lady).

It is an inspiration, an interior light, still confusing.

"How did you recognize her so quickly," I asked her.

"I don't know. Undoubtedly, it was given to me," she responded.

The second day, Ivanka (she who in the course of ecstasies has the most rapid reactions) is the first to question the Virgin about her mother who had died two months ago. She received, in response, these first words from Our Lady:

She is happy, and she is with me.

The Gospa opens the window of Heaven and the way which leads to it.

Know that if you humbly carry out your responsibility as human beings and Christians, that suffices to make you worthy of Heaven.

From that day, Little Jakov understood well both the Virgin and Heaven. He declares at the end of an apparition:

"Yes, now that I have seen the Gospa, I will never be sorry to die."

Vicka confirmed, that day, the identity of the apparition, which she sprinkles with holy water (as Bernadette formerly did, according to the same faith and tradition of the Church). Since the 26th of June, the apparition confirms:

I am the Blessed Virgin Mary.

And more specifically on October 12th, 1981:

I am the Queen of Peace.

Faith

The word "faith" is predominant in the messages of the first days:

"Why have you come here and what do you desire," the seers asked on June 26th.

And the apparition responds:

The reason is that here there are good believers.

Faith is obscure, austere. Those who surround the seers call for a proof.

"Ask her for a sign of her presence."

But, as Jesus refused the scribes a sign in Heaven, the

apparition refuses to give a sign on request. The signs will come later, freely and without warning. Our Lady returns to faith alone, through the very words of the risen Christ:

Blessed are those who have not seen and who believe.

These important words of Jesus, Our Lady repeats on Sunday, June 28th, in response to a new question on what she wants:

Let them believe as if they had seen. Let those who do not see, believe as you who see me.

At the end of the apparition of June 26th, she already gives "faith" as the means of reconciliation.

For that, it is necessary to believe, to pray, fast, and confess.

What does she expect of the Franciscans?

That they persevere in the faith, and that they help others keep the faith.

On June 28th, she insists:

Let the people believe and persevere in the faith.

What do you wish from our priests?

Let them be firm in the faith and let them help you.

Why don't you appear to those in the church?

Blessed are they who believe without having seen.

On June 29th, she likewise responds to a new question on what she expects.

There is only one God, and one faith. Believe firmly and do not fear anything.

And again:

That you may have a strong faith and that you keep the faith.

This faith, as in the Gospel, is tied to hope, which relies on God and dares to ask for the impossible. . . . in the sense of God's will, of course.

At the request of Dr. Darinka Glamuzina to the seers: "May I touch the apparition?"

The Gospa gives this gently ironic response:

There have always been doubting Thomases. Let her come. (June 29th)

That same day, the seers asked:

"Will we know how to bear persecutions?"

You will, my angels. Do not be afraid. You will be able to bear everything. You must believe and have faith in me.

Prayer

Prayer came into play before being the object of a message, and it did not cease to intensify during succeeding years.

At the first apparition, the visionaries spontaneously say the "Our Father," the "Hail Mary," the "Creed," perhaps nothing more.

On the next day, they receive advice from an old lady in the village who invites them to say, according to a local tradition, seven Our Fathers, seven Hail Marys, seven Glory Be. Since the first days, it seems the Virgin will ask them to have those prayers preceded by the Creed—always the faith!

"Her favorite prayer is the Creed," notes Vicka, on February 10th, 1982. "When we recite it, the Gospa does not cease to smile. I think that no one has ever seen her happier than during this prayer."

Fasting

From her second apparition of June 26th, Our Lady explicitly stated:

One must believe, pray, fast...

Fasting is tied to prayer. This message brings to life a local tradition which was on the way of disappearing. Fr. Jozo Zovko tried in vain to restore it. Since the 2nd of July 1981, without knowing the invitation of Our Lady it seems, he made the following proposition to his parishioners who had gathered at the Church:

"If you would like to, let us fast three days in order to ask for enlightenment." The agreement to do so was massive and unexpected.

The apparition was precise later:

Fast twice a week, on Wednesdays and Fridays.

On July 21st, 1982, in response to a question from Father Tomislav Vlasic, asked through the seers, she answers:

1. *The best kind of fasting is that on bread and water.*
2. *Prayer and fasting can put off wars.*
3. *It can alter the laws of nature.*

These last words illustrate the words of Christ on faith: *able to move mountains.*

Fasting has, as its function, to awaken the hunger and thirst for peace, justice and God Himself. This light privation stimulates the discovery of necessary uniqueness. Fasting establishes and confirms prayer.

Conversion

With respect to conversion (the starting point being the preaching of John the Baptist), the Gospa alludes to it since June 25, 1982.

Humbly accomplish your responsibility as human beings and as Christians, in order to make you worthy of Heaven.

The word appeared explicitly the next day, Tuesday, June 26th:

I desire to be with you in order to convert you and reconcile the whole world.

Conversion is the means of reconciliation which the world needs. To convert means a turning around, to turn back from sin in order to turn towards God. Conversion and reconciliation come through the Sacrament of Penance, mentioned the same day (or the 27th of June, because there is some doubt concerning the date of the words just cited):

It is necessary to believe, to pray, to fast, and to confess.

This call to confession will continue to renew itself later on, and to be heard by many people.

The apparition in the field of Gumno (200 meters from the house of Bijakovici) had ceased. Certain individuals had asked to touch the Virgin, but her white and shining veil became tainted, observed Maria belatedly. Marinko was struck by this and invited all to Confession. The Madonna is doing very well in Medjugorje since that time, where each day there is a need for many confessors, up to 150 on the 25th of June, 1987. And Jelena, at first embarrassed to go to Confession every month, (according to the invitation of Our Lady on August 7, 1982) because she had nothing to say, sees very well her faults today, in the light of a life closer to God. She now wishes more frequent confession.

God, Peace, Reconciliation

All these words (prayer, fasting, confession) refer to the same focus, to the same reality: GOD! He is the frame of reference. He is explicitly named since June 26th (or the 27th, according to some interpretations) in reference to the very finality of the message. Mankind must reconcile with God and with each other.

God is the source of all reconciliation, the starting point, and the end of all unity. The message of conversion, of prayer, and fasting, runs into this fundamental finality. The word "reconciliation" alternates with the word "peace," with which it is identified.

The word "peace" (in union with God), is the farewell of Our Lady at the end of the first apparition, Monday, June 25, 1981.

Go in the peace of God.

This formula will become the standard and the final words of each apparition.

Since the second apparition on the hill, June 26, 1981, the Virgin established, as we have already stressed, the bond between reconciliation and conversion, and its extension to the entire world. It is the essential finality of the message addressed to a divided world, because these divisions with God and among men, lead to ruin.

I desire to be with you, to convert and reconcile the whole world.

After the wish for peace, which ended the apparition to the six seers on June 26th, the Virgin returns to it with insistence, in the private apparition to Maria on the road when she returned. She told Maria then:

Peace, Peace, Peace! Be reconciled.

On June 27, the final wish for peace will carry some explanations and some variations. When the seers ask for a sign so that people would not treat them as liars or fanatics, the Gospa says to them:

Injustice has always existed, but do not be afraid.

The final wish for peace was given under two slightly different forms to the five seers who were together:

Goodbye, my angels. Go in the peace of God.
And to Ivan, who had the apparition alone, aside:
*Praised be Jesus. May peace be with you. Take courage.
The courage to cultivate and to achieve peace.*

The seers took these words very seriously. It is their preoccupation and their very life. At the time of the interrogation by the pastor at the rectory (June 30th in the evening), Mirjana spontaneously recalled the message of reconciliation in union with faith. The Gospa wishes to strengthen their faith. She said, *Reconcile them. It is why I am distressed, that people have come here to the hill this evening for nothing.*

C. COHESION AND LOGIC OF THE MESSAGE

The words of the message are linked according to the connections and multiple convergences which we have stressed. In the passage we don't find a summary statement of the kind, "Return to God (= be converted), believe, pray, fast, and you will thus arrive at peace and reconciliation."

Let us try to recapture this very simple chain of events, which is the result of scattered words. Conversion is a return to the Creator. He is seriously forgotten. This return is achieved by the means indicated, faith and prayer, along with fasting. Peace and reconciliation come in this way.

Genesis of Reconciliation

This progress, this consistency, is Christian doctrine, and scripture itself explains it to us.

The world is divided by sin. It is sin (contagious chaos), which causes and stirs up enmities, quarrels, wars, acts of violence. Men are divided among themselves because they are, first of all, divided in themselves. The incoherent, passionate impulses of sin turn them away from God and splits them apart, and this internal division abounds in exterior and collective oppositions.

The union with God, the Creator, remakes order and internal unity.

The "conversion" asked by Our Lady is then a return to God, with an understanding of the desires of God and of His loving will. That will is charitable for mankind and carries with it fruits of peace. At its peak, it obtains this a hundred fold which Jesus promised here below, to whomever gives nothing less than all. (*1 Mc.* 10:30) It is to this action that we are invited to reconcile with others, beginning with our reconciliation with God and with ourselves.

God The Creator

Be careful! In order to understand Him, one must recall first of all, what has been most forgotten. Our science knows everything about mechanisms and knows nothing of the "being" and the Creator.

God is the Creator. What does that mean?

That does not mean God has created the world *in the past,* like engineers make a satellite and place it in orbit where it will be able to turn indefinitely without them. God is not the mechanic of the world. He is its Creator. He makes it exist. He, alone, exists by Himself, necessarily. The other beings exist because of Him. He gives them, in every instance, existence itself. If God would stop wanting the world, creating it, this world would cease like a light ceases when the electrical current is cut.

But this superficial comparison gives only a weak idea of the Creator, because God does not give to the being mechanically. The characteristic of God is that He is faithful to His plan as Creator. It is thus that He makes the world exist according to an internal and coherent law. It is, finally, that He makes it exist in itself, and gives an autonomous and free existence to reasonable creatures whom He has invited to reign over this creation. (*Gen.* 1:27-28).

God creates man to His image. . .therefore, as a possible rival. He creates our very freedom. He makes it exist as freedom. In this domain, mankind has, therefore, many powers. Of course, we cannot be a creator in the strict sense of the word—make a radically new being exist. We can only distribute that which exists independently of us.

But man can be the primary cause of annihilation, because evil is less than a being, a failure of being, a deconcentration and a deviation from being. In this domain, human freedom can be a primary cause because God is never a cause of evil.

But God's creatures can be, and often are, a primary cause in the order of evil. They can also have the vertigo and the passion for evil, to present themselves as brilliant and sinister rivals of God, the Creator, capable of causing many catastrophies. Such was the original temptation, according to Genesis 3:5: *If you eat the forbidden fruit, you will be like God, knowing good and evil.* A tremendous illusion, because God has made of man something of an equal through freedom. But man lowers himself so that instead of accepting his loving relationship with God, he revolts against Him. God has not created man like a remote controlled robot in His service. He has created him with full power to forget God, to turn away from Him, and to turn against Him. But God does not forget man, He does not shut him out, does not destroy him. He continues to give existence to his protesting freedom.

God does not show Himself, His splendor, His beauty, His goodness. Because God is more beautiful than all the beautiful things of the world, and better than all the best things of this world, truer than the most authentic truths; our freedom would be pre-determined, if we could perceive Him such as He is.

He has filtered the mystery of His being, to which one has access through the gratuitous free ways of love. He is the hidden God, not by His smallness, but by His immensity. It is up to us to penetrate it, through the narrow way of persevering love.

The Free and Necessary Way of Love

Such is the law of creation, the law of freedom, because it is the law of love. God creates out of love in order to diffuse, to communicate, to share the good which is in Him, the good which is Himself, the community of love of the Three Divine Persons. It is not a mechanical diffusion, but a diffusion of love in which the only possible way is freedom, because there is no love without freedom, without choice, without a capacity to refuse love as did Lucifer, the supreme creature. Love does not have a price if it is free. It is not a true love without interior freedom. It is also the condition of love (with a capital L), that is God Himself.

Ecumenism

The Virgin gives this reconciliation an ecumenical dimension, which culminates in the message gathered by Monsignor Franic. The Gospa addresses herself thus to the Croatian Catholics:

Love your Muslim brothers. Love your Orthodox Serbian brothers. Love those who govern you.

These words are hard to understand for some Croatians. In the Balkans, so divided (more difficult than in Lebanon), the oppositions are felt with extreme intensity, stirred up by centuries of struggle.

The Muslims are Croatians who allowed themselves to be converted, or bought, at the time of the Turkish domination. Because of this apostasy of their fathers, they were not considered as brothers.

The Orthodox are the Serbians. The capitol of the federation is located in their area. There is still a hostility here of long duration. One does not marry between Serbians and Croatians.

With respect to the government, it is the atheistic Communist Party, under which the Croatian Catholicism and nationalism suffered.

The invitation to love these three catagories of persons is the affirmation of an ecumenism without limits. It is also the affirmation that unity will be achieved through love. Love is stronger than every division, strong enough to create unity.

This message surfaced several times under an ambiguous form, which provided the only serious doctrinal objection against these messages. But this ambiguity can be understood within the cultural context, which is foreign to us, and which required me to have long dialogues there in order to be able to grasp it. The explanation of this difficulty will be the object of Appendix 2 at the end of this volume.

The ecumenical dimension of the message of Medjugorje brings us back to the same profound explanation: the Creator creates out of love, for love, and freedom is the very condition of love. That is the reason why God has taken the risk of freedom. It carries with it serious consequences, sin, and the various divisions that result from it. The redemption must painfully go with this current; but love, the beginning and the end of all creation, is stronger than sin and all the forces contributing to division. It is from this concept that the ecumenical message surfaces.

It does not have a meaning of particular dialogue or diplomacy, or some concession, or even intellectual agreement on common formulas to live and let live. It is more profoundly that it become the bloom of all ecumenism. Unity comes from something more distant—from love. That will be the inspiration for the rest of the components.

This confusing perspective exposed itself to some objections and special misunderstandings. But it is well understood in the Medjugorje files through reconciliations, which have already been achieved:

> 1. The renewal of love which God has given in the parish has reconciled the villages of Medjugorje which formerly fought to the point of killing one another.

> Likewise, in many families and neighbors in each village, where some Muslims and Orthodox Serbians have come to Medjugorje, they have been very well received.

> Heaven has become involved in it to the surprise of the parishioners.

> On August 18th, 1982, the parish Chronicle observes:

> "The Mulsim Pasa Djano saw the light during an apparition of the Blessed Virgin to Mirjana, and at the time of an illness, she had an apparition of the Gospa. The Gospa confirmed the truth of her declarations to Mirjana, and praised this Muslim whose piety could serve as a model for everyone. This happened at Sarajevo." (Tomislav Vlasic noted that Mirjana had come to Medjugorje on August 18th).

> At Medjugorje, a child who was a Hungarian gypsy from an Orthodox family, was cured (probably in

- 1982). A Catholic priest was scandalized over it, according to the denominational hostility which was prevalent. Maria, shocked by the reaction of this priest, asked the Gospa and received this response:

> *Tell the priest and everyone, that it is you who are divided on earth. Muslims and Orthodox, like Catholics, are equal before God and before me, because you are all children.* (C.-128)

2. The attitude of the parish and the pilgrims, with respect to the police and representatives of the government, has also been most Christian. In this tense environment, there was no hostility against the forces of order, but obedience, courtesy, a constant understanding. Never were such large crowds so easy to watch over. From this fact, the Marxist government was brought to understand, contrary to all expectations, that Medjugorje was a movement strictly foreign to the ethnic and national confrontations, by no means political, therefore, legal.

If the benefits of the pilgrimages to the economy could facilitate this overture, it was surely not possible without a new attitude. Personally, in the early difficult years, I was forced to remain faithful during the legal proceedings which were brought upon me in Yugoslavia on December 27, 1984, and in humiliating procedures, (body search before a tribunal of 12 members.)

I invited them only to again find, as I had proposed from the onset, a common ground of friendship which was present between our two friendly countries. In spite of these horrible beginnings, this common ground was established, and my work there continued.

Thus, one understands the full sense of the message of Medjugorje. It is a reminder of the message of the Gospel. The secret of love and of happiness is conversion to God the Creator, by Whom we have been made. This conversion is the work of prayer. The prayer of the seers with the Gospa provides a constant and stimulating example.

Dimensions of Prayer

This prayer, and the spiritual order of things past, are represented through the acronym, ATPOR: A-Adoration, T-Thanksgiving, P-Petition, O-Offering, R-Resolution.

1. *Prayer* is, above all, adoration of the Creator— He who made us to be. It is a recognition of our truth as creatures. We owe everything to God, and still we are not totally dependent, because He gives us freedom itself. The most profound, most intelligent, and most productive act of our freedom is the adoration of God, our Creator; to recognize that we owe Him everything, to abandon ourselves to Him, and to deliver ourselves to His plan, to take up roots again in Him who gives us existence. It is to discover God more intimately through ourselves, than we are ourselves.

2. *Thanksgiving* is the logical consequence of adoration. If we were cognizant of the transcendental gift of God, existence and invitation to share His life, if we understood that everything is grace, we would only give thanks to Him who has given us everything. And to give thanks to God, the free author of all grace, is not to lose this grace which He "gives," but to achieve it and to amplify it in Holy Communion.

3. *Petition* would be for many, prayer itself and the only prayer, because we are motivated to speak to God when we lack something. It is then that we discover, "God exists. . . .perhaps. Let's try then." And we cry to Him, heart to heart, after having exhausted every other effort.

But the very function of prayer is less to ask, than to receive the gift of God; to learn to say, "Lord, what do You wish me to do? What do You give me to do? What are You telling me to do today?" God has something to tell us. It is our listening which is lacking.

Prayer is unfailing. It teaches Christ. *Everything*

that you ask the Father in My name, He will grant it to you. (Jn. 15:16). Unfailing? Yes, if we know how to discover what God wishes as good and better for us. For oftentimes, we would ask Him for something, not for our well-being, but for that which is evil; not what helps us, but what will destroy us. It is the folly of our desires and megalomanic plans. The petition should then be placed in trust, and trust in the plan of God conceived for our well-being.

4. *Offering* is essential to the petition thus understood. It is a gift of itself to God, who gives Himself, in return. We consecrate ourselves to God, who alone can consecrate us, fulfill us. But he can only do it with the loving cooperation of our freedom. It is in that sense, that one can consecrate himself to God, prepare himself, cooperate with the consecration, which is His work and His gift.

In this world of sin, this consecration passes through trials and the cross. It ends for each one of us in the holocaust of death, the last act, present throughout all of our life because it identifies us deeply with the Cross of Christ and extends into His victory and His life. Death, where we end our earthly milieu, is a new birth to the Divine environment and to God Himself—if we are prepared for it.

5. *Resolution* is the final act of prayer, for Christ has invited us tirelessly to "do the will" of His Father. Prayer is not the window shopping of Heaven, or imaginative effervescence on God or the beyond. It is a pledging of our will, called to take roots once again in God. It is to find inwardly (in love) the program and planning, enlightened by the Holy Spirit, which will engage God's function in our world.

THE FUNCTION OF FASTING

And Fasting? It has as a function, to nourish prayer. The satiated man who waivers between the fervor of his desires, and the stupor of satisfaction, should nourish his hunger and thirst for God. Those who are satisfied in this world are little open to God and to the great stakes of Creation.

Voluntary fasting hollows in us an overture to God. Well understood fasting does not stir up frustration, not even hunger. The person who fasts, who believes that he is hungry when he is fasting, is ordinarily a victim of a nervous illusion. The light "stomach cramp" which gets hold of him, lights a strong desire and sometimes he runs to the refrigerator to fill up this "small pit" which his psychism has hollowed.

If he does not polarize on this fleeting and insignificant sensation, if his spirit is occupied with prayer or something else, the deceptive impression of "hunger" is very quickly forgotten, even during a complete and prolonged fast.

True hunger, which almost no European or American knows, is a deep sensation which comes on like an alarm signal at the end of long fasting, where the absence places the organism in danger. Such was the case with Christ: *After 40 days he was hungry,* says the Gospel. (*Mt.* 4:2; *Lk.* 4:2). Such is the experience of persons after prolonged fasting.

Fasting accustoms us to curb our desires, desire for food, and at the same time, sexual desires, which carry with great intensity the same risks of nervous polarization and disorders everywhere. Man is a rational animal. He must control his appetite and his sexuality and no longer be a slave to them. To want to draw the maximum pleasure is a sure means of provoking exasperation, frustration, disgust, and bitterness. One does not leave these tremendous and anxious deceptions, except through a very narrow door. The Church widely requests it. The positive experience of so many of its celebate members attests to this profound truth, in spite of the failures which human frailty scatters along the route.[1]

Fasting is beneficial for one's health. During this time of reasonable privation, the organism eliminates its toxic waste and eats up its surplus. This blessing preserves health and

---

1. "La Croix" of March 1987 published a statistic according to which 20% of the U.S. clergy maintained homosexual relations, and 20% heterosexual relations. This statistic (which would need to be verified, but which no one has contradicted as far as I know) would not find in that 20%, 1% seriously engaged in fasting and in prayer.

prolongs life. It increases its efficiency, often disturbed by excesses.

Fasting from food is also the base of spiritual purification, and an overture to God which can progress through other ways. That is why Jelena, who has internal locutions from Christ and Our Lady, invites us to expand the field, fasting from tobacco, alcohol, television, and other superficial desires.

Fasting is a beautiful experience. On the suggestion of Our Lady of Medjugorje, hundreds of thousands of Christians persevere in it, and find themselves well, adapting a fast according to their situation, their vocation, and the advice of their spiritual directors.

Fasting nourishes prayer, a glow of enthusiasm toward God, toward peace, toward reconciliation, a pure echo of the Gospel. It places the body in unison with the soul, and it is the source of another reconciliation, that one an interior one.

CHAPTER 5

And The Secrets?

Conversion to God through faith, prayer, fasting, reconciliation and peace: Is that all the message of Medjugorje? It
seems to us that it is.

SENSE OF INADEQUACY?

Will some other words be added since the apparitions have
not yet terminated? No, it does not seem so to us. The message seems complete. The bottom line makes sense in reference to the Gospel which it recalls. It is complete with respect
to the word, but it remains to be achieved in action.

But then, what do the 10 secrets mean, the life of the Virgin, and the messages on the future of the world and the
Church, which the seers themselves guard? They express in
a very explicit way, the prophetic dimension of the basic
message. Our Lady shows us there, for what misunderstood
urgent reasons she visits us, what the current stake of these
messages is and who this messenger is, who has come
familiarly to the aid of mankind.

The 10 secrets are being revealed to the seers since 1981.
Mirjana received the 10th and final secret at Christmas 1982.
On November 5th, 1983, she gave an impressive synthesis,
of what could be unveiled, to Father T. Vlasic, who sent it
to the Pope on December 16th, (bottom of page 299). Ivanka
received the last secret on May 6th, 1985, with the notice
of the apparition as we have seen, (page 28).

Since August 26th, 1984, Mirjana has programmed the revelation, which will be confided to a priest. She has chosen

for that, Father Petar Ljubici, the youngest Fransiscan at Medjugorje.

In effect, it does not deal with confidences given to the seers for their personal guidance, as was the case of the secrets to Bernadette, but it deals with secrets destined to be revealed. Since everything is very strict with respect to the substance, the seers, in the meantime, have guarded well the nature and function of these secrets. They do not add anything to the message of the Gospel, not even to the message of Medjugorje, it seems. They state very specifically why Our Lady came, to remind us of the misunderstood urgency in a critical moment in the history of our salvation. We know the essential, in spite of our curiosity.

GRAVITY OF THE SECRETS

A grave situation motivated Our Lady's visit to Medjugorje. Our world has abandoned itself calmly to sin. It prepares thus its self-destruction.

"The majority of the secrets are grave, catastrophic," Mirjana has informed me.

The plans of the seers, the tears of some of them after having had the eighth, the ninth and the tenth secrets, assures us that these last announce the wages of sin.

These calamities seem inevitable, in part because one seems to emerge himself with impunity in self-destruction. The world, as every well-constituted organism, dispenses imminent justice. The alcoholic and the drug addict destroy themselves and destroy their posterity. Homosexuality was the determining agent in the spread of AIDS, an illness sexually transmissible, and which has spread principally through the disordinate and promiscuous exercises of sexuality. If well-intentioned priests try to put a mask on this scientific evidence, because it seemed "moralizing," or "prejudice" against homosexuals, their hazy ideas do not change anything in the predominant cause of the expansion of this illness. It continues to spread because, in spite of this message, many persons "do not change anything in their sexual practices," say the polls.

Of course, one must have compassion for those with such illnesses and take care of them as Mother Teresa has done in establishing a special clinic to treat the AIDS victims. It does not deal with not accepting persons among the sick who have contracted this illness through their own fault, versus those who are only the victims. But to love the sick is to treat the illness and help in preventing the causes, and not in justifying them, or supporting them.

Loving sinners is to want to free them from sin. One must be understanding and kind toward man, but not hide, through the goodness of one's heart, the signs of alarm. Doctors at the highest scientific level are surprised that people continue to deny statistical evidence that the pill multiplies cancers of the womb, and miscarriages (especially of young girls), the raid of cancer of the uterus. One avoids telling about it, in order not to create anxiety in people who abuse the pill, or have a miscarriage. Is this charity, which serves as an accomplice, well-placed?

CONTENT OF THE SECRETS

What are the secrets then? We do not know. But we can say something about them. The best guarded of all the secrets, the last secret of Fatima, was not completely impenetrable. The context indicates its outline:

> The Holy Father will consecrate Russia (which will be converted) to Me, and a certain time of peace will be granted to the world. In Portugal, the dogma of the faith will always be preserved, etc... Do not tell that to anyone.

The "etc." followed by two dots marks the place of the secret, which Lucy did not transcribe. The sentence which precedes "In Portugal, the dogma of the faith will always be preserved," is the beginning of the secret. It deals then with the future of Portugal, but also in contrast, with other countries, those which will lack fidelity.

In my chapter on the secrets of Bernadette, I indicated that one could draw conclusions from those responses which she had given to questions. Those secrets did not concern the world, nor France, but were meant only for her, etc. ("Lourdes, Authentic History." Vol. 3)

Likewise, at Medjugorje, the reactions of the seers and their evasive answers permit one to assemble the following observations. The first three secrets are of warnings, in order to invite conversion, before it is too late. They are undoubtedly, in part dramatic, in part positive. The first two warnings could be catastrophies (such as Chernoble, AIDS, or others) which would make one reflect on some misunderstood evidence, but also on positive facts encouraging one to believe.

The third is a sign of hope. According to the seers, it will be on the hill of the apparition, visible to everyone. It will be given to unbelievers as a last chance for conversion. Believers do not need it. The seers say that they know the date.

CRITICAL PERSPECTIVE

So much precision causes confusion, criticism, or doubt.

Such is the case with this information from Mirjana: The secrets are written on a document which the Gospa had delivered to her, not paper, not cloth. Her cousin, an engineer, was very impressed with this document, but since two other members of her family laughed at it, she no longer shows it to anyone, not even the priests of the parish. The message is written there, but it will be invisible until the day when Father Pero Ljubici will be authorized to read it in order to reveal it (after seven days of fasting and three days before the realization of each secret being forecast.)

All this resembles magic, more than customary laws of God. Reservation imposes itself then, as we await this revelation.

Certain pilgrims are waiting for the revelation of the sign as a marvelous proof which will convince the whole world. It seems more probable that it could deceive, and that its opponents will easily try to find excuses.

If the sign is a source of water, people will say: "Another source of water? Those who have revealed it knew it was there all along, and have brought it out at a most opportune moment."

If it concerns some intangible, people will say: "It existed before, and they have known to defer its revelation in order to have more publicity."

If people discover some hidden statue like that which deters the oxen of Betharam, they will say: "Same old tune."

If, on the contrary, it deals with a marvelous, spectacular, absolutely inexplicable sign (didn't one speak of a sudden rise of a church on the hill?), one would hesitate to recognize the action of God who usually manifests himself discreetly. Some would see only magic, indeed a sign of the prince of this world. Those who (without having ever been to Medjugorje) think against all evidence, that it relates to some diabolic manifestation, will triumph. Let us be on guard not to overestimate the secrets. We would risk being disappointed.

FUNCTION AND SITUATION OF THE SECRETS

All of this invites one to place the secrets in perspective. They are not the essence of the message. They are prophesies, words given in the name of God for the reality of the world and its future. Prophesies and forecasts have always played an important role, in order to guide the lives of the people of God—the Bible in our days, without discontinuance.

But one needs to be careful. Predictions are not made in order to satisfy one's curiosity. They are always given in clear-obscurity, or light and shade. That has the function of forecasting, a guide towards the future. In itself it is of the future, but a provision which cannot be history before the history exists. Further, it is incomprehensible before existing, according to all its cultural context. I understood it better in studying the exemplary prediction of Yvonne-Aimee de Malestroit. (O.E.I.L. Paris, 1987).

On the other hand, predictions, even those inspired by God, are not infallible, because they are subjected to human confusion on the part of the seers. The first Christians waited for the return of Christ in their lifetime, and He has not yet returned. In matters of the future and of prophecy, one must always distrust optical illusions which shorten delays. Mirjana underwent such an illusion in 1984, when she seemed to announce the realization of the secrets as near.

Besides, the seers have kept their secrets so well that they have not even discussed them among themselves. One then is not sure that the 10 secrets are the same for all. If that seems certain for the first secret, which had generally been received together, we are uncertain concerning the others.

The secrets then have one function. They motivate the urgency for conversion. Their general theme is well known. The world has peacefully abandoned itself to sin. It has wanted to live joyfully, "freely," without God, without faith or law. "New-look" prophets have announced the death of God, the death of the Father, as good news; and sexual freedom among others, as good news, but also freedom of the passions and human impulses of violence. The world is destroying itself. It is vehemently preparing its own destruction for having struggled, forgotten, or relegated the essential: God and His law of love, which the messages of Medjugorje recall.

WARNING TO A WORLD WHICH IS DESTROYING ITSELF

The ten secrets announce, to a large extent, the imminent destructions which are not extrinsic punishments, but imminent justice, the self-destruction of a world which entrusts itself to evil through deviation and frenzy.

The announcement of the threats which weigh on the world does not seem very evident, like their connection to sin. One thinks right away of war. The great military experts have not found another way to guarantee peace except through the equilibrium of terror. The two "greats" of this world share the same principle:

> If I want to maintain the peace, I must be stronger
> because in default, I would be attacked and defeated.

But this law of the jungle demands a scaling without end, and without a way out, which has already piled up more atomic, bacteriological, or chemical weapons than it needs in order to destroy all human life on this planet.

To achieve peace, it would be necessary to cease loading the two pans of the scale until it breaks, and instead to unload them. We are beginning to get there after 20 years of escalation without mercy. But a "retreat" of the destructive products would pose immense problems to which no one, as yet, holds a solution. Will so many prayers and sacrifices finally put us on the road?

The messages aim less at the so-evident danger of a world

conflict, than other more secret messages. Love is losing its strength in our world. Men seem to be less and less capable of assuming it in a durable manner. Marriage is collapsing in our societies to the benefit of free unions, which are not irresponsible and sterile. The "authenticity" of the moment eclipses fidelity. The creative plan and future of the world are threatened.

One observes a rise in blackmail, which is the outstanding way today, to obtain publicity, credits, satisfaction, whether one be a pirate of the skys, one who holds hostages, or just abuses an honest worker. Some do not know how to find other ways of obtaining justice, order, and development.

The increase in violence makes many cities insecure. One avoids going out in the evening. Terrorists and revolutionary organizations have acquired such a prestige, that young people from good families enter their schools to ransom some terrified quarters. Their irresponsible deeds of glory cause those interested, armed and helmeted, to have access to the honor of front-page newspaper coverage. Violence is ablaze in many parts of the world. Internal or external wars proliferate. Lebanon originally appeared during past years as a marvelous model of peace, amid differences of opinion: "The Switzerland of Asia." Who would have thought that it would come to this fatal, internal destruction, stirred up by so many external forces? One could continue with the sunny countries of Central America, or with the ethnic or racial conflicts of Africa, without forgetting the relentless repression of the Marxist countries (more than a third of the planet), against those who persevere against all assaults on their faith and their religion.

The secrets, as much as one knows of them, can then be taken seriously. The state of alert is recognized by great international experts who often become discreet, in order not to cause anxiety. A bad advice.

We will see whether the 10 secrets are really premonitory and to what extent they warn us of the perils so evident, but especially of the urgency to remedy them through the only way possible: A return to God, source of life and order, of reparation and protection.

THE "LIVES" OF THE VIRGIN

The *Life of the Virgin* has been revealed to the seers since January 7th, 1983:

to the end of April, for Jakov,
to May 22nd for Ivanka,
to July 17th for Maria,
to April 10th, 1985 for Vicka. This last revelation, which is the longest, has been recorded in three notebooks with a view to publication, when Our Lady will authorize it, under the responsibility of the priest which she has already chosen.

These revelations are for the moment, still more obscure than the secrets, and they leave us nonetheless perplexed.

In fact, history, the teacher of life, instructs us so. Several mystics of renown have already received some revelations, more or less detailed, about the life of the Virgin. After several instances in the middle ages, there was Mary of Agreda in the 17th Century; Catherine Emmerich in the 18th Century; and Maria Valtorta in the 20th Century. The publication of these "Lives" has always lent itself to criticism and objections. Mary of Agreda had been condemned by many universities. The work of Maria Valtorta: *The Gospel as it has been Revealed to Me* (original Italian title): *Poem of the Man God:* Editions Pisano, 10 volumes, more than 5,000 pages) was put in the index December 16th 1959. This was the last work recorded in the catalog (of approved texts) abolished by Paul VI toward the end of the Council. The prohibition was thus lifted, but not without problems. In a letter of May 30th, 1984, Cardinal Ratzinger stated precisely, that the reasons for placing it in the index guarded their value of dissuasion. Nevertheless, these reasons presented in *l'Osservatore Romano* of January 6, 1960, did not introduce any objective gravity, except for the apparent claim of its undertitle to be a *revelation* of the Gospel itself. One risks understanding a "fifth Gospel," more precise, complete, and less true, than the four Gospels, etc. This claim would be false and capable of being condemned.

Beyond the problem of authority, the "Lives" have always revealed their limits. Their chronologies are not in agreement on the date and the modality of the assumption, notably. Should one say that one of these "Lives" is authentic and the others are apocryphal? Or better, do they all err in different degrees, by approximation, whatever light they shed, and perhaps, by their fruits? One totally lacks, for the time being, a methodical study permitting an answer to these questions in a precise manner. But the "Life" revealed to Vicka would not escape the negative objections and reactions, which the preceeding ones raised.

THE FUTURE OF THE WORLD AND OF THE CHURCH

The messages, relative to the concrete future of the world and the Church, risk presenting the same limits and same problems. They were addressed:

> to Ivanka from May 22nd, 1983 to May 6th, 1985,
> to Vicka from April the 17th, 1985 to April 23rd, 1986.

The two seers have kept their secret in complete confidence. It would then be futile to stop there. Let us respect the hidden part of the iceberg, without departing from critical prudence, which is adviced by the Church on these matters.

Will these revelations by published one day? Will they be a beacon or a deception? They will not escape an answer and a discussion.

CHAPTER 6

The Signs

If we establish the relative importance of the secrets, shouldn't we also establish the relative importance of the signs? Of course, they are only signs. They have no other function than to return to reality, that is, to God. And it is this reality which counts. It is God which counts, not the fleeting ambiguity of the signs. These signs have exercised a considerable influence at Medjugorje and that merits attention. In fact, at the very time when daily preaching throughout the church finds so many deaf ears, why is it that so many Christians hear with so much joy, enthusiasm, and generosity, this same Gospel at Medjugorje? Why do they go to Confession *en masse* at a time when Confession is disappearing? Why do they profoundly change their lives? The reason is that these unexpected signs provide a remedy for the asphixiation of our critical abstraction. They arouse attention and restore conviction which had been asleep. God, who appeared distant, indifferent, indeed mythical, becomes present, credible and it is good news, whatever the relevance of the signs may be.

These extraordinary signs, which have never been lacking throughout the history of the Church, have had this function of awakening. It is in this spirit, that one should examine them.

A. THE APPARITION

The first sign is that of the apparition.

On the first day (June 24th, 1981), it was distant and blurred up there on the hill. This ambiguous sign made Ivanka and Mirjana flee; then Ivan, (the small one) while losing a sack

of apples. Fear vanished on the second day. The seers dared
now to climb the hill with extraordinary enthusiasm. It seemed
they had wings. They discovered then, a living presence near
and beautiful, no longer a hallucination which frightened, disunited, and destroyed them interiorly, but a real and tangible
person, respectful of their youth and of their rustic environment.
In spite of her fear, Ivanka had recognized the Madonna right
away, the first instant. Gloomy to see her on her return from
an escapade, it left her in a state of humiliation and remorse.

The Gospa had attracted them by her sweet tonic and therapeutic light. Just like at Lourdes, this light preceded her.[1]
She came in this light, which illuminated like an interior sun.
Christ himself illuminates the woman clothed with the sun,
according to Apocalypse 12.

The seers recognized the Gospa before she said her name.
Penetrated with this proof, they asked her for a sign for the
others so that they would be convinced:

"Without which they will call us liars, comedians, or drug
addicts." (L2-pg. 38)

They not only saw the Mother of the Lord, they saw Jesus
in her arms, on the first day, and almost at each feast of
Christmas. They saw His passion before Easter. Mary over-
whelmed them with her beauty, her smile, her affection, which
was immense and near; like that of a mother invested with
the very love of God, and for that reason, familiar like that
of a sister as much as a mother. It is the wonder of their
lives, a warm icon, a glance through which they see the invisible and transcendental glance of God.

B. THE CURES

The message of Christ, that of his apostles and their successors, that of Lourdes and other apparitions to this day, have been
accompanied by the signs of the power of God. There are, on
the first level, cures, signs which accompany the Gospel. Jesus,
who refused to give signs in the heaven, has multiplied them.

---

1. On June 30th, at the time of the apparition at Cerno, in sight of the distant
hill of the apparitions: "the light manifested itself before the Virgin, then
she appeared to us there (in the light), and she came as far as we were,
on a cloud," Maria declared to me August 14, 1986).

From When?

The first cure at Medjugorje was that of little Daniel Setka (three years old) who had septicemia since birth, and was not able to walk without assistance, or to speak. In this first case, it is not a case of a sudden cure, radical and total, such as the official records demand, but of a remarkable cure of which little Daniel's parents, and a number of witnesses, have given thanks.

Impressive, also, is the cure of Damir Coric, who had internal hydrocephelas, with a discharge of cephalo-rachidien liquid in the cavities of his cerebral ventricles. The surgical clinic at Zagreb had issued a somber prognosis. He was cured instantly at the beginning of the summer of 1981, at an unfortunately uncertain date because he spoke very little. A sick person cured by Our Lady in a Marxist country must be prudent. Damir Coric declined my invitations to testify on television, in spite of the grateful and shining memory which he has of the event. According to their legislation, religion becomes a crime if it ceases to be a private thing, if it becomes a public testimony. Whoever crosses this frontier takes incalculable risks.

"The Miracles of Numbers"

Since then, a flood of cures has continued. The parish records them objectively, on memoranda of a well-conceived model, and gathers the medical information which can be obtained.

I used to know this file, the existence of which the Bishop seemed to deny, although he had received it in the meantime. Also, when Dr. Frigerio, the person principally responsible for the Italian medical team, presented to me at Medjugorje in October of 1986, his program for recording the cures, I said to him:

"This recording has been in existence for years. It is only a victim of a conspiracy of silence."

Then I went to look for the file with Father Ivan Dugandzic, who discussed it with me with kindness. We examined it with Dr. Frigerio, in the small room which I occupied on the fourth floor of the belfry.

This file then listed 298 cures, spontaneously made public. It bears testimony to what Dr. de Saint-Maclou, (responsible for recording the many cures at Lourdes at the end of the 19th Century) called "The Miracle of Numbers." At Medjugorje the miracle is hidden in many ways, because the first two commissions were persuaded not to study this file, and some Yugoslavs, beneficiaries of the cures, had good reasons to remain most discreet. Dr. Frigerio then decided to study, first of all, the Italian cures, which were more freely able to be evalutated. "With that only, I will have more than four years of work," he said to me.

The phenomenon of the cures continues. The parish had registered 308 up to the 25th of June 1987. Still, this inventory of the cases made public at the presbytery is far from being complete. The most convincing cure, that of Diana Basile, does not figure among the 308 because she had been registered through other ways. At the time of this writing, the number of cases recorded has exceded 320.

Revising the Anachronistic Criteria

It is not a question of anticipating the medical study just begun. We verify only the universal fact, and it is not without interest. "The 'miracle of numbers' draws our attention," Dr. Mangiapan, president of the Medical Bureau of Lourdes, said to me, but the study remains to be done.

He has had the distinction of classifying and statistically evaluating the file of the cures, not officially recognized as miracles, which are preserved at Lourdes. This is over and above the 57 cases recognized officially by the Church. (I said 57 and not 64, as people continue to say according to an old error, because the first seven cures studied at Lourdes were not recognized by the Bishop, but only by Professor Vergez: ("Lourdes—Authentic Documents" Vol. 5 and 6).

Today, the unsuited criteria would seem to lead toward an elimination of the miracles, as Dr. Mangiapan has clearly observed in L'AMIL. Only one file currently remains waiting at Lourdes, in contrast with many which had formerly existed:—"the miracle of numbers."

The criteria for cures, judicially established on the principles of good sense by the future Benedict XIV in the 18th Century, were established at the dawn of our century, at a time when scientific rationalism prevailed, and they are tributaries of it. The scientists then said: "A miracle is rigorously impossible."

Their adversaries, at Lourdes and elsewhere, stated: "Let us prove only one miracle and science will fall to the ground."

Scientism and rationalism have today been overtaken by modern science. Apologetics does not dream any longer in looking for this kind of absolute geometric truths, which one tried to mobilize against the excessive claims from scientism.

The Church poses three questions for doctors:

1. Is there an illness, and what illness?

2. Is there an instantaneous, unexpected, complete, persistent, cure?

These two questions are well within the competence of their science. One adds to it a third question, which is conclusive and determinent:

3. Can this cure be explained?

This scientific official report of the unaccountable was the spearhead against scientism. The problem is that a positive response contradicts the basis of scientific research, indeed of scientific conscience. Modern science, which was established as such in the 16th Century, began to progress when it refused to give up before the unexplainable. Previously, it attributed it to irreparably unknown causes, or to God. "The Italian sickness" (the AIDS of the 16th Century) is a punishment from God," declared some scientific doctors. It was better to identify a germ. The short circuit through God was anti-scientific and detrimental to research in the coherent and verifiable order of second causes.

Doctors, then, are embarrassed with the third and final question which we pose to them. They answer it with evasions, which attempt to make things relevant or contradict their "yes."

"It cannot be explained in the current state of the art," they will respond in general terms.

But this restriction cancels out the positive response the Roman jurists have challenged for a long time, official reports which openly took into account these restrictions.

A testimony which includes such a loophole is without juridicial value, they would say, not without reason.

This alibi is no ground for prosecution. It is thus that the official reports of cures were followed for several decades in an ambiguity, in which one supports good as well as evil, but which contributes to the extinction of official reports of cures.

Signs and/or Wonders?

It is necessary, then, to return to criteria which would be more flexible, more in conformity with science, and with the very nature of the miracle, such as is defined by thoroughly understood scripture and theology. The Gospel designates them very often under the name of "semeia kai terata": "signs and wonders."

1. The word sign indicates that which means something other than self. Here, that which bears testimony to God. And that invites us to ask the following questions: Does the sign speak of God, His goodness and His mercy? Does it imply a message or language for the sick person who has been cured, for his environment, for the Church? Is it an answer to his prayer? Has the sign been fruitful for the sick person, his associates, or his witnesses? These questions are not indifferent. They are main things, and they are neglected.

2. The second word, "wonders," used by the Gospel, designates the territorialogical side of the miracle. It calls for another type of inquiry. Is this cure prodigious? Does it have an astonishing characteristic which leads astray, or contradicts the prognostication of reason? To what extent? Such are the questions doctors would have to answer. It would be necessary for them to give up asking a false question, or altering their skill and their process itself. Can it be explained, and/or make them state precisely in what sense this cure is unusual, extraordinary, prodigious, without science ever having to provide the mathematical proof for it?

It is here that the statistical argument, the argument of numbers (as the doctor from Saint Maclou stated), again finds meaning and importance. It is because the science of today, less ideological, less pretentious, less absolute, less hasty in saying "A miracle is impossible," begins with statistical arguments in terms of probability, including the physical sciences. Today's science has rejected absolutism. It integrates the concepts of relativity, uncertainty coefficients (Eisenberg), and the conclusions in statistical or probability terms.

In conformity with these more advanced criteria, it would not be necessary to reduce the number of official reports, or to shelve indefinitely the cures for which the smallest test is lacking, in the illusory concern of retaining only the absolute cure, the "cure crusher," against scientism. On the contrary, one would need to extend the information on the therapeutic effects reported officially at Medjugorje, as at Lourdes. The variety, and the details of the cures, do not permit one to reduce the cause to a simple factor, but invite one to take into account the gratuitousness, the freedom with which they bear witness, as well as an evident respect for nature on the part of the Creator.

The polarization over the official reports of the wonders, (and Dr. Mangiapan does not hide the fact that he would desire a revision of them) has diverted attention from the science immobilizing it, which is misunderstood independently from the sign aspect.

The official record of a "miracle," as a sign of God's action, belongs no longer to the doctor but to the Church. She judges it according to its religious context and its fruits.

The Crisis of Official Records

Cursiously, the exclusive polarization on the official medical records of the "wonders" make one forget the miracle as such, as a sign of God. When the International Medical Commission sends to the Bishop, the definitive judgment of a sick person who has been cured, established by leading authorities of world renown, the Bishop sometimes thinks that his task would be to control medical inquiry with local skills of lower quality, and sometimes to contest the conclusion scientifically established. The specific study of religious signs as such, has been forgotten more than once. The Bishop of Angers has fortunately broken with these troublesome practices in recognizing in 1979, the 64th and final miracle at Lourdes, the cure of Serge Perrin.

How To Get Out Of It?

The new Commission named to the study of Medjugorje can initiate its task in the understanding of this misunderstood evidence. The knowledge can only lead to three conditions: scientific clarity, Christian clearness, but also freedom of judgment. That is why Monsignor Franic asked that the Commission be formed at the international level. He did not succeed in this.

It is not a case of conducting a medical study, which comes back to the doctors. But it is necessary to situate the question and its criteria, and to mark out the study of the signs and wonders and their spiritual influence. It is vital because the cures have often been accompanied by conversion which one would have to take into consideration. They have transformed lives. There is the case of Agnes Heupel, cured in August 1986, whom I met at the end of December 1986 and the following April. They have transformed families, such as the case of Diane Basile, whose indifferent husband returned to a fervent and happy faith.

More Than 300 Cures

Without prejudging the scientific studies in progress, the situation is as follows:

The first two Commissions, established by the Bishop of Mostar, never made an inquiry on this subject matter. The Bishop was content to look among the sick, those who were said to have been cured at Medjugorje, or who had come to pray there for their cure, or those who had died. And he was able to find four of them, which he cites in different places of his *Positio* of October 30th, 1984. But that does not have great significance because Lazarus also is dead, and the sick cured at Lourdes and elsewhere finished by dying as well.

We have said that the parish has collected more than 300 cures. All that remains is to establish their files. To this effect, the Italian doctors of ARPA have given Dr. Antonacci a mission (April-June 1987) to establish a bureau of records and a plan of studies. Among the 300 plus cures inventoried, he discerned a dozen cases to be studied on a priority basis.

The case most studied is that of Diana Basile. Having a very serious case of multiple sclerosis for 12 years, she had most serious motor problems with four of her members. She was blind in her right eye, and had acquired a urinary and fecal incontinence, which had resulted in a skin disease of this entire area. She was cured instantly on entering the chapel of the apparitions on May 23, 1984. She experienced an interior warmth and saw, as in a film, some chapters of her life which had been completely forgotten. She was cured so completely that on the next day, she walked in her bare feet, without being carried, the 10 kilometers from her lodging at Medjugorje, and climbed the hill of the apparitions. Dr. Spaziante entered a file of 150 documents, including tests more numerous and more modern than the three multiple scleroses healings which were recognized at Lourdes. It is the most established case today. (For more details, we refer the reader to our "Medical Studies" p. 130-137). Agnes Heupel, cured on May 12th, 1986, also provided a very good file.

C. THE LUMINARY PHENOMENA

What do we think of the luminary and other phenomena which take place at Medjugorje?

They are often neglected or refused a priority, and one can understand that, because a number of exegetes avoid the reality of those which the Old Testament, and the Gospel, proclaim. They try to explain them, not as events, but as literary products of a purely symbolic order. And when Jesus promises "signs in the heavens," they ordinarily say: They are figures of semitic style which are to be interpreted allegorically.

The same principle causes the same thing to be said about the apparitions. The Bible narrates many of them, and exegesis usually explains them as the fabrication of a fictitious account destined to illustrate an idea inspiring fabrication. The writer, who is a believer, would fabricate a "theologoume-non," that is, an artificial account which expresses, in form of theological fiction, his faith and his spiritual experiences.

One excludes a premise that it can deal with the real experience of an apparition. Within this perspective, the message of the Annunciation would not at all be the account of an experience of Mary, but a fiction in a primitive community. But for Bernadette, Lucy of Fatima, and the contemporary seers whom I know (including Medjugorje), the apparitions are certainly not a literary phenomenon. They are an experience, repeated each day, and capable of being controlled by its precise physical effects: (change in cerebral rhythm from alpha-beta mingled in alpha pure), a fixation of the eyeballs, loss of contact with the external world, and insensitivity to pain, etc. For the seers, it is a real event, the most real one of their lives, ardous in other respects, and they testified to it with courage and realism, in face of intimidations from the clergy or the police. This was at the risk of their life and their freedom.

At Medjugorje, luminary phenomenon is also a fact, an experience. Some people try to attribute it to subjectivity, and this explanation can be justified in certain cases. A difficulty, however, arises for this type of explanation (which has been scaled down). Sometimes cameras record these phenomena. Or course, we have to be skeptical of these recordings for solar phenomena, since a part of the striking luminary effects can be explained through the effect known as back lighting (radions of the sun and bubbles), or by the unsteadiness of the photo electric cell pointed at the sun. It is important to distinguish the phenomena of an optical and mechanical nature from the perceptions unique to the witnesses of the facts. To this is added an annoying uniqueness. In a crowd's testimony of several "solar miracles," the majority see the phenomenon, but some do not see it, even though a camera recorded it.

Several types of phenomena have occurred at Medjugorje.

The Sun As In Fatima?

First of all, there were some "signs in the sun," which illustrate the word of Christ in Luke (21, 25), and confirm what was seen at Fatima October 13, 1917.

The first took place the 2nd, 3rd, and 4th of August, 1981, and several testimonies were written about it. These testimonies are reasonable and balanced. Those who have seen them have been surprised, have tried to overcome them. But this does not concern a scientific analysis at all.

Since that time, the signs in the sun continued to multiply consistently.

On this subject we need to eliminate the most frequent series. If one looks at the sun a little before it sets, one will normally observe an impressive but natural phenomenon. It can be seen as well in America, or in Britain (as I have seen it), as in Medjugorje. If one watches the sun near its setting (dazzling and not yet turned red), it ceases to dazzle at the end of a second. The center becomes dull in color, "like a Host," say those who are religiously struck by this sign, while the periphery stays luminate and radiant. Those phenomena do not require supernatural explanations at all. Some witnesses have interpreted them in a religious and fruitful manner, like an icon of the Eucharist and of the light of God. It is thus, a "speaking" sign. It is not a "wonder" at all.

But the solar signs, described or recorded on a video tape recorder, are far from being always reducible to a phenomenon which can be explained. They are produced at times, and under conditions, where this explanation is not applicable at all.

I collected important material on it (date, testimonies, pictures, video cassettes), and I am waiting for a team of specialists, both competent and open to the supernatural, who would be able to exercise a judicious judgment on the matter.

You cannot exclude that some signs in the sun have been given at Medjugorje, as at Fatima. Would they be explainable? Preternatural? Supernatural? To what extent? It is not my place to anticipate this conclusion. But honesty, which forbids premature favorable conclusions of a file which has not yet been clarified, forbids likewise, negative conclusions, a premise supported by explanations which are purely verbal in nature, as so often happens.

The Cross At Krizevac

Other phenomena have taken place around the cross at Krizevac, beginning October 22, 1981, then again on the 26th of October, the 19th of December, etc. (There is a list in the notes in the index, Chapter 3, Luminary Phenomenon.)

The phenomena includes forms which are relatively varied:

The cross disappears. Sometimes there is a disappearance, pure and simple.

Sometimes, the cross becomes a column of light which forms a "T" on certain days.

Sometimes it is, in a striking manner, a shining silhouette, a human form, feminine, resting on a flat globe. This icon in the heavens is analogus to the Miraculous Medal where the Virgin rests her feet on an earthly globe. Several video cassettes permit the study of this phenomena, for which no convincing explanation has ever been proposed.

Some have had on these occasions, a more distinct vision of Our Lady, to have distinguished her face; whereas for others, the small luminous silhouette, registered by the camera, is indistinct.

When Father Yanko Bubalo, armed with binoculars, sees along with 70 persons, a shining silhouette on the hill at Krizevac on the 22nd, 23rd, and 24th of November, 1981, he has the seers ask if it was really the Virgin who had appeared to them.

The seers received this response:

Why do you ask me, my angels? Did you not see me?
(L2-pg. 125)

One can quibble at this response.

Peace

To that may be added a different phenomena of equal value.

At the end of July 1981, many saw the word MIR (peace) written in the heavens of Medjugorje. A Polaroid picture had been taken of it, but it was confiscated by the police August 17, 1981, with a collection of other data. (K.58) And it is thus that the exact date of the phenomena, which took place between the end of July and the 6th of August, cannot be firmly established. But the witnesses are numerous, and were thrilled by this inscription of the message.

Stellar Signs

To that may be added the nocturnal signs, stars and lights not identified with other heavenly bodies, which have been seen and filmed repeatedly.

Picture Miracles?

Is it necessary to add here the file of pictures, some striking, which a number of pilgrims have sent me?

There are some thrilling effects of light, some pictures of the Virgin, more or less visible, more or less convincing, which the pilgrims of Medjugorje had the surprise of finding in their negatives.

This topic is very complex and would require the examination by persons competent in photographic and optical material, etc.

The most explainable are the pictures of cruciferous radiance, in which beauty can be enhanced through rainbow-colored bubbles. But one is dealing there with spectacular effects of light, which filmmakers in photographs of post cards know how to capture and edit, in mountainous countries. With respect to the rainbow-colored bubbles, which decorate the effects of radiance, the more one closes down the lens, the more effect can be produced, especially with the wide-angled lens which causes a larger defraction. A back focus diaphram stop is favorable to such optic effects. The statue of the apparition, which was venerated in the Church for a long time, and which, on orders from the Bishop was consigned to the former chapel of the apparitions until April 1985, presents some reflections which show a very beautiful crucifix on the dress of Our Lady. It is surprising that these reflections are produced with very different lighting (flash in front, or diffused surrounding light), and what cannot be explained, would call for a study. But the basic phenomenon prevents us, for the time being, from making an argument.

Part of these documents is somewhat convincing in any case, even without controllable scientific value. Some see on the wall of the chapel of the apparitions, or of the church, in their own perspective, the figure of Christ or the Virgin, the object of all their attention. But it is an ambiguous figure, such as one could find through the game of ink spots dear to Victor Hugo. These signs can talk to "believers." They don't have objective or conclusive value at all.

The picture of a sweet and beautiful Virgin in the style of the *Seicento* had circulated in 1984. It was the most aesthetic among those which people have sent me. But the seers said they did not recognize the Gospa, and the priests of the parish put an end to the career of this picture, which had been attributed to an Italian handicapped person, whom I was not successful in contacting.

What follows surprised me, and indicates the complexity of the phenomenon. In 1986 some pilgrims were returning from Cairo where the apparitions of the Virgin, visible to all, were sometimes photographed. They mailed me a picture authenticated by the Coptic patriarch there, but one could recognize in it a facsimile of a negative attributed to a handicapped person of Medjugorje well before the apparitions of Cairo had taken place.[2] The seal of the patriarch on this negative wanted thus, to guarantee that the negative came from a witness in good faith. But something was wrong in his testimony, if the negative, supposedly taken in 1986, came from that which circulated in Medjugorje in 1984.

Since, I have received beautiful negatives of this Virgin crowned with roses, but those had been taken, someone tells me, at the apparitions of Necedah (USA, 1950-1952), the object of a negative judgment by Monsignor John Tracy, Bishop of La Crosse, dated June 17th, 1955. In any case, the seers rejected this picture and several others. They say with pity: "The Virgin in much more beautiful. No relation."

It is necessary then to maintain a critical spirit, and not

2. This is not in relation to the apparitions at Zeitoun (1968), but those which began in Cairo in 1983 and became more frequent in 1985.

be so easily content with apparent guarantees. If God Can speak to a believer through the insignificant signs of his daily life, it would be grotesque to establish "as proof" these intimate communications.

It would be anti-scientific to declare these negatives to be miraculous, en masse, or to declare them explicable, without a rigorous and justified examination. But criticism sins as well, just like illuminism. Often it is through the same type levity, or lack of open minds.

These luminary phenomena have not stopped the critical spirit of the pilgrims at all. Those who discern illusions or exaggerations tell about them energetically. Those who have documented such phenomena speak generally without exhaltation, and in an objective manner, without overestimating their observation or their conclusion.

Briefly, even here, one must distinguish between signs and wonders.

The antennae which cause one to catch hold of the sign of God in daily life are not without value because *the heavens and the earth proclaim the glory of the Creator* (Coeli enarrant gloriam Dei: *Ps.* 19:2). And it is regrettable that we do not know how to discern the natural signs of this presence better than we do. Those who identify them excessively are closer to the truth than those incapable of seeing them, and ready to exclude them.

If contact is established with God in this way, it matters little whether the sign is prodigious or ordinary. Signs from Heaven are not mathematical proofs at all, nor magic prowess. The signs from God are generally discreet. They are given in a light and shade to human freedom, to the love of mankind.

As concerns the phenomena of Medjugorje, it is then necessary to know how to distinguish the scientific study rigorously conducted, before stating whether it is a "wonder" or a miracle. The language of God can pass through ordinary signs in prayer.

So as not to play only on the "wonder" scene, one dodges the religious phenomenon (in the etymological sense of the word, "religion" means "to bind again"). These mysterious bonds between God and man are nourished with signs now natural, and now supernatural, difficult to separate because the supernatural is not an element which is put on (like a hat on one's head). It penetrates nature and fulfills its potentialities.

It will be important to know how to distinguish the more or less probable proofs and the perception of a *language from God,* which permits itself to be seized by these discreet and varied signs.

D. PROTECTIONS

Under the heading of "protections," which many people believe to experience in their lives; for example, on being unharmed in an accident where their car is in pieces, there arises certain questions. Where is the risk? The coincidence? Providence? The miracle?

It is not one of the most important questions, but one cannot ignore it, or hastily reduce it to one of these mere terms.

CONCLUSION

Today's theologians are largely influenced by rationalism and the concern for mathematical proof, according to scientific presuppositions, which scientific progress has largely revised. For more than a half century, commissions of inquiry have examined apparitions of the last 50 years, and have not recognized any of them (except in Latin America). With difficulty, it could have been otherwise, since the criteria and presuppositions have been given.

"I think that it is in spite of the miracles, and not because of the miracles," Professor Pierre Mauriac of the faculty of Bordeaux, told me at the Mariological Conference in Lourdes. So have many others with him, and since then.

Vatican Council I had reminded us that miracles and signs are an important and normal vehicle of the faith. The systematic and suspicious elimination of all signs has been weakening for Christianity. Faith was nourished, up until now, with signs of all kinds of which the spiritual made a judicious discernment. Today, every positive judgment seems forbidden, is ridden with guilt or ridiculed. But a faith which refuses signs (faith without religion) becomes, very often, asphyxiated. The rational animal, which is man, has a congenital need of tangible signs.

There remains the sacramental signs. These are natural signs. Christ has chosen elements of the world: water of baptism, oil of unctions, gestures and human words. But the ecclesiastics, inclined to play the role of angels, have usually reduced these signs to a minimum. After the Council, one has eliminated the salt from baptism, has made different unctions disappear. The water of Baptism, in which one had previously been "plunged," (as the Greek word—baptizein [to baptise] means), is reduced to the parcimonious use of a few drops. Is it a compensation that here and there some icons begin to drip with perfumed oils at times today?[3]

Man, deprived of religious signs, looks for signs elsewhere; sometimes in fetishism, credulity, sexuality, a sign which is easily accessible.

"He who wishes to be the angel, becomes the beast."

The spiritual angelism of so many Christians, be they priests or theologians, has sunk in compromise, where the protagonists of a "faith without religion," very often slip. It is a move backwards, because the religious signs, such as were received in the monasteries or the novitiates by spiritual people endowed with judgment, were received with a justified observation in accordance with the essential, and often in the humor of God. God does not lack humor in His familiarity with man. He gives Himself to him without reserve, and this treatment is not lacking in Medjugorje.

One finds today, not only a climb of the irrational in a rationalistic civilization, but a return of signs among Christians. That explains, in part, the interest which Medjugorje and other apparitions arouse.

After excessive weaning, Heaven seems to come to the aid of those who are hungry, and many begin their lives again, thanks to the aid of these signs. We shall then keep this file open with the required prudence in waiting for qualified specialists capable of verifying them with the same seriousness as the medical aspects of the esctasies.

---

3. The miraculous icon of Mary, Gate of Heaven, and its replicas. But the icon of Damas spread an oil of olive, which was not perfumed.

Another series of facts posed a question: Does God defy the *wisdom of the wise* at this point? (*1 Cor.* 1).

These documents reopen an apparently closed question. Does God show signs in the heavens and elsewhere? To what extent are these signs natural, providential, or prodigious, preternatural or supernatural?

PART II
The Teaching

R. Lejeune

The dates of messages cited, which are given in parenthesis, permit us to find the context in the chronological index.

CHAPTER 1

Mary—Educator

If these apparitions in Medjugorje had, as a goal, only to recall the Gospel, then just the first apparitions would have sufficed; plus a few weeks for the signs, (cures, bright phenomena, etc.) which awaken the spirits and dull hearts.

But the seers and those receiving locutions (Jelena and Marijana) continue to receive a number of messages which guide the prayer groups (Jelena, Ivan) and the parish (Jelena then Maria).

SOME OBJECTIONS

This fervor provokes a smile among the wise and the learned.

"These messages are banal, repetitive, nothing extraordinary. The fervor of the seers suffices to produce them," they say.

Most certainly, these messages do not bring anything extraordinary. But extraordinary is not the principal criterion which creates the value of a message or a sign. Its Divine origin is not measured by the lure of the extraordinary or the inexplicable. This would be the specific remedy of magic. The messages often repeat the same words: God, faith, conversion, prayer, fasting, peace, reconciliation.

A PEDAGOGY (Teaching)

These repetitions have, as their sole function, to make the substance of the Gospel enter into daily life: faith in God, conversion, prayer, etc.

The best criterion to appreciate them is neither the extraordinary nor even the novelty, but the fruits, which are ample and marvelous. It concerns a teaching, which gradually forms the seers, the parish, and the pilgrims. This chapter has as its objective to present this pedagogical dimension.

MESSAGE AND MATERNAL RELATIONS

Banality and repetitiveness, which is criticized, have another explanation. A comparison at the human level will help one to understand. Let us suppose that a psychologist, concerned with the study of the relations between mother and child, takes the trouble to record everything which a mother tells her child during the first three or four years of its life. These recordings would last thousands of hours, and their transcriptions, some tens of thousands of words, from the first internal communication of the mother and the child until the first stuttering and dialogues. On reading these elementary notations, the wise and the learned would say, "All that is banal, insignificant, totally repetitive, uninteresting."

And yet, without this daily and banal dialogue, the baby will never learn as an adult. There was a tragic experience in the 30's. The unilateral polarization on species led to the establishment in America of model clinics where babies were raised under a glass bell, cleaned and nourished by hospital nurses wearing masks and gloves. The experience was a disaster. They died like flies or became idiots for want of affectionate contact, deprived of language and human relation. It became necessary to eradicate these methods and to provide each infant with a nurse, who obtained for him, maternal contact necessary to his development (kisses, caresses, scoldings) because affection, love and contact are as essential to life as are milk and bread.

The insignificant prattle of the mother with her infant arouses and establishes the very fundamentals of all human life. Through this daily contact (both physical and verbal) the infant learns to recognize others, to communicate with his equals. The first "equal" is the mother, who has made her child to her image. She teaches him how to smile, to talk. He learns, thus, her language—maternal, the only language that he will speak without an accent. And no professor, be he qualified and well-armed with perfected methods, will ever attain, except in the rarest occasion, such perfect results. Dialogue will also mold the child to all kinds of customs, rules and practices, which will remain the basis of his human life.

Such is the marvelous role of mothers (so forgotten by certain feminism)[1]. This is most indispensible in this world and what establishes the human quality of each child ("accomplished in communicating by age four," say the psychologists).

A KEY WORD: TO EDUCATE (educere)

It is with the inexhaustible patience of a mother, that Mary undertakes the education of the seers beginning June 25, 1981; then that of the parish, beginning March 1, 1984.

The key word here is "educate." It came into existence at the end of the 14th century coming from the latin "educere" used by the Vulgate in *Jn.* 19:3: *the Good Shepherd "leads His sheep out."* The word "educate," created from that time, has since been replaced with other terms ("instruct" or "form"). In that time of crisis, when the traditional values were hardening or the morals were relaxing, and when skepticism was expanding, a monk created this word like a program, facing the anguish of the time, the black death which decimated Europe. The word "educate," then, has been created beginning with Christ, the Good Shepherd, who leads his sheep out of the darkness toward the light, out of sin toward a life of grace, out of the grasp of Satan toward the freedom of the Kingdom, out of the conditions of an orphan toward that of a child of God, a son and daughter of the Father of the Heavens. Jesus burns with the desire to lead all souls to His Father.

There is only one teacher, the Divine Shepherd. When His disciples carry out instructions they do it in the name of Jesus, in His place. The Christian teacher is one by delegation. At every moment, in every circumstance, he is moved by the Spirit of Jesus.

Thus it is well that Mary acts in displaying her efforts of

---

1. A certain American feminism fails to recognize and fights this essential dimension of women. The feminine model, they say, is not maternity, it is homosexuality, it is abortion, the liberator of women.

teacher at Medjugorje. To educate the seers and the parish is to lead them to her Son. Her maternal voice which counsels, exhorts, beseeches, reprimands and encourages, *borrows* it from Jesus. Likewise, her hand, which blesses. Likewise her heart, which loves. Mary has only one goal, *Pray so that my Son will triumph*. (Sept. 13, 1984).[2]

Every form of education presupposes a pedagogy. If education is walking side by side with the Good Shepherd and His sheep, pedagogy (teaching) is the way in which the Shepherd leads it on this itinerary, the method used to "educate it."

—

2. The dates of all the messages cited, which are given in parenthesis, permit us to find the context in the chronological record which appears on pages 149 to 298.

CHAPTER 2

Prayer

At the heart of the educational plan: Prayer!
It is in walking alongside the Good Shepherd that one gets to know Him. The Shepherd and His sheep move together, hearts beating in love. Through prayer, the sheep are united to the Shepherd. To pray is to talk with God. It is to enter gradually into His intimacy until there is total, filial, abandonment. It is to imitate Jesus in the absolute need of prayer, in which life attests. Isn't it also astonishing that prayer is found in the very heart of the educational plan of Mary? *Pray,* she repeats constantly. *Pray, I will take care of the rest.*

All arguments aside, Mary has this distressing, decisive word: *Pray, I don't know anything else to tell you because I love you.* (Nov. 15, 1984). She states one of the reasons for her presence in Medjugorje: *I have come to earth in order to teach you to pray with love.* (Nov. 29, 1984). It is likewise the reason for the length of time of this presence: *You will understand why I am visiting you for such a long time. I want to teach you to pray.* (June 12, 1986).

PEDAGOGY OF PRAYER

Pray with love, says the Holy Virgin. What does that mean?
When one asks a favor, or thanks a loved one for some good deed, or praises an artist for the beauty of his work, one would not do it with indifference, absent mindedly, without feeling deeply within himself the very sentiment that he has expressed. The request, gratitude, or praise, demand the participation of the heart, the place where the human being

83

becomes involved completely.

To ask, to thank, to praise while in prayer, is to have access to the God of love and mercy. Can this intimacy be anything else than an outpouring of feelings and of warmth? To pray with love is an act similar to the secrets of the wife for her beloved husband. It is like the prattling of the little infant who is very happy on the lap or in the arms of his mother. To pray is to call on God for help in time of suffering, and to send Him a cry of distress.

Now, what does the believer often do when he prays? In "reciting" a prayer, his mind wanders elsewhere. In his dialogue with the Lord, he remains distracted, unconcerned, impersonal. He does not know what to say to his Creator. A number of the faithful are content with "reciting" some prayers or even refrain from praying at all. *Many people do not pray, they do not know what to say when they pray.* (Jan. 15, 1984). Or, they just keep asking for some favor: *One prays erroneously, in only asking for material favors.* (June 7, 1984). Worse still, is if one remains indifferent. And, in our relationship with God, to refrain from praying has its consequences: *Through their indifference, many persons destroy prayer and peace.* (June 26, 1986).

In order to "pray with love, to pray with the heart," there is only one way: "The Holy Spirit, who prays in the faithful. He is the fountain of water gushing forth through eternal life." (Vatican II, Lumen Gentium 4).

Pray so that you can receive the Spirit of truth, who will inspire the spirit of prayer. (June 9, 1984). Mary requests to the seers that they follow this way: *Do not cease to pray to the Holy Spirit,* she repeats. (Jan. 2, 1984). Sometime previously, she summarized in a vigorous way the benefit of this prayer. *Pray to the Holy Spirit. Those who have the Holy Spirit have everything.* (Oct. 21, 1983). From the spirit of prayer, from this gift of the Spirit of Love comes forth the prayer of love, par excellence. It comes forth more freely in union with Mary:

> *Consecrate yourselves to the Immaculate Heart.*
> *Abandon yourselves totally. I will pray to the Holy*
> *Spirit, pray to Him yourselves.* (Aug. 2, 1983).

Our Lady invites us to a prayer of our entire being, body and spirit. For the seers who gazed upon her, Mary expressed herself with great dignity. Each time that she says the "Our Father," she raises her hands with palms open toward Heaven. In her prayer of supplication, she gets on her knees, her arms raised. These gestures are a teaching. The body must participate in the sacred act of dialogue with the Creator. The language of the body magnifies the love of interior exchange between man and his Lord. In return, prayer represents a service for the body. The brain enters into alpha rhythm, that of the repose or rest for our being, of contemplation, of interior peace. It is that which Mary says in her message, in these words: *What is most important for your body is prayer.* (Dec. 22, 1983). Or yet, *With prayer, body and soul find peace.* (Feb. 4, 1984).

She stresses that prayer is not a matter of quantity: *I do not need a hundred or two hundred Our Fathers. It is better to pray one, but with the desire to encounter God.* (March 9, 1985). Above all, to pray is to contemplate God, to enter into His presence.

PRAYER OF THE HEART

Prayer through love, which Mary teaches us, can be silent adoration, mute contemplation, or a spontaneous movement of the soul. It can use every liturgical or traditional form of prayer to express itself. It can be the Eucharistic prayer or that of the Rosary; community prayer or phrases of repeated chantings as in the Christian Orient.

Mary uses the expression: "Prayer of the heart." *I invite you to prayer of the heart, do not pray in routine fashion.* (May 2, 1984). A little later she returns to it more vehemently: *I invite you again to prayer made from the bottom of the heart. Let it become your daily bread* (May 30, 1985). It is bread of the body, and bread of the soul.

Above all, Mary uses the word "heart" in its Biblical meaning. Through this word, which reappears *hundreds of times,* Scripture defines man in his capacity to express feelings and to allow himself to be guided by reason, which is enlightened by the faith. The heart is the place of the knowledge of good and evil. It can, alas, "harden" (*Ex.* 7:22), transforms itself into "rock" (*Ezech.* 11:19). It is to the "heart" of Israel that the Lord speaks in the desert. *It is in her heart, that Mary, retained...and meditated on the events.* (*Lk.* 2:19; 2:51).

In prayer of the heart, the entire being vests itself in the joy and the sorrow, the supplication and the action of grace or praise. Body and soul! At Medjugorje, Mary gives the perfect example of this prayer, when she speaks to her Son, on her knees, with arms raised and hands turned toward Heaven, in a gesture of imploring.

These effects of the prayer of the heart are irresistible: *If you pray with the heart, every obstacle will disappear. Conversion will be easy for all those who want to receive it.* (Jan. 23, 1986). Just like the rain which comes and makes the earth fertile, likewise, man will open up to God, thanks to a prayer which has come from somewhere else. A just person can save a city which has floundered in sin. Prayer of the heart pours forth from the bosom of the Church, militant with such power. It is so indispensable that Mary, Mother of the Church, goes so far as to stress her own helplessness if she is not supported by the prayer of her children: *Without you, I cannot help the world. Let your prayer come from the heart.* (Aug. 28, 1986). Helplessness likewise, for the needs in the parish: *Without your prayer, I cannot help you, so that the message which the Lord has given me for you will materialize.* (Oct. 23, 1986).

What is prayer of the heart to us? It is not necessarily a prayer which involves feelings. It can be pure commitment of faith, an act of the will, a desire to dialogue with God, without being carried by an emotional impulse. Some saints have "prayed with love" while they crossed the desert. (The night of the senses.).

The Christian Orient possesses an old tradition which is called precisely, "the prayer of the heart." They are not trying to express themselves through a diversity and beauty of words, addressed to God, but of conversing freely with the Creator like the child with his father. The person who prays limits himself to repeat untiringly one invocation, inspired by the cry of the blind man who asked Jesus to cure him. (*Lk.* 18:38). In talking through the beads of a cord with a hundred knots, and in following the slow rhythm of breathing, these words execute to perfection, one by one, as dew drops:

"Jesus Christ, Son of God, have mercy on me, a sinner."

At the hundredth knot, the rosary begins again. This prayer of the heart, also called "the Jesus Prayer," repeated some thousands of times every day, ends by permeating the entire being. The later is immersed in a profound eternal peace. At times this peace, this long repose of the human being, is crossed by an intense, indescribable joy.

The pious Oriental tradition of prayer of the heart goes back to the sixth century. Those who practice it proclaim its marvels. It was practiced originally in the monasteries of Sinai. However venerable it may be, it is not the only form of prayer of the heart. Another method consists in repeating slowly during long moments, likewise to the rhythm of breathing, the names of the most Holy Trinity in the primitive language which was revealed to man: "Abba, Jeshova, Rouah," (Father, Jesus, Spirit). In the prayer, it begins with the name of the Spirit, because, *No one can say Jesus is Lord, if it is not through the Holy Spirit (1 Cor.* 12:3). The name of the Spirit is followed by that of Jesus repeated as in a celestial chant. This name alone opens the way leading to the Father of the Heavens; in fact, *no one comes to the Father except through Me. (Jn.* 14:6). Through the names of the Most Holy Trinity, alternating in the secret garden of the soul like the sun and the heavy shower, the individual ascends up to the very heart of God, to the place where love becomes fire, in order to communicate itself with all of Creation.

There you have two forms of prayer of the heart, among others. In summary, every prayer springs forth from an authentic faith. Every prayer which subscribes itself to the affectionate and trusting dialogue of the creature with its Creator, to moments of peace and joy, even spiritual dryness and pain and depression, merit the name of prayer of the heart.

THE ONLY WAYS OF PEACE

Mary constantly insists upon the extraordinary effects of prayer inspired by love. From the beginning, she speaks of this invincible force. *Through prayer, one obtains everything.* (Feb. 1, 1982). To a world in conflict, she shows the way, the access to the precious good, which it is so lacking. *Prayer is the only way to peace.* (Oct. 29, 1983). Negotiations, conferences, international meetings are, of course, useful. But they will not lead to peace, nor even bring us together, unless they are accompanied by prayer of the people of God.

No peace without prayer. (Sept. 6, 1984). It is the same with respect to the plan for individuals. Mary asks the seers to pray, because she desires to see, *a great love, a great peace flourish in them* (Dec. 12, 1983). It concerns the entire being, not only the spiritual dimension. *With prayer, soul and body find peace.* (Feb. 4, 1984).

Prayer is, after all, the universal remedy. With what insistence does she communicate this to the parishioners? *I feel pressed to address to you, this invitation. Pray! Pray! In prayer you will find the solution for every situation, even if it is unsolvable.* (Mar. 23, 1984). It is prayer that gives life. Jesus is life. And when Jesus lives in the heart, how can an unsolvable problem remain there? *Draw your life from prayer,* (Jan. 27, 1984), she recommends to the seers. She likewise invites them to pray so that Jesus, *May be born again, not in a manger, but in your hearts.* (Jan. 5, 1984).

Prayer is not a matter of available time, reserved for hours of rest and freedom. Regarding the great tasks in the fields, to which the inhabitants of Medjugorje devote themselves until they are exhausted, Mary gives the parishoners some exceptional advice: *Prayer will be joy and repose for you.* (May 30, 1985).

The word, joy, she also uses in relation with prayer. The reason for this is simple: *Prayer is the joy of an encounter with the Lord.* (Aug. 14, 1986). She herself, is very happy to share the joy of her children in seeing her efforts bear fruit. *I received your prayers joyfully.* (Feb. 23, 1984). *I am happy because of your prayers,* she repeats to them. (Apr. 4-10 and Apr. 28, 1984). Above all, happy to see her action succeed, she said: *Rejoice, a part of my plan has been realized. Many are converting.* (Mar. 23, 1984). To the entire parish community, she gives this astonishing, if earthly, message and which is necessary to grasp in its heavenly perspective: *When you pray, you are very beautiful. You resemble flowers after a snow, vivid with beauty in their indescribable colors. After prayer, you display better before God that which is beautiful in you, in order to please Him.* (Dec. 18, 1986). It is a mysterious transfiguration, which escapes the limited range of our senses.

A "CATHOLIC" PRAYER

Since prayer is a dialogue with God (to whom one owes everything, and from whom one expects everything), Mary teaches the seers and the parish the way to pray as an intercessor, which one can associate with prayer. Her teaching takes place in the ecclesiastical tradition of universal prayer; it converges on sin and conversion. *The world has been caught up in a large whirlpool; it is swallowed up in its sin. I need your prayers so that it can be saved.* (Feb. 17, 1984).

In her teaching on prayer, she is not happy with simply exhorting the seers, but she transforms everything into a prayer of supplication before God. The day of the Feast of the Immaculate Conception, she prays on her knees with extended arms:

My beloved Son, I beseech You to want to forgive the world its sins, through which You have been offended. (Dec. 8, 1981).

The Immaculate Conception, unique creature preserved from sin, extends her prayer to the dimension of the world. She invites her children to give to their prayer this same "Catholic" dimension: *Include the entire world in your prayers.* (Nov. 13, 1983).

Prayer is all the more fruitful because the instrument is more efficacious. It is humility which brings to prayer its full effectiveness. To the request of praying for peace, Mary joins that of attending to the humility of heart. (Feb. 10, 1984). She points out the road to approach: *You cannot become humble except through prayer and fasting.* Humility is very necessary for the success of the mission which Our Lady has confided to the seers. *The Spirit of truth is indispensable for you in order to transmit the messages as I have given them to you without adding or deleting whatever it may be.* (June 9, 1984).

Humility is a rare and precious gift, among others of the Holy Spirit. The Holy Virgin continuously returns to the dispenser of all gifts: *Ask for enlightenment by the Holy Spirit.* (Apr. 11, 1985). *Aspire to the descent of the Holy Spirit on you and for His outpouring in you,* she tells them a month later on the approaching Feast of Pentecost. (May 9, 1985). And in order that the graces, which have been obtained in abundance by the innumerable pilgrims, can be diffused beyond the parish without limit, she asks the parish community to pray, in order to be her witnesses: *Pray so that you can obtain the gifts of the Holy Spirit which you need in order to be witnesses of my presence here,* (Apr. 17, 1985), to be witness among others, through the unity of the parish. The Lord is very anxious for the unity of His disciples. He can only work through them as a community, when they are united. *Pray for the unity of the parish; my Son and I have special plans for it.* (Apr. 12, 1984).

Beyond the prayers for the Church militant, Mary also invites us to remember the Church suffering. The souls in Purgatory have more recently been present in the prayer of the faithful. Universally, we currently stress the solidarity of believers with those who suffer here, notably victims of injustice. It is indispensable and pressing prayer, but should not lead us to neglect the souls which are enroute to purification from those with which we are equally in communion. *Pray for the souls in Purgatory,* the Mother of God asks us. (Jan. 10, 1983). Vatican II has also strongly reminded us of this responsibility. (Lumen Gentium 51).

"PRAY WITHOUT CEASING"

At Medjugorje, the teaching of prayer calls for numerous precise details; both for times when it is convenient to devote oneself to it, and the moment to which one *must* dedicate to it.

At first, Mary is very demanding. She asks that prayer groups pray three hours a day, including 1/2 hour in the morning and 1/2 hour in the evening. (June 26, 1983). In May 1984, she told Jelena herself, *I know that every family can pray four hours a day.* And then to her objection, Mary responded, *That represents only 1/6 of the entire day.* She adivses us to pray before going to bed and explains the reasons for it (Oct. 30, 1983); to pray also before we begin a task or after we have finished it (July 5, 1984). She insists repeatedly on the virtue of prayer in the family unit, especially in the evening, and she asks us to pray for the conversion of sinners (Oct. 20, 1983 and Oct. 8, 1984). She rejoices when she says that prayer has taken root again in the homes of Medjugorje. (Mar. 9, 1982).

With respect to the form of prayer, Mary gives us some instructions. At least five minutes should be devoted to the Sacred Heart: *Every family is an image of it,* she adds (July 2, 1984); *meditate at least a half hour.* (Jan. 21, 1984). Often, she comes back to the virtues of the rosary (Jan. 27, 1984, Aug. 14, 1984, etc.). She expresses the desire that the recitation of the rosary be considered a responsibility to be accomplished, and a joy (June 12, 1986).

It is true that the most pressing requests are addressed to prayer groups, whose members have freely committed themselves, and in full knowledge of their cause. At the time of the establishment of the first prayer group, the Blessed Virgin made known on June 14, 1983, the rules to be followed with regard to prayer. They are as restricting as those of a monastic community.

On the contrary, when she mentions four hours of prayer per family, surely it is not four hours of formal prayer which she is talking about. It is a time of a conscious presence before God; a union of the heart with our Lord. That is possible in work, while driving a car, during meals, and even during moments of relaxation. Prayer does not necessarily have to be expressed through words. It can rely on the movement of the heart, a brief lifting of the soul (at the beginning of a task, for example) which consecrates it. The past practice of ejaculatory prayer responded to this need of direct and frequent contact with God throughout the day. Mary confirms the need of this kind of permanent prayer: *Let your day be only prayer and total abandonment to God.* (Sept. 4, 1986). She goes as far as repeating the very words of the apostle (*1 Thess.* 5:17): *Pray without ceasing.* (Jan. 1, 1987).

What this "pray without ceasing" means, Mary clarifies in her message of March 1, 1984: *To pray more, does not mean an increase in the amount of prayers, but a more intense desire for God.* In this sense, the "pray without ceasing" of the apostles means a permanent longing for God. However, formal prayer (said at precise moments during the day) ought to play a significant role in the life of the Christian. *You will not have an exact awareness of the value of prayer as long as you do not say to yourself, "now is the moment to pray." Nothing is more important at that moment and no one is more important than God.* (Oct. 1986). Three years earlier, she had already confided to the seers, *The most important thing in life is to pray.* (Dec. 27, 1983 and Dec. 28, 1983).

Important, likewise, is every person who prays: *You have forgotten that you are all important,* she reminds the parishoners (Apr. 24, 1986). That day, she stresses the eminent role of old people, who pray in the bosom of their families.

Regarding an obstacle mentioned by the seers, the Virgin comments, *Pray to me to take care of the rest,* (Feb. 3, 1984). In prayer, the Christian is aided by the Mother of God, especially in the prayer of adoration before the Most Holy Sacrament, (Mar. 15, 1984).

Yes, prayer must really be the daily bread of the disciples of Jesus. To pray is to recognize their helplessness and their poverty before God, but it is also to put the available Divine help into action. Many, many important events in the history of the world have come about because of hands in prayer, rather than hands which have been armed. Prayer is the sword of the spirit. And this sword is of fire. *I want to permeate you with prayer,* Mary tells us. (Jan. 23, 1984). It is a principle message of Medjugorje.

"I COME TO CAST FIRE ON THE EARTH" (*Lk.* 12:49)

The teaching of prayer, put into words by the Mother of God at Medjugorje, has produced exceptional results. It suffices to watch the visionaries lives, to begin to listen to their comments on prayer. Remember that these are young people taken "from the crowd" and not exceptional human beings. Young people nevertheless, who, during long years, have had the extraordinary privilege of being molded, formed, taught and insturcted by the Mother of Jesus. She has taken them at the level where they were and spoken words which they could understand and integrate into their internal universe.

Above all, over a long period of time, she has won over these six children and adolescents, effectively and patiently answering their questions (sometimes trivial and simple) like those which are asked of a mother by children their age.

She has used a progressive method. It has evolved from the daily concrete experience of the beginning, up to the ascetic and mystical spirituality of these later years. She has maintained a simple language accessible to everyone, the language of the Gospel. She speaks not to writers and doctors, but to children, and through them, to all those *who are ready to become children, in order to be able to enter into the Kingdom of God (Matt.* 18:31). She is a mother, full of care and of tenderness. A mother who, in need, does not lack firmness and even strictness at any one time. It is this same simple observation we must concentrate on in the messages of Medjugorje. What annoys a learned theologian in these messages is precisely its incomprehensible price—their humble simplicity, the role of virginal innocence with which they are clothed.

The maternal presence of Mary, and her words, are a matter of love. It is to original purity that love reduces everything. Love is never complicated. How many times this admirable mother pours our her Heart!

> *If you would know how much I love you, you would cry.* (Mar. 1, 1982).

I love you, you cannot love me as much as I love you, she continues to declare three years later, (Feb. 1985). She lives in the brightness of the Most Holy Trinity, who is LOVE. She still knows, however, that on earth love is a demanding asceticism, a rooting up of the old man attached to this world through all the fibers of his being. *I invite you to a greater sacrifice,* she tells the seers during Holy Week, *the sacrifice of love. Without love, you are not able to transmit to others your experience.* (Mar. 27, 1986).

In order to teach these young people in her ways, she needs time. That is the reason for the long duration of her stay on these high Dalmatian lands.

TO PRAY AS ONE BREATHES

The results of these efforts among the visionaries have been prodigious in the proper sense of the term. Here are some of their comments with respect to prayer (1984):

Vicka (born in 1964): "I recite the Rosary more than any other prayer though it makes me very happy to speak spontaneously to the Lord. Certain days I pray more, other days a little less. In comparison with the way that I used to be, I love to pray, and I say that I really pray from the bottom of my heart.

"In a very special way, the Virgin encourages us, during this period of Lent, to live deeply the way of the cross. If we do not do it well, she will tell us at once: 'Today, I am not happy with you. Try because you can do a lot better.' And above all she encourages us to continue on the way in which we have committed ourselves, and not to wait for her exhortations." (F2, p. 48-49).

Maria (born in 1965): "I do the housework, I take care of the sheep, I work in the vineyards and in the tobacco plantations. I try to find some time for my personal prayer. I take part in two prayer groups. But at this time, the Virgin wishes for us to meditate on the five wounds of Jesus. I do it with a lot of fervor. Every time that I pray, I try to have a crucifix near me. I gladly recite the rosary, but I prefer to meditate. I love all forms of prayer, but I prefer to read some verses from the Bible, and then to meditate. I feel that is exactly what I like.

"Every time that I do not want to pray, I think of Our Lady, then it is no longer difficult. Our Lady says, 'Pray.' If you would only be able to hear the way in which she says it, you would then be able to understand me perfectly." (F2, p. 55-56).

Ivan (born in 1965): "In the morning, I get up at 5:00. I pray for a half an hour. At noon, I pray for an hour. Three times during the week, after the evening Mass, we pray together in the prayer group until 9:00 p.m. During the other days, I withdraw to my room. I find relaxation in prayer.

"What helps me the most is the Bible. I read a passage or a Psalm, and I take great joy in meditating on it for a

long time. Often I stop on the word 'Jesus' or 'Abba.' I also
have some prayers which the Blessed Virgin has taught me.
I meditate on them likewise. When I pray, it is not I who
prays, but someone else who prays in me; Jesus.

"On praying with the Bible, I have had the experience with
the Lord, an experience which I would wish for all those
who pray. On meditating on the Bible, while fasting and in
doing penance, everyone can grow and lead a Christian life
full of reflection." (F2, p. 43-45).

Jakov (born in 1971): "When I wake up in the morning, I pray
a little bit; then I go to school. When I return home, and
also during the day, I pray. In the evening at home, we recite
the rosary, the seven Our Father, Hail Mary and Gloria. Then
five Our Fathers.

"At school, we all pray together. On Friday, our class re-
cites the rosary. (Prior to his entering secondary school).

"Prayer is never difficult for me. Sometimes, when there
are a lot of people here, I am distracted. But I try to be patient. Prayer is what is most precious for me in my entire life.

"I read a passage of the Bible, then I reflect. God gives
us His message and I have to meditate on it. After that, I
thank God for all that He has done. I think that all prayer
is a heart to heart conversation with God. I would really want
for all young people to pray. It is the most essential thing."
(F2, p. 51-51).

"SOME GREATER WORKS..."

What an agreement within the diversity of these testimonies! A rising call to prayer from a 14 year old youth to his
friends. A day of a young man 19 years old who adopts the
ritual of monastic life demanded by prayer. A 19 year old
girl who, already, has attained higher levels of spiritual life.
Another one, a 20 year old, very familiar with prayer of the
heart.

When Father Faricy, the American Jesuit, interviewed them,
they had already been under the direction of Mary for three
years. Under these conditions, one would say that the results
could only be exceptional. That has little regard for the freedom of the individuals. Surely, these young people had been

radically transformed by Mary. However, they have freely accepted to be transformed in this manner. And they paid a high price for it, through a rigorous discipline of life, self-denials and numerous sacrifices. But, on the contrary, this does not mean a life without joy.

Nevertheless, we might believe that such transformation is unthinkable, if it were not for the Mother of God herself who brought this about. She guided these young people on the road to conversion. Nevertheless, isn't it possible to apply to this situation, the words of Jesus, *Amen, Amen, I say to you; he who believes in me will also do the works which I do, and he will do even greater works because I go to the Father. (Jn.* 14:12).

In order to succeed in this apostolate, as Mary is on the point of succeeding at Medjugorje, one would have to fulfill three conditions:

1. Believe in Jesus;
2. Transpose in our own life the Gospel messages of Mary, which are markers on the road to sanctity;
3. Draw inspirations from the methods of instruction applied by Mary, including the teaching of prayer in the heart, itself an educational project of apostolic effort.

Prayer actually encounters its own end in itself. Through it, mankind finds his Creator. And the beloved Mother wishes for this encounter; *to be a source of joy for him who prays.* (Aug. 14, 1986). Through prayer, "The ecclesiastic community still exercises a true maternity, to lead souls to Christ." (Vatican II: Presbyterorum ordinis, 6).

The most immediate effect of prayer is the strengthening of faith. Mary insists on this aspect. *Prayer must fit into the daily life so that faith may take root.* (Sept. 8, 1981). Prayer and faith are interdependent. She reminds us that: *when one prays for a sick person, the most important thing is a solid faith.* (Feb. 9, 1982). It is an echo from her Son with respect to the daughter of Jairey, *Believe only and she will be saved. (Lk.* 8:50).

Consolidation of faith, likewise, becomes both the goal and the reception of the spirit and abandonment to God. *Open your hearts to the Holy Spirit and offer your life to Jesus . . . . so that He will strengthen you in your faith.* (May 23, 1985). Mary goes as far as to give a sign to a group of young people, among whom is Ivan, in order to strengthen their faith (end of August 1982).

MARY AND THE BIBLE

With respect to prayer, a special mention should be made concerning the Bible.

Mary calls repeatedly for the reading and meditation of Holy Scriptures. With respect to the prayer groups in particular, she says: *Have them read the Bible and meditate on it,* (Feb. 28, 1984). Less than two months later, she comes back to it with exceptional vigor. She uses the teaching process for a preliminary awakening of interest. *I am going to reveal a spiritual secret to you.* Her confiding of a secret has made their ears perk up, their hearts open up more willingly. *If you want to be stronger than evil. . . .* Who would not want to be, in the midst of such groups formed of ardent souls who are submissive in love, regardless of the demands! There is an urgency to prayer and intercession for Christians facing the devastation of evil in the world.

Mary continues: *Develop a plan of personal prayer. Take some time in the morning, read a text from Sacred Scripture. Anchor the word of God within your heart and try very hard to live it during the day, particularly in time of trials. In this way, you will be stronger than evil.*

Precise instructions, which nevertheless leave a good part to personal initiative—the content of the plan, and the choice of texts. And always, the same bursting forth of prayer from the heart. To anchor the word of God in the heart is to permeate it for your entire life, both its most significant aspects as well as those which are apparently insignificant. The word becomes our power and direction, the comprehension of the present, and a guide toward the future. Under the leadership of Mary, the disciple of Christ is an intimate friend of the Bible.

Mary gives two stipulations to the parishoners of Medjugorje: the daily reading of the Bible, and a place of honor reserved for the book of books within the household. *I invite you to read the Bible every day within the family. Display it so it will incite you to read and to pray* (Oct. 18, 1984). It is not a book for a shelve in the library or to be kept in the bottom of the drawer, but a sacred object, precious among others. Display it in an area which will give it its due importance, in the center of the house. Invite someone to use it every day.

Four months later Mary again expresses her concern for the spiritual growth of the family. She suggests two ways. *Every family should pray together and read the Bible.* (Feb. 14, 1985).

Man is free to receive or not receive the word of God. It is the same with the family to whom the Holy Virgin gives this advice. She also insists: *I wish, dear children, that you would listen to me and that you would live my messages.* Alas, it is not the same for some, and she expresses her sorrow over it. *The entire parish does not accept the messages and it does not live them. I am sad.* Simeon's prophecy did not only concern Mary's life on earth. (*Lk.* 2:34-35). The sword pierced her soul throughout the history of mankind, of which she is mother. The tears that flow in our time, from the humble statues and images of the Virgin, are a poignant reminder of it. The heart of a mother afflicted by the failures of some of her children is consoled by the generosity of other children. It is thus that in reading the Bible every day, and in anchoring the word of God deep in their hearts, Christian families can dry the tears and eliminate the sadness of the Mother of God, and of the Church.

We have seen to what extent the seers follow on their own. The pressing advice of Mary, concerning the daily attendance to the word of God in the Holy Scripture, is their constant companion.

CHAPTER 3

Fasting

Faith and prayer, rooted in the living tissue of the soul, causes the sustained ascent or climb toward God. Mary asked that prayer be associated with fasting. It is a Biblical reality, which has long been forgotten. Prayer and fasting are often found in the Scriptures like twin virtues, two stimulates of the spiritual life called to work in concert.

The messages of Medjugorje deal with the subject of fasting at least thirty times. It emphasizes the importance which Mary attaches to this practice of asceticism. The daughter of Sion reminds us of the spiritual experience of the people of Israel at the time when the law of God awakened their liberty, to make it a Holy nation of the alliance.

Where does fasting come from?

In ancient times it was practiced by philosophers such as Pythagore, Socrates and Plato. The reflection was particularly vivified. Different oriental religions practiced fasting like an ascetic act, the training of the spiritual athelete. One would find there the attachment, the vision, an inner search into the secret spheres of knowledge.

For Israel, fasting was something else entirely. It was a sign of repentance, auxiliary of the prayer addressed to God, sustinance in the preparation of an important mission. It bears witness to the dependence of man in rapport with God. In order for it to be agreeable to the Lord, fasting must be sincere, humble, discreet. It demands solidarity, acting with the oppressed and the poor. (*Is.* 58:3, 8)

Two types of fasting of long duration came about at decisive moments in the history of Isreal. Moses had to receive the tables of the Law and to seal again the alliance with the Lord. In these important circumstances, he gave himself up to a complete fast of forty days. (*Ex.* 34:28). At the end of this experience, his countenance reflected the Divine Light intensely. The same with Elias who fled into the desert. He found there the strength necessary to carry out his terrible mission—to restore the alliance between the Lord and the people of Isreal, which had fallen into a proud self-sufficiency and into paganism.

Jesus prepared himself for what was to lead Him to the paschal mystery, through a fasting of forty days, a sign of complete abandonment to His Father.

The first Christians prayed and fasted before undertaking important decisions: with the Church at Antioch, and at the moment of sending Paul and Barnabas on their mission. In the course of their journey, the two Apostles fasted and prayed with the newly founded communities at the time of their appointment by the ancients. Thus, the latter confided in the Lord. The Apostle Paul fasted frequently, from his very first mission. (*Act.* 13:2; *2 Col.* 6:5 and 11: 27).

Biblical fasting stimulates humility, hope, love and total abandonment to God. The fathers of the Church are witnesses of these effects. Saint Athanase summarizes them in these words: "It cures the sick, dries up bad moods, drives away the demons, expells evil thoughts, makes the spirit clearer, purifies the heart, sanctifies the body, and transports man to the foot of the throne of God. Fasting is a great force, it leads to great victories."

With varying results, fasting was maintained in the Church throughout the centuries. It fell into disuse in our time. Mary stresses this error: *Fasting has been forgotten in the bosom of the Catholic Church in the course of this last quarter of the century.* (May 1984). The Church has maintained but two symbolic days of obligatory fasting. One kind of fast remains very moderate with a "complete meal and a light meal."

In Medjugorje, Mary takes up the exhortation of the Angel to Tobias: *To prayer, it is good to add fasting.* (Tb. 12,8) In the second day of her dialogue with the seers the Madonna mentions fasting at the same time that she mentions faith, prayer, and reconciliation (June 26, 1981). These are the basic elements of her message. Following her invitation to do penance, fasting begins to be practiced in the parish, since the first weeks of the apparition. The question is then raised: "How does one fast?"

The best way to fast, Mary responds, *is on bread and water.* (end of August, 1981). This method of doing penitence deals with an old tradition in Hercegovina. "The Medjugorje Fast" spread from that moment on, among the parishioners of the village, and including the young people. From then on, in these succeeding years, through the intermediary of pilgrims who have come, this means of fasting has spread to a large number of countries. It is a means of communication of the message of Medjugorje.

A MYSTERIOUS POWER

A year later Mary expresses her gratitude for the effort which has been accomplished. She asks for perseverance in prayer and in fasting, then she adds: *May you wait patiently for the realization of my promises. Everything is unfolding according to God's plan.* (June 25, 1982). A few weeks later, she has a surprising message which should challenge the Christian conscience:

Prayers and fasting can prevent war and natural catastrophies. (July 21, 1982).

Neither prayer alone, nor fasting alone. Prayer and fasting together. A distant echo of an exceptional response from Jesus: *This kind of demon can only be driven out through prayer and fasting.* (Mk. 9:29; cf. Mt. 17:21)

In order to express the mysterious, extraordinary power of fasting, Tertullien wrote toward the end of the second century: "Fasting succeeds in taking away from God, a part of the mysteries which have been hidden from the eyes of men." (De Jejunio).

Mary's frequent appeals to fasting, her reminders of the extraordinary virtues of fasting, inspire a large number of people, who are listening to the messages of Medjugorje, to integrate weekly fast in their lives. "Friday on bread and water," has made the rounds throughout the world.

We cannot forget that fasting exists at both the physical and spiritual level: *True fasting consists in renouncing all sins, but one must renounce oneself and make the body participate in it.* (Dec. 1983)

All of 1983 was placed under the sign of fasting and prayer. On December 31, 1982, there was actually this special message for the year which was just beginning: *Pray as much as possible and fast.*

If Mary insists so much on fasting, if she has chosen it as a password for 1983, together with prayer, it is that she wishes to utilize its irresistible power toward a very precise goal: the conversion of sinners. Fasting, in effect, constitutes a powerful help in the efforts of Christians to lead the world to conversion. A means, however, totally neglected by a large number of them.

The world is sinking proudly in sin.

The latter drags it to the brink of the abyss. The urgency must be great in this year of 1983. On April 25, the Virgin beseeches: *Be converted.* In the message confided to Jelena, 11 years old, she uses the words "convert" and "conversion" twelve times. She insists: *I need your prayers and your penance.* A plague must be threatening humanity or at least a part of it. In this same message, Mary speaks of "punishment," a word which the rationalist mentality of this period rejects with disdain. *I will pray to my Son to spare you the punishment. Be converted without delay,* she adds in a very pressing manner.

Bible history—and a very short history—shows that "punishment" of a people has never been an arbitrary act of a vengeful God. It is always, and without exception, the logical consequence of individual and collective sins. Because of their enormity, they have attained the breaking point within the natural order of things in the "universal law," which is applied to mankind as much as to the vegetable and animal kingdoms. Just like a dam breaks at the moment when the pressure of the waters exceeds its capacity of resistance, in the same way the natural order of things bursts under the pressure of the cold and proud scorn by mankind of the universal law of God. This scorn of the natural order, a terrifying illness, has drawn from the recent apparitions a devistation possibly attained in the course of the next decade; catastrophic proportions surpassing the black death in the 14th Century.

Punishment is the logical consequence of the disordered state of man's morals. This natural dignity is immeasurable, because we are created in the image of God. (*Gen.* 1:26).

THE THURSDAY'S SACRIFICE

In the course of the year 1983, Mary encourages her children to fast for the conversion of sinners, because the disturbances of sin caused great threats which weigh on the world. At the beginning of the month of July, she asks for fasting twice a week, so that the major obstacle to the spreading of her message may disappear. On the 27th of July, she particularly invites the young people to do penance. It is a word which is hardly heard anymore in relation to youth, in a society where a boisterous, restless and superficial force extolls, without end, in favor of licentiousness and good times.

On October 29th, 1983 she encourages all those who follow her insistent advice; *If you pray and fast, you will obtain everything that you ask for.* Consequently, probably noting the spirit of egoism which ventures to introduce itself to some of them in the practice of fasting, she becomes more specific: *If you wish to obtain from the Lord a grace through your fasting, let no one know that you are fasting.* It is a direct echo of the words of Christ: *When you fast, groom your hair, wash your face so that your fast may not be known by man, but by your Father Who is present in secret. And your Father, Who sees in secret, will reward you.* (*Mt.* 6:16-18).

With her celestial glance, the Mother of God, and Mother of the Church, gazes at a garden in bloom, a multitude of souls who in obedience to her repeated requests, devote themselves to prayer and fasting. *I wish that your hearts blossom through prayer and fasting,* she says January 17, 1984. She permits the addition of a third day of weekly fast to those who are particularly eager to fulfill her wishes.

On Thursday, March 1, 1984, a memorable day when she gave her first weekly message to the entire parish, she expresses a new wish—that everyone try to make a simple sacrifice on Thursday, a gesture such as giving up smoking, drinking alcohol on that day, avoid getting angry, giving up television, or try to be particularly kind.[1]

In brief, it is a return to the ancient asceticism of "sacrifice." It is something we have abandoned in teaching and in the pastoral, in order not to create frustrations, or going against the current of modern practice which is the result of a hedonistic and materialistic vision of existence. The sacrifice freely agreed to, and offered with love to the Lord for the same reason as fasting, gives evidence to our dependence in relation to God.

Mary returns consistently to the teaching of sacrifice. It is thus that at the beginning of Lent, 1986, she says to the parish: *May Lent incite you to change your life. Begin right now. Disconnect the television, put aside useless things. I invite each one of you to conversion. This is your time.*

Every customary practice is simply sheer habit. It is the same with fasting. One finishes by getting used to it, and frees the spirit. On September 20, 1984, Mary reminds her children of this demand: *Fast with the heart and not through sheer habit.* And she adds an unprecedented form of fasting, and indeed remarkable at first sight—the fast of thanksgiving. She asks the entire parish to fast, *To thank God for having permitted me to stay here a very long time.*

On January 10, 1985, she once again thanks the entire parish for the sacrifices which they have agreed to do. She adds: *Offer them with love.* This dimension of love makes the sacrifices more precious in the sight of the Lord; just like a wedding ring set with a diamond increases its price. That is what she calls: *living the fast* (Sept. 26, 1985). The same day she reveals the exceptional, even astounding importance, attached to fasting. *Thanks to fast,* she says, *You will realize*

---

1. In December 1983, Mary put us on guard against this modern form of leisure at home: *Before anything, abstain from television programs. They represent a grave peril for your families. After you have seen them you are not able to pray anymore.*

God's plan in Medjugorje. And she adds these touching words:
That will be for me a great joy.

A WEAPON OF LIGHT

Mary continues unceasingly to involve her children in the
asceticism of penance. The stakes are very high. Prayer, fasting and sacrifices are some irresistible weapons of light, which
Christians can set up against the powers of darkness, who
are at work throughout all of humanity.

Fasting is truly a privileged weapon of light. It is up to
us to discover it. What Saint Athanase has written about it
has no grandiose purpose. It is necessary to take it literally,
as we previously stated. Fasting leads to a purification of the
soul, of the spirit and of the body. For the soul, it arouses
an invincible force which the Christian, in the example of
Moses and Elias, can use in the re-establishment of the alliance between God and men. Thanks to fasting, unsuspected
new perspectives of renewal open up for people as well as
for nations. The Lord God of Hosts can then lead to combat,
a people who pray and who fast, for the restoration of the
alliance. He needs instruments pure and simple like the blade
of the sword. Fasting forges such instruments.

As for the body, fasting creates the conditions necessary
to its regeneration, particularly a fast which is prolonged. The
organism absorbs the reserves accumulated in the tissues; it
is able to benefit from a thorough cleaning. The cells are
purified, the blood is cleansed, the skin rejuvenated; thus the
body support of the spirit permits the latter to function better.
In effect, the spirit becomes more lucid, memory improves,
judgment is sharpened, and the perception of things darkened
by the bodily weight, becomes more beautiful and productive.

Fasting is an act of asceticism. That is why it is necessary
to have humility rather than personal force: *Be humble through
prayer and fasting.* (Feb. 10, 1984) But once one has entered
the rigid edifice of fasting, one discovers there magnificent
marvels. It is necessary to have experimented, in order to
be able to admit that fasting is, in reality, a feast for the body
and the spirit, a feast which prepares another. "Purify and
regenerate your body through fasting," said Soloviev, "in order

to better prepare you for the transfiguration of the universal body." Fast, in order to help save the world, for this is a feast of inexhaustible love.

At Medjugorje, a new appeal resounds for our era, the old Biblical invitation to fasting, matched with fantastic promises:

> *Pray and fast, and you will obtain everything that you ask for,"* (Oct. 29, 1983). *Fast and God's plan will be realized.* (Sept. 26, 1985).

God has, in fact, a plan for humanity. Its realization is not automatic. It needs the cooperation of all His children. It needs an active cooperation, submissive to the injunctions of the Spirit, and accompanied by prayer and penance. For it deals with a struggle.

CHAPTER 4

Against the Power of Darkness

THE WOMAN AND THE DRAGON

A bitter struggle against the forces of darkness occurs throughout the history of mankind. Having started from the beginning, it will last, the Lord has told us, until the last day. (*Mt.* 13: 36-43). "Engaged in this battle, man must fight without ceasing. . ." (Vatican II, Gaudium et Spes, 37).

In effect, this struggle will cease when the Son: *will restore royalty to God the Father, after having destroyed every domination, every authority, every power. For it is necessary that he reign until he has subjected all his enemies under his feet.* (*1 Col.* 15: 24-25).

In the meanwhile, every human being is drawn into this merciless struggle; and he freely chooses his field. Jesus was there before us. He has personally attacked Satan and his legions. He has conquered the *Prince of this world (Jn.* 12:31); he, who continues to be against mankind. A large number of people permit themselves to be lead astray by him, whom John the Evangelist calls, the *father of lies (Jn.* 8:44), *the murderer of man since the beginning. (Jn.* 8:44).

The New Testament reveals the tricks of this personal and invisible being, completely devoted to evil and seeking without respect, the loss of man, who is the image of God. Scripture indicates to us likewise, the means by which we can protect ourselves from the attacks and snarls of Satan.

At Medjugorje, Mary becomes the echo of the warnings of the Bible. Combat against Satan is so important for her that she mentions it some forty times in her known messages.

Just shortly after the beginning of the apparitions, she places, through a powerful sentence, the present day importance and seriousness of the confrontation between the Light and Darkness:

> *A great struggle is about to unfold, a struggle between my Son and Satan. Human souls are at stake.* (Aug. 2, 1981)

In the modern world, there is disbelief concerning the personal existence of Satan, "the Adversary"; a disbelief shared by some theologians and some priests. Mary affirms vehemently that *Satan exists. He seeks only to destroy.* (Feb. 14, 1982).

In his strategy for the conquest of souls, the Devil launches some punctual offenses aimed at certain places and particular individuals. It is thus that Mary warns the members of prayer groups: *Be on your guard. This period is dangerous for you. The Devil tries to lead you astray. Those who give themselves to God will be the object of attacks.* (July 26, 1983). Three weeks later, the very day of the Assumption, she calls attention to the particular targets aimed at: *Satan is furious against those who fast and those who are converted.* (Aug. 15, 1983). It is precisely at this time that, "the Medjugorje fast" began to spread, through the pilgrims, to several countries. It was in 1983 that Mary had given it its slogan—*prayer and fasting.* (Dec. 31, 1982).

"The Prince of this world" aims not only at persons, but also at communities of life and of faith, the parish among others: *Satan attacks the parish insidiously; do not fall asleep in prayer.* (Jan. 17, 1985). *Satan is very active these days in the parish. Pray. . .that every trial of Satan be transformed to the glory of God.* (Feb. 7, 1985). A week later, a new warning (Feb. 16, 1985). Consumed with envy, the Devil is set on attacking those with whom the joy of Christ resides: *You have savored these days, this sweetness of God; thanks to the renewal of the parish. Satan attacks you violently in order to tear away this joy.* The feelings which reign there, where he is at work, are those of trouble and confusion. *Every trouble comes from Satan.* (Aug. 25, 1983). *Satan is enraged against you. He seeks above all to plunge you into confusion.*

THE OASIS AND THE DESERT

Mary designs the most effective weapons for the combat against the Powers of Darkness. First of all, there is prayer: *I invite you to engage in battle against Satan through prayer. Because you know he is active, he also wants to intensify his action.* (Aug. 8, 1985). *It is only through prayer that you will conquer the influence of Satan, wherever you may be.* (Aug. 7, 1986). In this regard, on the Feast of the Ascension, Mary stresses the value and the function of the Eucharist: *I invite you to a more active prayer, more particularly, to Holy Mass. I wish that the Holy Mass may be for you an experience of God.* (May 16, 1985).

To have recourse to prayer is an act of free determination. From this choice emerges the fight against Satan, where prior to that, there was passivity before his schemes: *I am with you,* says Mary, *but I cannot deprive you of your freedom.* As a result, prayer produces the flight of Satan. *Pray that Satan will withdraw from this parish and from every person coming here.* ("Here" is the parish of Medjugorje.) *I love this parish.* she added. *I will protect it with my mantle against the works of Satan.* In the final analysis, it is the intensity of prayer which succeeds in driving away the evil one. *Pray more, then Satan will be kept removed from this place.* (Sept. 5, 1985).

In this struggle, the rosary is a formidable weapon. *Arm yourselves against Satan with the rosary in hand.* (Aug. 8, 1985). Mary advises also to have recourse to the sacramentals, blessed objects worn on the person and placed in the homes. These objects have somewhat fallen into disuse in our times; causing reservation and even a kind of distain. Only icons escape this rejection.

Holy objects do not have any power in themselves. They represent several aspects of the paschal mystery, of the death and resurrection of Christ, source of all holiness. The human being is not a pure spirit; what is sacred touches him because it is tangible, either by way of intelligence or by faith. It nourishes itself through some important object. Meditation can freely rely, at least among some, on a holy object from which contemplation leads beyond the thing represented, to the indescribable, the unbelievable.

I beseech you, she tells the parishioners, *put more holy objects in your homes. Let every person carry with him a holy object. In this manner Satan will tempt you less because you have an armor against him.* (July 18, 1985). Already two years before, the Blessed Virgin had counseled the seers. *Place an image of the Hearts of Jesus and of Mary in your homes.* (Nov. 11, 1983).

Mary says so much on the presence of Satan, and on the struggle which one must consciously, deliberately, lead against him. It is because "the red fired Dragon" stationed from the beginning *before the woman who was giving birth (Apoc.* 12:4), has *set off in pursuit of the woman who sent to the world a male child. (Apoc.* 12:13) She reminds us at Medjugorje: *Whatever be the place where I appear, my Son comes with me, but so does Satan.* (Jan. 28, 1987).

In the meantime, there, where the Mother of God appears, an *oasis of peace is built* (Aug. 7, 1986). Every oasis is encircled by the desert, sterile and evil: *Outside of the oasis, there is a desert where Satan is and where he tries to tempt you.* (ibid.).

We must multiply the oasis of peace, inhabited by beings praising God, in a total abandonment to His holy will, in order to hasten the coming of His Kingdom. There you have God's plan for mankind in the immediate future. It goes without saying that Mary's projects are an integral part of this plan.

At Medjugorje, she often mentions God's plan and her own plan; and most of the time it is in relation to the tricks and the snares and machinations of the original tempter: *Satan is set on thwarting God's plan.* (Dec. 7, 1984). *Satan is trying to destroy my plans* (July 12, 1984). *Satan continues to hinder my plans.* (Apr. 9, 1984). Later she must state with sadness that he has succeeded in his perverse undertakings. *Satan has taken hold of a part of my plan, he is trying to take it over for himself.* (Aug. 1, 1985). The more Satan's relentlessness increases, the more the maternal tenderness and vigilant protection of Mary intensifies: *I protect (this parish) with my hands like a little flower,* she confides with an emotional tenderness to the parishioners. Alas, her efforts are sometimes doomed because of the free choice of some of her children, who yield to the seductions of the Tempter. The beloved Mother is profoundly afflicted over it. *Wipe the tears from my face which I shed in seeing you act this way.* (Jan. 28, 1987).

On the contrary, what joy on seeing a victorious combat: *Thank you for having resisted Satan. I am happy with your prayers.* (Aug. 2, 1984). To know that one can contribute to the happiness of the Mother of God, what a marvelous stimulus in this unceasing battle between the Light and the powers of darkness, in which each one is engaged. *You are the Light of the world* (*Mt.* 5:14), said Jesus in asking his disciples to reflect their own Light on others. The Mother of Jesus reminds them of this mission: *Light and darkness are fighting each other. Many live in darkness and suffer. Show them the Light.* (Mar. 13, 1985).

We know that the answer to the maneuvers of the Prince of Darkness is prayer: *Help Jesus, through your prayers, to realize His plans and to thwart Satan.* (Jan. 9, 1986). It is a plan for an intentional, determined and persevering prayer: *in order to receive from God the grace to conquer.* (July 12, 1984). A *prayer of the heart* (Aug. 9, 1984) with the spirit: *of abandonment to God* (ibid.), because: *in your hearts God is conqueror* (Dec. 7, 1984).

Asceticism (which is to prayer what perfume is to the flower) should accompany it always: *Offer your sacrifices to Jesus so that he can realize his plans.* (Jan. 9, 1986). Not only the general plan with the parish of Medjugorje, the Church and the world, but also the special plans with each soul that wants to abandon itself to Him. *God has a plan with each one of you,* she insists. *Without prayer, you will not be able to understand it.* (Apr. 25, 1987).

The absolute weapon against Satan's undertaking is love, which is God Himself living within the heart of man: *Let love be your sole means. With love you will be able to convert into good all that Satan tries to destroy and to take for himself. In this way, you will be mine, and I will be able to help you.* (Jul. 31, 1986).

Satan (Hebrew: Satan, the Adversary) appears with extraordinary force in the messages of Medjugorje, as the subtle and evil antagonist of Jesus Christ. The Mother of Sorrows, whom the dragon follows, reminds us insistently of this irreconcilable antagonism. Christians, particularly the pastors of souls, must again become more conscious of the doings of the evil one in the world, and in each one of us. The present generation has passed over it in silence. There is no longer any teaching about Satan and his works in our churches. In doing so, we render him the greatest service, and permit him free reign to his devastating action.

The voice of Mary at Medjugorje must have strong repercussions there, where the Church is at work. The urgency to conquer Hell, unleashed over the entire Earth at this time, is greater than ever. Conquer it: *by the blood of the Lamb and the Word.* (*Apoc.* 12:111). To be stronger in this struggle, one must not forget that at every moment: *in his rage in the encounter with the woman, the Dragon carries on the struggle against the rest of her descendants—those who observe the commandments of God and keep the testimony of Jesus.* (*Apoc.* 12:17).

HELL

Whoever says Satan, speaks of Hell. Mary does not avoid the terrible and agonizing reality of "Hell," the place of eternal damnation. The biblical reality of Hell is unbearable to modern sensitivities, and this comprises a large number of Christians. It is most often passed in silence in catechisms and homilies. The scriptural texts which speak about it are presented as symbolic, and analogical, as figures of style, relevant to the oriental psychism. Isn't it also astonishing that only a minority of Catholics continue to believe in Hell?

At Medjugorje, Hell is mentioned insistently in the messages. On November 6, 1981, Vicka notes in her diary that the Blessed Virgin has given the seers a vision of Hell. She describes, in simple words, the terrifying spectacle which she has seen. On January 10, 1983, the seers questioned the Blessed Mother about Purgatory. From her response, it is evident that one must pray for the souls who are there. The message concludes: *The majority of souls go to Purgatory, many go to Hell. A small number go straight to Heaven.*

This same day, Mirjana, troubled and somewhat shocked, asks Mary why God is so hard with sinners. Her question reflects the sensibility of our times concering Hell. The Madonna tells her that it is not God who is hard. Those who are condemned have given themselves up to evil forever. They have: *made a decision to live in Hell.*

Mary's teaching is that of truth. Hell does exist. If the Old Testament speaks about it only occasionally (cf, *Is.* 66:24); the New Testament abounds with passages which mention it. Thus, Jesus speaks of *Gehenna, where the fire is never extinguished. (Mach.* 9:48). He describes the last judgment, the terrible words which await those who will be condemned by their merciless selfishness, disdaining the distress of the poor, the hungry, the stranger, the sick, or the prisoner. *Depart from me ye cursed into eternal fire, which has been prepared for the Devil and his angels. (Mt.* 25:41).

By what right do we deny Hell? How do we justify the silence of our time on this subject?

In the example of Mary, we must restore Biblical truth, in the teaching of faith; restore truth, including that which does not adapt itself to our psychic world. The latter is not exempt from ideological influences of the environment. With respect to Hell, it is sufficient to recall it in the words of Scriptures. All talk which is added to it is useless. The existence of a place of eternal damnation, if it represents a demand for justice, remains only one of those mysteries which will be explained to us in Heaven.

It is always a fact that the word of the Lord, testimony of Divine justice and mercy, takes over the diffused and disturbed sensibilities of our time. To deny Hell is to favor the power of darkness, from whom the Heavenly Father has rescued us in order to take us into the Kingdom of His Son. (*Col.* 1:13) Mary's messages recall these Biblical realities.

CHAPTER 5

A Mother's Love

AN EVENT WITHOUT PRECEDENCE

To repeat these truths, however terrible they may be, to unveil the combat between Light and Darkness (of which we are the stakes), to expose the tricks and evil spells of the adversary, to arm her children in order to confront him victoriously, these are some of the more important aspects in the teaching of Mary at Medjugorje. It is a teaching that goes against the current that is commonly practiced in our times. Today one gladly interprets the manifestation of Satan as some pathological disorder.

Mary is our Mother. She has been shepherdess of Medjugorje, since March 1, 1984, when she confided to the seers a message unprecedented in history; a message in which no one measured, at the moment, its full significance:

> *I have especially chosen this parish, because I would like to guide it. I watch over it with love...*

It is the first message that she addresses through the intermediary of the seers, to the entire parish of Saint James in Medjugorje. For the Croation parishioners, the news which came from Heaven is staggering. For the Church, at the dawn of the third millennium, the initiative of the Virgin Mary could very well have incalculable significance.

Why this initiative, this coming? What part does it play in this calling, this mission of Mary of Nazareth, Mother of God, and Mother of the Church?

Her ultimate objective, it seems, goes beyond the six, then

the eight young people, whom she has maternally gathered in order to teach them. The evening of March 1, 1984, just before the Eucharistic Celebration, she unveils a new dimension of her mission. She offers herself as shepherdess of the entire community of Saint James. Here is the Mother of the Church who has become a guide to a parish, deliberately, openly. It is really an event without precedence in history.

Just as she undertook the education of the group of children from this parish beginning the 25th of June 1981, now, on this great day of March 1st, 1984, she takes up the guidance of the entire parochial community. After two and a half years of patient efforts since the first apparition, she has succeeded in leading a small group at a level of spirituality which enables them, at different levels and in shifts, to serve in the new phase of her action—the community, the parochial stage of her plan.

Since that day, as Shepherdess of Medjugorje, Mary initiates a pastoral, the principal aspects of which are analyzed here. Does it concern a pastoral testimony, or an exemplary pastoral? The future will tell. It is certainly a fact that the fruits have been constant and superb. Just as the young seers and others, through different prayer groups, have been so active for the community, and in the very heart of the entire parish, likewise Saint James Parish itself is susceptible to becoming a force for renewal in this pastoral for the entire Church.

THE SHEPHERDESS, DAUGHTER OF SION

In the next world, a human being who enters into the glory of God, is not deprived of his own character. He maintains his personality throughout all eternity. It is simply purified; glorified in his meeting with God.

In the bosom of the Most Holy Trinity, where she is a daughter, spouse, and mother, Mary remains the person she was at Nazareth, the Daughter of Sion, who gave birth to the Saviour of the world, the "Shepherd of Nations."

In the world of Israel, the symbolic tradition of the shepherd is one of the oldest. The supreme Shepherd of the people is God. The visible shepherd, by Divine right, was the king, since David, who had been shepherd of the flocks of his father in the region of Bethlehem.

Mary of Nazareth is an authentic daughter of this people, of whom sociology has produced a beautiful image of the shepherd. It is a very rich symbol of the relationship between God and man. It has provided Jesus the subject of one of the most beautiful parables, a symbol all the more admirable through which he defines Himself. (*Jn.* 10).

His Mother, in her turn, henceforth becomes shepherdess: *I have particularly chosen this parish, because I want to guide it.* Like a shepherd who leads his flock.

The image of shepherd of his people had been reserved for the King of Israel. And here it is that Mary, daughter of Israel, assumes this pastoral function in a parish of Hercegovina, which she has chosen. Isn't Mary the Mother of the King of Kings? Isn't she Queen? Hasn't she been introduced in Medjugorje, under the most noble, the most urgent title of "Queen of Peace?" She comes to a world in which weighs the very great threats of physical and spiritual destruction.[1]

After March 1, 1984, with the regularity which the function of shepherd demands, Mary addresses the parishioners of Saint James with weekly messages, until the 8th of January 1987. Thereafter, they are monthly, beginning the 25th of January 1987. They are truly pastoral letters, in the great tradition of the Church, destined to guide the people of God on the way to eternal salvation.

This role of shepherdess of a parish, would it have been possible a generation ago? The concept of a clerical pastoral is transferred, thanks to Vatican II, into a very living reality—that of an ecclesiastic pastoral, only in conformity with the great priestly and royal dignity of everything Christian. It is the pastoral of the people of God, among whom its members are "all responsible in the Church."[2]

Many trials and errors, some more or less opportune initiatives, accompanied the first steps of this change so successful

---

1. In April 1982, the Virgin expresses her desire that a feast of "QUEEN OF PEACE" be established, and that it be the 25th of June, anniversary date of the first contact with the seers, the 25th of June, 1981.
2. "All responsible in the Church," title of the declaration of the Plenary Assembly of the French Episcopathy, Lourdes, 1973.

in itself, so painful sometimes in its concrete manifestations. Mary comes with her maternal responsibility. She undertakes the pastoral of a parish. In the simple language of a mother, she returns insistently to the essential point. At the heart of the pastoral is "prayer." The quality of everything depends on it.

The psychology and psychoanalysis, of materialistic tendency, exercise an almost universal dominion, and it involves a good number of Christians. They seem transformed by the human sciences, then challenged by the radicalism of the Gospel. One is almost tempted to research new pastoral methods along these proceedings and techniques. Surely, psychological knowledge is useful for all pastoral. But it should be in the light of faith, especially for pathological cases, which are more and more frequent in our time.

It seems that attracted by some purely human formulas, we lose sight of the fact that the up to date source of grace is prayer. Mary reminds us of it unceasingly at Medjugorje. She speaks of the Gospel. She teaches by example for a determined return to the Biblical and ecclesiastic tradition. Prayer, fasting, penance, reconciliation and conversion form part of the prophetic plot.

CONVERSION

The Biblical and ecclesiastical tradition, initiated by Mary's pastoral at Medjugorje, calls everyone to conversion.

Mary has: *come to convert and to reconcile the whole world* (June 26, 1981). She confirms this, a year later, with particular solemnity: *I have come to call the world to conversion for the last time.* (May 2, 1982). These words express the urgency to return to God. In her message of April 25, 1983, entirely devoted to conversion, and which resounds as an anguishing appeal, Mary uses the words "conversion, convert" twelve times. *Don't wait for the sign in order to convert, that will be too late,* she adds.

What exactly does "to convert" mean? In the Bible it relates to a change of direction, a turning around on the road which one has taken. This change implies repentance, a change in the mentality we have bred, on the road to sin.

God does not cease to call Israel to return to Him. John
the Baptist, proclaiming the immenence of the reign of God,
calls mankind to conversion. He enunciates the two conditions which they must fulfill in order to attain it—recognize
their sins, and change their lives. Then he baptizes them with
water. And when the Kingdom of God is revealed in Jesus,
conversion is at one and the same time, more radically new
and simple. In order to convert, it is to "Him" that one must
go. His person becomes the expression of the change of direction. It is to God, that one returns in Jesus. In Him one receives
the baptism *in the Holy Spirit and fire* (*Mt.* 3:11). To convert
to Jesus is to find the freshness of youth, the simplicity and
the transparency of the child. (*Mt.* 18:3) One turns away from
the way of sin, where there is nothing but chaos, torment,
and perversity, in order to borrow that which culminates in
perfect joy, which no one can ever take away. (*Jn.* 16: 22-24).

Like John the Baptist, Mary cries for the urgency of conversion. For John the Baptist, there was urgency because Jesus
was going to appear, in the presence of men. Mary becomes
insistent, because she knows God's plan for mankind today:
This is a time of grace and conversion. Use it well, she says.
(Oct. 25, 1985).

If God grants special graces, the reason is that there is real
urgency. Humanity is placed at a very important turning point
in its history. God has a plan for mankind. Mankind is free
to accept it or to reject it. If this plan fails, the reason for
the rejection is because of the hardening of hearts, given to
sin. For lack of conversion, God's plan is at a stalemate, not
without deadly consequences. Just as conversion leads to the
joy of Christ, likewise, obstinacy in sin leads to individual
and collective catastrophe. The seers had the vision and the
realization of the first secret; a spectacle of desolation which
brought tears to their eyes. (Oct. 25, 1985).

The catastrophe is not inescapable. Mary has taught the
young seers personal responsibility. She unveils for them, the
power of their prayers: *I need your prayers and your penitence.* (Apr. 25, 1983). Their prayers—our prayers—reinforce
Mary's prayer. *I do not dispose of all the crisis,* she says
with humility, *I receive from God whatever I obtain through*

prayer. (Aug. 31, 1982). She does not cease to appeal to prayer. One must, on his own, storm Heaven in prayer. United with fasting, it possesses an extraordinary power: *Fasting and prayer can prevent wars and natural catastrophies* (July 21, 1982).

It is not surprising, under these conditions, that the young seers were converted; that they adopted the spirit of prayer, and that they gave themselves up to penitence and to fasting. And with them, was a large segment of the parish of Medjugorje, along with large numbers of souls throughout the whole world.

CONFESSION, THE SUPPORT OF CONVERSION

Conversion is not a unique and isolated act. It is a permanent process; a sure way which permits one to stay on this road to conversion. This change of spirit which never ceases to aspire toward perfection, is the sacrament of reconciliation.

Mary insists on the regular practice of this sacrament: *One must invite the Christians to confession every month, especially the first Saturday of the month.* She most particularly recommends monthly confession to "the Western Church," as a remedy for the evils from which it is suffering (Feast of the Transfiguration, 1982). She likewise advises confession on the eve of a great feast, thus on the threshold of a new year, *even if one has confessed just a few days ago.* (Dec. 31, 1983, Mar. 24, 1985) She insists on a sincere confession which nourishes the faith and makes one progress in his change of life: *Do not confess through sheer habit, in order to remain the same after it. No, it is not good. Confession ought to give new life to your faith. It ought to stimulate you and bring you back to Jesus. If confession means nothing to you, really, you will convert with difficulty.* (Nov. 7, 1983).

This last message is marked with severity and sounds like a call to those who, in our day, put off the sacrament of reconciliation. Unfortunately, they are numerous. They neglect this privileged means offered by the Church in order to periodically re-focus our lives on Jesus Christ.

In the teachings of Mary, confession represents an important element in conversion. Vatican II had recalled of this sacrament, "the immense benefit for the Christian Life" ("Christus

Dominus" 30). John Paul II stresses its extraordinary value; he invites the faithful to regularly receive the sacrament of reconciliation.

ON THE ROAD TO SANCTITY

To convert, to be reconciled with God, after having sinned against Him, is to enter into His holiness. It means to be able to maintain oneself in it. To be Holy is to reflect the unique holiness of God. "You alone are holy" we sing in the Gloria.

At Medjugorje, Mary frequently calls us to holiness with great insistence, since the beginning of 1985: *Without holiness, you will not be able to live.* (July 10, 1986). That is what Cardinal Newman vehemently expressed through these words: "To live is to change, and in order to be holy one must change a lot."

Mary's constant concern is to "clothe with holiness" the faithful in the parish, to whom she became shepherdess. She shows the way: *If you would live my messages, you would at the same time, live in holiness.* (Oct. 10, 1985). When she realizes that her calls to holiness have found an echo in the heart of the parishioners, she is filled with joy: *I am very happy with all of you who are on the way to holiness.* (July 24, 1986). She also mentions one of the privileged places, where she wishes to see the growth of holiness. *Let your family be the place where holiness is born.* This is not a withdraw but a support and a sharing. *Help yourselves to live in holiness, specially in the midst of your families.* (ibid.). The message of October 9, 1986 is completely devoted to holiness. Mary stresses it in two fundamental aspects.

The approach to holiness proceeds from a free choice. There is no possibility of constraint by force. The greatness of the human condition rests on freedom. Secondly, holiness is not built on extraordinary acts and events, but through an everyday life led in the sight of God. ("The Little Way" of St. Theresa toward holiness). Life is studded with little sacrifices, modest signs of our dependence on God, and our abandonment to Him in poverty and in love. It is thus that one grows in holiness. It is within the reach of everyone, from the smallest to the greatest, from the weakest to the strongest. The beloved Mother confirms it in telling the parishioners, of whom she is shepherdess: *I wish that every one of you would become holy* (Oct. 9, 1986). She wishes for every one of them *to come to paradise with this special gift,* which she will give —*holiness.* (Nov. 13, 1986).

BENEDICTION (Blessing)

Holiness is a gift from God. Mary, daughter of Sion, knew this gift to its highest degree. She wishes to share this Divine favor with the greatest number of souls. That is why she never stops blessing us. A blessing is the opposite of the Divine curse which Adam and Eve attained, after they had turned away from God through sin. It is a gift which restores holiness, and which permits one to reflect the sole holiness of God. God's blessing given to Abraham reflects on each believer. Mary, whose "Blessed Fruit" sums up every blessing, gives her blessing abundantly. *Today I bless you. I am anxious to tell you that I love you,* she says to the parish on the feast of her Assumption, the 15th of August 1985. *Today I bless you with a solemn blessing which the Almighty has permitted me to give you.* On Christmas, a day to which the Mother of Jesus Christ shows great tenderness, she gives: *a special blessing to all the mothers.* (Dec. 19, 1985).

You must ask for the Divine blessing, everyday of your life. *You cannot grow without God's blessing. Ask for it everyday, so that you can grow normally.* (Apr. 10, 1986). In her example, one must bless others, without excluding anyone. One of the essential characteristics of the Christian is the obligation to love his enemies. *Bless them,* requests Mary (Jun. 22, 1983). An enemy is also a child of God. It is not our duty to judge him. (*Lk.* 6:37). It is one of the highest forms of blessing. The most perfect is that of the Eucharist, which has come from the Son, Whom she has given us.

Mary happily blesses the humble objects which the faithful present to her. These objects, such as rosaries, medals, images or books, do not receive a magic virtue. Blessing falls on those who use them with faith in God and in His blessing, the fruit of the Spirit. (Mary also requested these objects receive the blessings of the priests, empowered for this purpose.)

A blessing is also a gift from God. It is abundant; it is received in many places. To a prayer group which had gathered on Krizevac (among them Ivan and Maria), Mary confided: *You are on a Mt. Thabor. You receive blessings, strength and love. Take them to your families and homes. To each of you, I am giving a special blessing.* Finally, the blessing is an expression of love, a jesture dictated by her: *I pour out to you my blessing, because my heart wishes to be with you.* (Oct. 26, 1983).

As a sign of the blessing received, and as an expression of the will to preserve this Divine gift, Mary asks her children *to consecrate themselves to the heart of Jesus and to her Immaculate Heart.* (Oct. 20, 1983 and Aug. 2, 1983). The families consecrated to the Sacred Heart are an image of it. In order to make them sensitive to the blessing flowing from this consecration, she advises: *Put a picture of the hearts of Jesus and Mary in your homes.* (Nov. 11, 1983). Thus, these simple objects which have been blessed, and which we carry with us, or which adorn our homes, are a sign and constant reminder. On seeing them, our thoughts are raised toward those whom they represent. That is the unique function. And that is the reason that Mary includes these pious traditions in her teachings.

Thus through the instruction which she gives, the Mother of God and of mankind pursues a two-fold objective. She teaches, vividly reminding the teaching of Jesus and of His Church; and she guides, transforming little by little, the interior spiritual development of her children. In turn, she asks them to become the instruments of the Blessing of God. Thus, to the conversion which emerges in holiness, and the blessing which maintains it, she accomplishes her mission—so strongly brought to light at Medjugorje—which is to lead her children to the Father, through her Son.

A TRUE MOTHER

To lead her children to the Father, through her Son; that is Mary's entire plan. In this sense, her presence at Medjugorje is completely a matter of "education." In the meantime, there is an abundance of details in the messages, which are more directly pedagogical. They tend to create little by little, through a system of repetition and permeation, some behaviors among the seers and the parishioners, all in conformity with God.

Prayer, fasting, conversion, holiness, Satan, Hell: The Mother of God is not content just with educating on the truths and asceticism of faith. Like every Mother, she also includes in her instruction, minor aspects of life. The accumulation of these details provide the orientation of customary behavior of the child.

She frequently gives advice of a general nature. Repetition establishes the awareness of having to act in conformity with the desire of so loving a Mother.

Remain united as brothers and sisters. (Feb. 14, 1982). *Be generous, persevering.* (Nov. 5, 1983). *Be courageous, do not fear anything.* (Feb. 25, 1982). *Give up disorderly passions.* (June 16, 1983). *Do not believe everything told you; do not weaken in your faith* (Nov. 20, 1983). *Be well mannered* (Feb. 19, 1982). *Be humble through prayer and fasting.* (Feb. 10, 1984).

Practical advice is not lacking: *Fall asleep in prayer,* she says (Oct. 30, 1983), in explaining to the children the advantage of winding up a day through prayer. *Read the Bible in the morning, anchor the Divine word in your heart and force yourselves to live it during the day.* (Apr. 19, 1984). *Force yourselves to overcome a weakness each day.* (Feb. 20, 1985). *Each day prepare your hearts for Christmas.* (Dec. 4, 1986). *Every evening make your examination of conscience.* (Feb. 24, 1985). And above all, she teaches her children not to let themselves be concerned with worries, not to be preoccupied with the tomorrows. She recommends insistently weekly meditation of the passage in the Gospel which gives this liberating advice. (*Mt.* 6:24-34).

Like every mother, she reproaches the seers and the parishoners, when she has to. *Stop slandering,* she tells them, always exhorting them to prayer for the unity of the parish (Apr. 12, 1984). *Do not quarrel* (Feb. 14, 1982). *Do not ask any more that type of question.* (Feb. 23, 1982). *Stop your chattering at Mass.* (Feb. 19, 1982). *Don't grumble because of the rain.*

Thank God through prayer and fasting. He sends the rain which makes the earth fertile. (Feb. 1, 1984). A light reprimand which comes back many times: *You have not yet understood what is meant to pray. I wish so much that you would understand it.* (Jan. 23, 1984).

Mary is very attentive to the prayer of thanksgiving. The day after Christmas, she reproaches the children: *No one withdrew to his room to thank Jesus.* (Dec. 26, 1983). The reproaches are made with discretion. When she reprimands one of the seers, the others do not hear what she is telling them; a maternal tenderness which avoids hurting needlessly. *I have often reprimanded you,* she tells the group one day. *Pray with me,* she adds, as though she is trying to do away with the least conflict or annoyance which may have resulted from it, in order to lead the souls to the fullness of peace.

In order to teach the mastery of themselves, Mary educates them with respect to sacrifice, self-denials, and the asceticism of the entire being. The sacrifices, freely consented to and offered with love to the Lord, form a precious contribution to the conversion of sinners, and through which, to the salvation of the world: *Pray, fast, ask the Holy Spirit to renew your souls and the whole world.* (Mar. 5, 1984).

This advice of a general and practical nature, including calls to penance and correction of their faults, had been very frequent in the course of the first three years. It is during this period that the seers have visibly developed from young people (like their friends in most everything, with little concern at this age for their spiritual lives), to become authentic individuals of prayer, a testimony of an exceptional religious fervor. With respect to the parish, it did not distinguish itself from the community of Christians of Hercegovina, a province well anchored in sociological Catholicism. Now, in just a few years, it has become one of the most fervent Catholic communities in the entire world.

If the advice and the reprimands are frequent, the expressions of gratitude are even more so. At the end of each apparition, Mary thanks the seers and parishoners with great tenderness. Her acts of thanksgiving are often bound to the spiritual progress which she enhances. *I am happy today; I thank you for your prayers.* (Aug. 2, 1984). *I am happy for your participation at Mass. Continue as you did this evening. Thank you for having resisted the temptation from Satan,* she tells Jelena the same day. *Thank you for having offered me your suffering, now that the Lord is trying you.* (Oct. 11, 1984). *Thank the people in my name for their prayers, sacrifices and penances.* (June 25, 1982). *Thank you, thank all of you,* she uses Jelena to say to numerous persons who have come to church one evening during a great cold spell, (Dec. 2, 1983). *Thank you very much for all that you have offered my Son, present in the Most Holy Sacrament. That touches me deeply.*

At the end of every Thursday message, Mary kindly thanks the faithful: *for having responded to my call.* To her gratitude, Mary willingly adds some encouragement, so important in education, and so often neglected or scorned. *I know, my children, that you have worked and prayed well today. . . . Be generous, persevere.* (Nov. 5, 1983). *The faithful are beginning to be converted. They are praying again in the homes where they no longer prayed.* (Mar. 9, 1982). *I am anxious to tell you the happiness which your prayer has given me.* (Oct. 4, 1984). *Ivan prays and obeys well, he follows my recommendations,* she tells those who remained at Medjugorje, regarding the seer who entered the seminary (Mar. 7, 1982).

Their participation in Mary's plans receives a new impetus when she confides to them: *A first wish of my plan has been realized.* (Mar. 22, 1984). She calms and assures the children that their extraordinary spiritual adventure has lead them to some difficulties, and submitted them to continuous pressure: *Jesus is your great friend. Do not fear anything in His presence. Give Him your heart.* (Nov. 29, 1983). *I am the Mother, that is why I have come. You should not have fear, because I am here.* (Nov. 25, 1985). It is the language of a mother to her little children. Throughout the centuries, Mary has not ceased to exercise this maternity to which she has been called by her Son, even at the most tragic moment of the life of the Saviour. She tries to arouse in each of her children the feeling of their uniqueness, of the irreplaceable role which each has to fulfill: *I have chosen you.* (May 25, 1984). *Jesus confides in each of you a mission. He wishes to receive something from each of you.* (Nov. 21, 1983). It means, *Let each one of you work according to your own capacity.* (Oct. 31, 1984).

The maternity of Mary is not dis-incarnate, distant, symbolic. It is authentic, caring, attentive to the details of the real life, happy, like the one which she lead at Nazareth. She has the experience of a mother, an experience stamped forever on the heart of every woman who has had the privilege of giving life. Universal maternity, to which Mary had been beckoned at Golgatha by her Son nailed to the Cross, is not simply a collective maternity, a mass maternity exercised through proxy. It is not even priestly, solemn or abstract.

Jesus confided Mary to John, and not to a collection of apostles. He confided to His mother, the apostle who best understood His plan of love for humanity. John became the representative of the community of mankind. His personal choice symbolizes the individual character of the exercise of Mary's maternity. Having become the mother of John, she offers every disciple of Jesus a maternity which does not impose itself, but which is freely accepted or rejected. In the spirit of mankind, the mother personifies to a high degree, the most fundamental, existential reality—that which gives birth and life, and which is at the very source of the hope of immortality, "love."

"I LOVE YOU. LOVE ME. LOVE ONE ANOTHER."

Above all else, Mary speaks her love. She repeats it insistently. She requests, she almost begs to be loved in return. She adds to it the second commandment of the Lord, the love diffused, the product of the love received and given. The message of October 5, 1984 gathers in a few words the effusive and diffusive characteristics of love: *I love you. Love me. Love one another.* A perfect expression of the supreme law, destined to realize on earth the Kingdom of Heaven. Men have tried, especially in our century, to define numberless plans for society. When the message of October 5, 1984 becomes a reality, a new world will unfold, that of the "civilization of love."

A utopian world? No! Does mankind have the capacity to make it a reality? Of course not, if he relies completely on himself; and especially, as long as we remain in sin against the Spirit. But, *to God, nothing is impossible. (Lk.* 1:37). Consequently, it is necessary for believers to pray untiringly to the Holy Spirit for the Kingdom of the Father to come, in order to finally establish on earth, the civilization of love. *And does not God do justice to His chosen ones who cry to Him night and day, so long as He exercises patience for their cause?*

If there is a domain at Medjugorje which Mary tackles with constant insistence, and with extraordinary fervor, it is really that of love. From her messages on love, one could conclude a true strategy for the realization of the new world. Above all, she speaks her love with an overwhelming force, insistence and fire. *I love you, you cannot love me as much as I love you.* (Feb. 1985). *If you would know how much I love you, you would cry.* (Mar. 1, 1982). *I love all of you in the same manner.* (Oct. 31, 1985). *I, your mother, love you...I never tire of it. I call on you even though you may be far from my heart.* (Nov. 14, 1985). How she would like to spread this fire which consumes her. *I wish to engrave in each heart the sign of love.* (Jan. 16, 1984). Whoever carries this sign, will act only through love in everything.

Yet, love is not only a sweet communion of hearts, an irresistible attraction that unites people, it is an affectionate solidarity, which unites members of a family. Love is likewise a sacrifice: *I invite you to a very great sacrifice, that of love...Without love, you cannot transmit your experience to others.* (Mar. 27, 1986). The "sacrifice of love" is her practice in conformity with the definition which the apostle Paul has given. (*1 Col.* 13:4-7).

It is impossible for mankind to live this kind of love without Divine grace. But when, with the help of grace, the Christian gives evidence of love, he becomes a living tabernacle. He makes Jesus live again in the sight of others. It is then that he realizes that "transfiguration" which St. Paul has expressed in his immortal phrase: *It is no longer I who lives; it is Christ Who lives in me. (Gal.* 2:20).

"LOVE-SACRIFICE"

The most cruel and ruthless aspect (from a purely human point of view) of that which Mary calls "the sacrifice of love," is to have to love him who despises you, hurts you, brings misfortune to you or hates you. *Love your neighbor,* says she, an echo to the Gospel (*Lk.* 6:27), *especially those who harm you.* (Oct. 7, 1985). *Love your enemies, bless them.* (June 22, 1982). Love a malicious, rancorous and aggressive person with whom I am bound to live? Love a neighbor who persecutes and slanders me? Love at work an unjust and miserable boss who harrasses me and encroaches upon my rights? Love the hoodlum who has rendered me infirm in attacking me to steal from me? The drunken driver who has made of me a paraplegic for life? Love the unfaithful husband who further discredits and mistreats me? Yes! To be a Christian, it is at that price. But such sacrifices are not in vain. *With love, one turns into a good thing, that which Satan tries to destroy.* (July 31, 1986). And, in loving thus: *God will fill you with great gifts.* (Dec. 19, 1985).

How does one create the new world, the civilization of love? *If you love only those who love you, what reward will you have? Don't the Publicans themselves do as much?* (*Mt.* 5:46). Christian love knows no limits. It is not selective. It includes the friend and the enemy, black and white, rich and poor, the native born as well as the immigrant. It is that love "which flows out from itself," and "love-sacrifice;" both that which is natural to man, and that which demands mortifications of himself. Jesus gave as a law to His disciples the extreme case: *Amen I say to you: love your enemies and pray for those who persecute you so as to become children of your Father, Who is in Heaven.* (*Mt.* 5: 44-45). At Medjugorje, Mary emphatically repeats this basic truth of the Gospel, which Jesus practiced as an example, up to the supreme sacrifice on the Cross.

A TEACHING OF LOVE

If it is enough to simply follow the movement of nature with little effort (to love the spouse, the child, the friend, every lovable person) then the love for the stranger, for the miserable and perverse individual, for the adversary and for the enemy, is a grace which is obtained through prayer and fasting.

Like all grace, it is given as a seed. God does not transform man into a robot. He has given him intelligence and freedom. On applying these gifts to love-sacrifice, one causes the growth of it like the rain causes the blossoming and growth of the seed. In that sense, every effort enjoys Divine blessing. *Grow in love. The flower does not sprout without water. You cannot live without God's blessing.* (Apr. 10, 1986).

Mary shows the practical method of growth in love. Twice, she proposes a week of exercise in love. *During this week, live the words "I love God."* (Feb. 22, 1985). The love of God is inseparable from the love of neighbor. *If someone said: I love God, and he detests his brother, he is a liar. He who does not love his brother, whom he sees, would not know how to love God, Whom he does not see.* (1 *Jn.* 4:20).

As Christmas neared, a feast which particularly touches her heart as mother, she gives instructions to the parish: *Let this week be one of apprenticeship in love.* (Dec. 13, 1984). Apprenticeship, above all, in love-sacrifice. It is in this sense that she once again asks the parishoners to prepare themselves for Christmas through their, *works of love.* (Dec. 5, 1985).

The love of neighbor (whoever they may be); likewise the love of events, of circumstances in life (whatever they may be): *Pray so that you may be able to accept the illness and the sacrifice with love, as Jesus accepted them.* It is on the occasion of the Feast of the Holy Cross (September 14), that Mary gives this counsel. She adds: *I wish that the cross may bring joy to you also.* (Aug. 11, 1986).

She invites us to love in everything that we do. To teach this love constitutes one of her objectives, one of the reasons for her coming to Medjugorje: *I am your mother...I have come to earth to teach you, to listen, to love, to pray through love.* (Nov. 29, 1984). In fact, listening to this quality of the messages of Mary, necessarily implies the determination to live them through love. And the prayer of the heart, as we have seen, surmounts all the obstacles. Love is the basic energy, the universal force of the world. In order to grow, the plant needs sun and water. In order to live and to blossom, the human being needs love. He is a monstrance with the Spirit of love in his heart, like a host. If the Holy Spirit, Who is love, is not there as that host, it will not be long before the vacant place is occupied by the adversary. Every destiny, every drama of mankind is there. If he escapes the Divine call, through his freedom, he is reduced to his natural strength— easy prey for the tempter. If he is docile to the commands of the Spirit of love, he is on the same wave length for which he was created. He is in harmony with himself and with others, in harmony with the universe. He is a parcel of the civiliza- tion of love, of the community of mankind united under the crook of the Good Shepherd. It will be that someday.

In the creation of this new world, priests (through their vocation) play a significant role. "Living in conformity with Christ through Ordination, they are participants in His priest- hood and in His authority. They exercise the responsibility of Christ, priest and shepherd, and act in the name and the place of the Lord Jesus." (Vatican II: "Ministry and Life of Priests").

For all of these reasons, priests are particularly dear to the heart of Mary. She dedicates to them the message of May 30, 1984 with some urgent advice: *Priests should visit fami- lies. More particularly, those who no longer practice and who have forgotten God. Priests should carry the Gospel of Jesus to the people, and teach them the way to pray. And priests should, themselves, pray more and also fast. They should give to the poor what they don't need."*

When the Good Shepherd is truly able to depend on a large number of priests to guide His flock as He wishes; *then the conquest of the world will be accelerated for there will be only one flock and one shepherd. (Jn. 10:16).*

"APOCALYPTIC" PRESENCE

Medjugorje sometimes has an Apocalyptic (even eschato- logical) flavor. Mary has come "for the last times," and she has announced a time of grace and of conversion, which she invites us to use well. Many signs in the sky at Medjugorje confirm these messages, which have been transmitted by the seers. A great sign, permanent in nature, has been announced. Mary asks us to be patient in waiting for it. Terrible trials have been unveiled. If a huge mass of sinners does not convert, these trials will occur as surely as night follows day. It deals with an entirely secular based society, which has deliberately turned away from God. It makes up its own law of life and death, reduces love to perversion and fleeting emotions, lives in amusement, approves the unjust death of millions of hungry children each day without reacting. It tries to forget the chaos of morals, and wears itself out in the unrestrained pursuit of a technological progress without end.

The weight of collective and individual sins is so great that the dikes of Divine mercy threaten to break. If this harm should come about, then the unleashed torrents would carry off everything in their way. It is to avoid this harm that Mary calls the world to conversion. She tries to lead an idolatrous society out of the road to perdition. She instructs her children in prayer, the spiritual and physical asceticism in love, the first and ultimate force of life, of every life.

Without love, you cannot do anything. she cries. (May 29, 1986). And with an agonizing insistence, which should upset us if we did not have hearts of stone, she cries out to us, *Listen to my maternal appeal. Live it. I say it to you out of love in order to be able to help you.* (Jan. 16, 1986). In challenging us in this way, she fulfills her obligation as Mother of God and mother of mankind, a double bond which has given her a share in the history of the alliance. *I act as mediator between God and you. I invite you to live in that love which God is asking of you.* And she shows us the sovereign way of this existence, in conformity with the will of God: *Live the messages in humility.* (July 17, 1986).

To successfully carry out her task as teacher, Mary needs time. All teaching requires time before it is able to produce results. Some people are astonished at "apparitions of such long duration, accompanied by numberless words." Are not permanence and repetition expressions of maternal power, which is the power of love? At Medjugorje, Mary fully exercises her maternal role. *This long period which I am with you is a sign of the immense love which I have for you.* And she adds, in order to recall the parable of the lost and found sheep (*Lk.* 15: 3-7): *I wish that every one of you would become holy.* (Oct. 9, 1986). She does not want to lose a single one of those who have been confided to her.

If these words are intended for the parish of St. James at Medjugorje, they are likewise addressed to all of those who listen to Mary's messages; and those who try to conform their lives to her evangelical exhortations.

A CHRISTIAN ACCORDING TO THE HEART OF MARY

It is Vicka, who notes in her diary: "When I see the Gospa, nothing else exists. My eyes become emerged in hers," (Mar. 4, 1982), or Maria rediscovering her fervor, only in the tone in which Mary says: *Pray.* The seers live directly in her immense love. They have seen her, and have understood because of infinite tenderness: *I hold you in my arms. I need your prayers for you to be all mine and I all yours* (Feb. 23, 1984). *I love you, I hold you on my knees.* Words of an exquisite sweetness of every mother in love with her child.

At Medjugorje, Mary reveals fully to what extent she is in love with her children. Captivated, filled with wonder by her dazzling beauty—(the hallmark of such a love)—little Jelena asks her with childlike candor, (in April, 1984): "Why are you so beautiful?" And she receives this extraordinary response, which crystallizes all the dynamics of the existentialist of man: *I am beautiful because I love.*

Yes, love is the creator of beauty—for the plans of nature, of the person, and of society. When mankind understands that, that will be the coming of the Kingdom of Heaven on earth. Mary has come to educate us to this understanding. She shows us the way: *Open your hearts to the Lord of all hearts.* (June 20, 1985).

That, without precedence, is the objective of the teaching endeavor of Mary at Medjugorje. To accomplish this objective, she establishes a pedagogical system which has born incomparable fruits for the young seers, as well as for the parish community; and now, for numberless pilgrims who have come from all over the world.

In following the track or method of education by Mary at Medjugorje, in analyzing the pedagogical system which constitutes the implementation of this method, (the way in which the Shepherdess leads her sheep), one can design the profile of the Christian, and that of the Christian community; Christians as Mary desires to model them, in order to lead them to her Son, and Jesus to His Father.

Who is this Christian? What is this. Christian community according to Mary's heart? How does her teaching define it?

UN-OBTAINABLE FINALITIES

To consider him in his real life and behavior, from a general point of view, this Christian is very different from that produced by the educational systems which are popular in the world today.

The 20th Century has been called, and with good reason, "The Century of the Child." Never before has one accumulated so many studies and experimentations, so many systems of education and teaching methods in bringing these systems into operation.

And yet, at the end of this century of excess, one should acknowledge that, after having traveled through it, he is not able to find any worthy finality of a good healing condition. In the light of the education at Medjugorje, it is not difficult to discover the cause of these "un-obtainable finalities." The predominant currents of the century produce beings who are truncated, uprooted. And when one considers the future, the very same errors reproduce themselves. What will the man of tomorrow be? It will be a man "in full bloom physically and intellectually; a man who is independent, creative and socially acceptable." (Bertrand Schwarz: "Education Tomorrow"). He is a man who has been amputated, cut-off from God. Where is the part of the immortal soul in all of this, the soul made to the image of God?

At Medjugorje, Mary shows the way of the true education of mankind. It is the way of the Gospel, which the Church has never ceased to follow. But it is a way which has been obstructed by incessant ideological movements; and more particularly, in this century, by passive Christians. Some Christian schools have permitted themselves to be abused by these currents clothed with novelty. Mary not only shows the only new way—the Christian way of always—but even takes charge of the formation of a group of adolescents and young people, then of the teaching of the entire parish. The results are convincing. They go beyond everything of that sort one has been able to observe.

Since the first years of this formation, we have seen a maturation among the seers, a reflection of their interior growth. The repetitive method constitutes the leverage of this maturation. In the course of the first month, the plans of the adolescents were often familiar and naive, but likewise, sometimes inept and foolish. The questions dealt with the daily banality. From time to time, they brought mere curiosities, especially with respect to the promised sign. It is true that these adolescents were the prey of a multitude of people who tried to use them to obtain the clarification of problems of a personal nature, or of mysteries. *Do not ask any more that type of question*, the Holy Virgin finishes by telling them. Later on, the exchanges are progressively established at the level of the essential.

Like every mother, Mary uses repetition abundantly. The more important the element of the spiritual life, the more she insists on recalling it. Prayer comes largely to mind. It is through it, that a direct bond is established with God, and which is also used to maintain it. Our Lady speaks to the children in a language which is simple, immediately comprehensible, and which can be assimilated. One would hardly imagine Mary speaking to the adolescents in a language of theologians, even if it is deprived of every scholarly device. It is not in the nature of the mother. And these young people, from a rural environment, would not have been able to either retain the messages, nor especially, to assimilate them. Reduced to a crystalling simplicity, the words of Mary penetrate right into the hearts of the seers. They are thus accessible to all, elementary and university students, children and adults, in a world of images, impoverished with vocabulary. The last objection which one has a right to make of the messages of Medjugorje is their simplicity, their repetitive nature. These characteristics contribute to their incomparable value.

Following the best maternal teaching, Mary encloses and maintains spiritual advice for effective purposes. She deliberately creates an atmosphere of joy, to which the young people are particularly sensitive. Through Mary, their mother, the group of young people easily make up a family. This is quickly identified at the exceptional event, which they are in the process of living. In speaking with this so loving a mother, and in the affectionate reception of her messages, the seers are gradually immersed in a new system of values. A personal, living faith is substituted for the traditional religious practice of their environment. In testing this system, one can observe their development. Body and spirit, heart and soul, it is a full use of the human faculties.

Spiritual formation is the full support of this integral development. No abstraction! It concerns the real spiritual person in a personalized approach. Mary speaks to all together, and to each one in particular. The supreme value of this system of values, is love. It is of the Father, extended into our lives by Jesus in the Holy Spirit. This love is grace. Mary serves as mediatrix of it.

In analyzing the pedagogical method of the Shepherdess of Medjugorje, one can draw up the profile of the Christian according to the heart of Mary. All the details of this profile are directly borrowed from her messages.

All in all, the Christian, according to the heart of Mary, is in constant union with God—from the moment he wakes up to the moment when he goes to sleep, everyday of his life. There is a state of total abandonment to the Holy Spirit, and to Mary, in order to be led more securely to Jesus; and through Jesus, to the Father of the Heaven. Under this guidance, he is moved by an intense and fervent spiritual life, based on an effective and psychic life of peace and joy, and sustained by a characteristic forged day after day through a demanding asceticism. Character, affective life, and spiritual life, form a totality, from where the profile of this Christian and this Christian community breaks loose.

First of all, the character. The Christian entirely abandoned to God is without fear. He is free and responsible. He is courageous and strong in his determination. He is polished, well mannered, without credulity in his relationships with others. Conscious of his faults, he makes an effort to eliminate them systematically—one by one; in taking one of them as a target during a given day, in order to be able to fight it deliberately. He does not tolerate any resentment in his heart, for he knows that does not help anything. On the contrary, his objective is to turn evil into good, in loving him who does him evil. He is detached from material things and radiates with joy, having been inhabited by the Spirit of Jesus.

"YOU ARE MY SECURE SHELTER" (*Ps.* 71:7)

In regards to his affective and psychic life, the Christian (according to the heart of Mary) finds himself in total existential security. The fact is, he feels loved by the Mother of God, protected by her. He knows that this so-loving a mother is happy with him; that she is happy near him, as he near her. Certainly, he is a sinner. He is sorry for his past sins, but he is relieved of the feeling of remorse for he knows that he is pardoned through the infinite mercy of God. Rooted in the messages of Mary, he progresses knowingly in holiness, because these messages show him the way to it. It is in the bosom of family that he draws the strength for this march. In the same way, he is harmoniously put in a parish, entirely listening to the Word of God. There, one sees a habit, the gesture of love, like the flower which is placed near the nativity scene at Christmas time by each person.

All of that makes him feel as though he is in an oasis of happiness. He knows that this oasis is surrounded by a threatening desert, but thanks to his total abandonment to God through Mary, he goes through life with the feeling of being sheltered in absolute security, like one who fights from an impregnable fortress. Character and affective life are not superficial expressions of his being. They are the reflection of an intense spiritual life modeled after Mary.

Spiritual life is founded entirely on prayer. This is not a passing, but a permanent dialogue with the Lord, in all circumstances, for the Christian lives constantly in the sight of God. Prayer of thanksgiving, of petition, of intercession. To pray for the conversion of sinners is particularly urgent because of grave threats which weigh on the world. Prayer brings about many conversions. It can also turn away these threats. Together with fasting, it contributes to the realization of God's plan. The Christian is thus able to utilize an invincible weapon.

Prayer itself is nourished through the Sacraments. The Eucharist, daily if possible, and monthly Confession, constitute the major signs of the spiritual life. Adoration of the Blessed Sacrament is also of prime importance. The Cross (instrument of salvation) is the object of great tenderness. It invites us to penance, to humility. It facilitates acceptance of suffering. It shows us the way to conversion, to change of heart, to a new life. And the Cross is, paradoxically, the source of joy because it is bound to the Resurrection, like a flower to the seed which has produced it.

This spiritual life is totally penetrated with the beatitude of pure faith. It is conscious of its poverty, and comforted by the ocean of grace, which God opens to us through Mary. The faith of the Christian adheres to the whole doctrine of the Church. It does not discard whatever is troubling. Hell and Purgatory, temptation by Satan, as well as God's wrath, are realities which are humbly accepted.

This faith is Biblical in essence. The Christian, according to the heart of Mary, is a fervent reader of the Bible. It is his daily bread. The Biblical version, reaffirmed by Vatican II, establishes it in the bosom of the people of God; people chosen, which know no frontiers, countries, continents or racism. Thus the Christian is strongly conscious of his adherence to a universal Church, and circling the totality of mankind. His intentions of prayers are often inspired by this universality.

The Christian, according to the heart of Mary, follows with an attention full of tenderness, the great stages of the liturgical life. His year is punctuated with solemn feasts. Christmas, Easter, Pentecost are just some of the peaks. He prepares for them with a great fervor, notably through Novenas. For their celebration, he is in communion with the earth and Heaven. The feast days of Mary are also great.

The Shepherdess of Medjugorje has expressed the desire that the feast of "Mary, Queen of Peace" be added. She would like to see it celebrated on June 25th, anniversary day of the first dialogue between her and the seers. She also stated that August 5th of the year 16 before Christ (B.C.) was the real day of her birth.

TO TAKE UP EVERYTHING IN CHRIST

Having involved body and soul in the struggle of Light against the powers of Darkness, the Christian (according to the heart of Mary) knows that he is a part of the Divine plan for the salvation of mankind. He knows that he plays an important role in the realization of this plan. Brought together in the unique Body of Christ, the people of God, (of whom He is a fervent and active member), he progressively builds the temple of the Holy Spirit.

This struggle, both the personal and community task, leads to salvation, and has reached a critical point. Signs in the sky confirm the urgency of an increased participation of man in God's plan, through prayer, fasting, penance, conversion. One confidently awaits the great sign. It will confirm for the eyes of the world in a powerful manner, the authenticity of the message of Medjugorje.

In this spiritual combat, the Christian, far from being on the defensive, is (on the contrary) continuously on the offensive, with his weapons of light—humility and charity. His love is not selective; it extends to all mankind, to his enemies in particular. He is a communicating vessel. What happens in him arouses immediate repercussions on the outside, even to the confides of the world to which his prayer extends.

It is thus that through spiritual power, and not through a vain and ridiculous activism, he contributes to the building of the Kingdom of God, to the reign on earth of the Father of Heaven. Taught by Mary, the Christian is, at the same time, the witness and a protagonist of the Kingdom, which will take up every being and everything in Christ.

Why has Mary come to earth at the end of the century and millennium, at the juncture of two worlds?

Humanity has forged the weapons of its own destruction, and has devoted colossal resources to it. It has even lost the remembrance of its alliance with God. It despises the natural law, rejects inalienable moral values. A large part of the world goes as far as to deny the spiritual dimension of mankind. The part of humanity which has developed materially, is engaged in a frenzied course of technological progress without end. At the same time, hundreds of millions of inhabitants of poor countries swallow bitter tears over their distress, instead of being able to eat the bread of fraternal sharing. This world is, before the common Father of mankind, in a state of mortal sin.

Facing torment and facing threatening plagues (fruits of sin without repentance), there is no longer any issue other than prayer of supplication, reinforced by fasting. At Medjugorje, Mary does not stop imploring, sometimes with tears:

> *Pray and fast. Pray without ceasing. Without prayer, you are not able to do anything. There is no peace without prayer. If you pray, I will be able to protect you and remain with you. Pray. . .I will take care of the rest.*

The duration of her presence at Medjugorje has also been conditioned by prayer. *As long as you pray, I will have words for you.* (February-March 1985). The place from where this prayer must proceed, is the heart—the place where love is born and displays itself.

If Christians obey in large numbers to the supplications of Mary, the Mother of the Church, then the menacing catastrophies will be avoided. The example is Ninive, spared because its inhabitants followed the reproach from Jonas and repented. How does one make Christians understand that nothing is more urgent to the current state of mankind than prayer, penance and conversion? It is the time to chose between the "Light of the world" and the "Prince of Darkness;" peace or new catastrophies affecting entire regions of the world. It is the hour of Christians, of all men of good will.

There you have the substance of the message of Medjugorje.

Christians, permit yourselves "to be educated" by the Queen of Peace and begin, finally, to listen to the Good News of Jesus Christ, unique source of a just and responsible world.

A message without precedent in history. (Apr. 4, 1985). Mary calls: *the world to conversion for the last time. I will not appear anymore on earth,* she reveals (May 2, 1982). These words are grave, imploring and dramatic. Is it the time of *the seven bowls of God's wrath (Apoc.* 16:1) provoked by Babylon, in which *spells led all the nations astray? (Apoc.* 18:23).

Nothing is fatal, or final. *Evil will come if the world does not convert. Call the world to conversion. Everything depends on your conversion.* (Dec. 15, 1983).

God continues to offer His alliance to mankind. The Shepherdess is of Sion, and invites all to follow it through her Son, in order to seal again this alliance of love. Since 1981, the invitation has become an active teaching. Its fruits are of an exceptional abundance. Medjugorje constitutes a model. Shouldn't parishes be everywhere in the world be inspired by it?

Mary states that at Medjugorje, things have begun to develop in a good direction. *Rejoice with me. A part of my plans have been realized. Many are converting.* (Mar. 25, 1984).

It really depends on us to speed up this movement. Each one of us has been chosen by God to be *used for His great plan of salvation of mankind.* (Jan. 25, 1987). *You cannot understand how great your role is in God's design,* Mary adds in this same message.

May those who let themselves be led by this mother, in love with her children, be more and more loving. A mother never abandons her little ones. *I will stay always near you.* (Nov. 11, 1981). She is burning with the same desire for each one of us, to see us undertake the road to sanctity. *Begin to live a new life, from today on.* (Jan. 25, 1987).

How one must thank her for having come to tell us all of this at Medjugorje, at a moment in the history of mankind, when the extreme urgency of the return to God manifests itself!

CONCLUSION

After the message of Our Lady, after her teaching, let us not forget what stands out, because it is the very finality of the message—the fruits which have multiplied themselves in a marvelous way, and which are very well cultivated by the priests at Medjugorje.

They never abandoned their ideas nor their methods, not even the proper techniques to Charismatic Renewal (which only Fr. Tomislav Vlasic knew, but it doesn't matter at Medjugorje). They were the pastors attentive to another tradition and another grace.

From the beginning, Father Jozo Zovko channeled this exceptional grace toward the Liturgy and the Eucharist. He thus avoided every disassociation between the Charismatics and the fundamental life of the Church. He has succeeded in having all nourish and stimulate themselves reciprocally.

After his imprisonment (August 14, 1981), Father Tomislav Vlasic, who succeeded him, paid particular attention to enlighten, stimulate and coordinate the charisms (prayer, recognition, service) which were born here. In effect it was an overwhelming task and threatened from all parts. It is an exemplary, historical fact, and a rare performance to have attained this harmony, because apparitions often give way to tension and misunderstandings within the Church. When the charisma of the visionaries, and the authority of the pastors, are disunited, the former deviate and the latter become tense. They are conflicting and destroy one another. That can lead the former to disintegration or schism; the other to a sterile authoritarianism. Just like at Lourdes where so many things were exemplary, the priest, held by his responsibility for caution with reference to the apparitions, kept this movement to himself, not without some inconvenience. Thus, exaltation appeared at the grotto itself where an epidemic of visionaries raged. That is what would happen at Medjugorje, without the spiritual quality of the parish, and enlightened pastors. As good gardeners, they did not try to create their fruits (the fruits of their ideology, of their knowledge or their technique), but nourished the fruits which God gave them. These fruits were propagated happily and intensely, step by step—from the visionaries, to the parish, and to the pilgrims, as we have seen.

In Lourdes, from the testimony of her confessor, Bernadette was, "the best proof of the apparition." In Medjugorje the seers have become a convincing proof as well, not only through their testimony and their charisms, but by their whole life, which shines over the parish and beyond.

The parish on the other hand, has radiated this grace over the pilgrims. A praying Liturgy, reception, testimony of prayer and of fasting given by the hospitable families, have all been a constant moving force of this spiritual growth.

Finally, many pilgrims radiate this same grace in many prayer groups and communities, which developed in so many countries.

This beautiful response by mankind is not insignificant, because God, author of every grace, has needed mankind. He founded a Church, its mystical body, so that life may propagate itself actively through the Sacraments, evangelization and pastoral work, listening to God under so many forms.

To describe in detail this pastoral and its admirable fruits would exceed the dimensions of the present volume. Someone may want to undertake this complimentary study, in spite of the great difficulty. This domain remains, to a large extent and for the best, the secret of God.

At the end of this conclusion (and a suggestion to read the messages) it is important to call to mind these fruits which are the end result of the messages, and the sign of their authenticity. They have even been imposed on adversaries themselves. Msgr. Zanic, an avowed adversary of the apparitions, recognizes these fruits, making every effort to explain the causes as ordinary. This fundamental subject has enlightened our reading of the message and constitutes the foundation for the future.

One must add: Though the response to this grace of Medjugorje may have been admirable, everything comes freely from God. Everything leads to God—the origin and the source of all grace. It is to Him, then, that we must give thanks, with Mary, for this prophetic message which has paradoxically awakened so many Christians.

PART III
Chronology Of
The Messages

Acknowledgments

We would like to thank all of those who have preceded us in this study of the messages of Medjugorje, each according to his own grace, particularly:

Father Y. M. Blais, author of the first comprehensive work on the subject: "500 Messages to Live" (a very eloquent title), Montreal, 1986. He gathered nearly 350 messages, of which some are repeated several times because they relate to different themes, which justifies the number as announced in the title.

Fr. Robert Faricy, Professor of Spirituality at the Gregorian University in Rome, who examined closely, through interviews, the testimony of the seers and the spiritual dynamism of Medjugorje.

The titles of his works: "Medjugorje, Mary Queen of Peace," (Tequi, 1984, 108 pgs.) "At the Heart of Medjugorje—Mary Speaks to the World," (Fayard, 1986, 198 pgs.)

Also the irreplaceable spiritual commentaries of Fathers Thomislav Vlasic and Slavko Barbaric.[1]

Our book has been assigned an appropriate and complementary task: to assemble into a "corpus," according to chronological order, all the available messages, (more than 500), to categorize them theologically and pastorally; to dispell apparently annoying objections, and thus to clarify their sense or meaning through the teaching of Our Lady.

---

1. This daily pastoral from Frs. Vlasic and Barbaric has been published in four volumes, edited by the "Friends of Medjugorje" via Nirone 9, 20123 Milano, Italy.
    Volume 1—*Open Your Hearts to Mary, Queen of Peace.*
    Volume 2—*Abandon Yourselves Totally to Me.*
    Volume 3—*Pray With the Heart.*
    Volume 4—*I Beseech You, Listen to My Messages and Live Them.*

Chronology of the Messages

It was necessary to collect all the messages known at Medjugorje, according to the only possible objective order: Chronology. That puts a limitation on this file because the apparitions are not yet finished.

Another reason is because these texts have been transmitted in very different ways: through oral or written translation, immediate or delayed, direct or indirect, date or non-dated. We have presented, at the end of this file, the texts which apparently were not dated.

We will keep these characteristics in mind as well as the functional diversity of these messages. The six visionaries say they understand them as a normal conversation. Jelena and Marijana receive "internal locutions" through their heart.

All this seemed discouraging and dissuasive. But since so many Christians follow these messages, "Live them" (according to the beautiful formula of Father Blais), in a fruitful manner, and that so many leaflets, bulletins, books and telephone calls transmit them from day to day, it became necessary to collect these messages attributed to Our Lady. She does not impose them, but she proposes them, to the entire freedom of each person. Those who have found a home there—who live them—will benefit from them. The continuation, and the conclusion of this message, which is still unfinished, will come in its own time.

In order to show the non-official character of the apparitions, (since the Commission of Inquiry of the Bishops' Conference has not completed its work), and in order not to anticipate the conclusion of these tasks which are being accomplished in discretion, Cardinal Kuharic has asked the pastor of

Medjugorje on September 17th, 1987, that the messages not be proclaimed from the altar, and that they not have official dissemination. Private dissemination of these messages, which everyone agrees to acknowledge to be orthodox and fruitful, remains authorized. The publication of this corpus maintains this private character.

It brings a service to those whom these apparitions have converted, or involved; and to the studies of the Commission, a publication which is better organized, better dated, more exact, and thus an historical and theological clarification, useful to dispel the ambiguities of the transmission.

It is in this spirit that we dedicate this file to the Commission, and to its president, who has indeed offered thanks for my private work as an expert to the service of the common ecclesiastical research for truth.

One will find the abbreviations of the references at the end of the volume, on page 354.

Publisher's Note

In Mary's appearances to the seers prior to March, 1984, the beginning salutation was usually: *Praise be Jesus*. In leaving the children, the ending words were usually: *Go in the Peace of God*.

Beginning in March, 1984, the messages were usually given for the parish, (and the world), and the opening salutation from the Madonna was usually: *Dear Children!* In leaving, Mary almost always thanked those involved with: *Thank you for having responded to my call*.

These salutations are normally omitted in this text, and in the index of messages at the end of the book, but it should be noted that they constitute part of the messages, even though it is not necessary to print them for every message stated.

It should also be noted, that in some cases these messages have been translated among three or four different languages. As a result, certain words may show slight variation, or phrases could change within the sentence structure.

CHAPTER 1

The First Apparitions

MARY ON THE HILL

(June 24-29, 1981)

WEDNESDAY, JUNE 24TH

A silent and distant apparition of the white silhouette on the hill of Cronica; the first time in the afternoon, the second time, towards 6:00 p.m.

THURSDAY, JUNE 25TH

The date of the first apparition for the group of six seers, who see the Gospa nearby on the hill:

Praised be Jesus! (DV.1).

Ivanka: "Where is my mother?" (Her mother had died two months previously.)

She is happy. She is with me. (A variation on this wording is) *She is your angel in heaven.* (Lj.15).

The seers: "Will you return tomorrow?"

The apparition acquieses with a nod of the head.

Mirjana: "No one will believe us. They will say that we are crazy. Give us a sign!"

The apparition responds only with a smile. Mirjana believed she had received a sign. Her watch had changed time during the apparition. (Bu 24; D4; K21).

Goodbye, my angels. (BU.24).

Go in the peace of God. (DV.1).

FRIDAY, JUNE 26TH

In the presence of a crowd of 2,000 to 3,000 people, drawn there by the luminary signs coming from the hill of the apparitions, Vicka sprinkles the apparition with holy water and says:

"If you are the Gospa, stay with us, if not, go away."

The apparition only smiles.

Ivanka: "Why have you come here? What do you desire?

I have come because there are many true believers here. I wish to be with you to convert and to reconcile the whole world.

(According to others: *To convert all of you.*) (K.26).

Ivanka: "Did my mother say anything?"

Obey your grandmother and help her because she is old. (K.26; Lj.16; BU.28).

Mirjana: "How is my grandfather?" (He had recently died.)

He is well. (K.26).

The seers on a request from the crowd:

"Give us a sign which will prove your presence."

Blessed are those who have not seen and who believe. (L.2,24).

Mirjana: "Who are you?"

I am the Most Blessed Virgin Mary. (L.1, 37).

"Why are you appearing to us? We are not better than others."

I do not necessarily choose the best.

"Will you come back?"

Yes, to the same place as yesterday. (L.2, 25).

On returning to the village after the apparition, Maria sees the Virgin again, in tears, near a cross with rainbow colors:

Peace, Peace, Peace! Be reconciled! Only Peace. (D.7). *Make your peace with God and among yourselves. For that, it is necessary to believe, to pray, to fast, and to go to confession.* (F.2, 126; D.5).

SATURDAY, JUNE 27TH

Praised be Jesus!

Jakov: "What do you expect of our Franciscans?"

Have them persevere in the faith and protect the faith of others. (DV.1).

Jakov and **Mirjana:** "Leave us a sign because the people treat us as liars."

My angels, do not be afraid of injustice. It has always existed. (L.2,33).

The seers: "How must we pray?"

Continue to recite seven Our Father's and seven Hail Mary's and Glory Be's, but also add the Creed. (B1.12).

Goodbye, my angels. Go in the peace of God.

And to **Ivan**, alone, aside:

Be in peace and take courage. ("And what a beautiful smile when she left me," noted Ivan.) (L.2,33).

SUNDAY, JUNE 28TH

The seers: "What do you wish?"

That people believe and persevere in the faith.

Vicka: "What do you expect from the priests?"

That they remain strong in the faith and that they help you.

"Why don't you appear to everyone in church?"

Blessed are they who believe without having seen.

"Will you come back?"

Yes, to the same place.

"Do you prefer prayer or singing?"

Both, pray and sing.

Vicka: "What do you wish from the crowd which has gathered here?"

This question remained without any response except for a glance of love, with a smile, said the seers.

Here the Virgin disappeared. The visionaries prayed so that she might return because she had not said, *Goodbye, my angels.*

During their song, "You Are All Beautiful," she reappears.

Vicka: "Dear Gospa, what do you expect of this people?"

She repeated the question three times and finally was given this answer:

That those who do not see believe as those who see.

Vicka: "Will you leave us a sign so that people believe that we are not liars nor comedians?"

No other response, only a smile.

Go in the peace of God, she said, as she disappeared.

(The responses for the 28th of June were taken from the tape recorder of Grgo Kozina.) (L.2,37-38).

MONDAY, JUNE 29TH

The seers: "Dear Gospa, are you happy to see so many people here today?"

More than happy ("She smiles," writes Vicka).

"How long will you stay with us?"

As long as you will want me to, my angels.

"What do you expect of the people who have come in spite of the brambles and the heat?"

There is only one God, one faith. Let the people believe firmly and do not fear anything.

"What do you expect of us?"

That you have a solid faith and that you maintain confidence.

"Will we know how to endure persecutions which will come to us because of you?"

You will be able to, my angels. Do not fear. You will be able to endure everything. You must believe and have confidence in me.

Here Vicka writes a question from Dr. Darinka Glamuzina: "May I touch Our Lady?" She gives this response:

There have always been doubting Thomases, but she can approach.

Vicka shows her where to stretch out her hand. Darinka tries to touch her. The Gospa disappears, then reappears in her light. (L2,33).

The parents of a three-year-old child, Daniel Setka, who had suffered from septicemia since the fourth day of his birth, asked the seers to intercede for the handicapped child. "Dear Gospa, is little Daniel going to speak some day? Cure him so that they all will believe us. These people love you very much, dear Gospa. Perform a miracle...It is watching...it...Dear Gospa, say something."

They repeated this petition and conveyed the response:

Have them believe strongly in his cure. Go in the peace of God. (L.2, 42-43).

CHAPTER 2

The Hidden Phase

(June 30, 1981 To December 31, 1981)

During this period, the Gospa appeared where the seers (who were being tracked down), discreetly awaited her, away from the patrols of the police.

TUESDAY, JUNE 30TH

Apparition at Cerno. (L.2,40-41).

Mirjana: "Are you angry that we were not on the hill?"
That doesn't matter.
"Would you be angry if we would not return any longer to the hill, but we would wait in the church?"
Always at the same time.
Go in the peace of God. (L.2,50).
On that day, Mirjana thought that she understood that the Gospa would return for three more days, until Friday. But it was only her interpretation.

WEDNESDAY, JULY 1ST

Apparition in the van (L.2,56: no words were reported).

THURSDAY, JULY 2ND

Jakov: "Dear Gospa, leave us a sign."
The Virgin seemed to acquiese with a nod:
Goodbye, my dear angels. (L.2,60).
The apparitions from the 3rd to the 20th of July, 1981, have left few traces, almost uniquely the diary of Vicka (July 21-29,

Aug. 22-Sept. 6, Oct. 10-Dec. 24), and the parish Chronicle (which begins Aug. 10, 1981).

FRIDAY, JULY 3RD

Apparition at the rectory. No message was preserved.

SATURDAY, JULY 4TH

The seers believe the apparitions had ended, but the Gospa appeared to each one of them separately, where he or she was. No message was preserved.

TUESDAY, JULY 21ST
(27th apparition, according to Vicka's diary).

Just like every day, we spoke with the Gospa. At 6:30 when she arrived, she greeted us:
Praised be Jesus!
Then we asked her if she would give us a sign. She said yes. Then we asked her how longer still would she come to visit us. The Blessed Virgin responded:
My sweet angels, even if I were to leave the sign, many people will not believe. Many people will only come here and bow down. But people must be converted and do penance.
Then we questioned her on the subject of the sick. For some, the Gospa said that they would be cured only if their faith was strong; and for others, no. Then she prepared to depart. Upon leaving, she said to us:
Go in the peace of God. (DV.1,2).

WEDNESDAY, JULY 22ND:
(28th apparition, 6:30, according to Vicka's diary). (DV.1,2).

On arriving she said:
Praise be Jesus Christ.
All of us questioned her on the subject of some sick people who had been recommended to us. Then we prayed with the Blessed Virgin. She only said the Our Father and Glory Be, and during the time that we said the Hail Mary, she was silent. The Gospa told us that:
A good many people have been converted and among them some had not gone to Confession in 45 years, and now, they

are going to Confession.

Then she said:

Go in the peace of God.

She began to depart and, while she was departing, a cross appeared in the sky.

THURSDAY, JULY 23RD

(29th apparition, according to Vicka's diary.) (DV.1,2).

Vicka only mentions the greeting from Our Lady:

Praised be Jesus Christ.

FRIDAY, JULY 24TH

(30th apparition, 6:30, according to Vicka's diary). (DV.1,2).

Today, also, we went to the place of the apparitions about 6:20, and while praying and singing, we waited for the Blessed Virgin. At exactly 6:30 we saw the light which slowly approached. Then we saw the Blessed Virgin and heard her customary greeting.

To our questions, relative to the majority of the sick, the Gospa answered quickly:

Without faith, nothing is possible. All those who will believe firmly will be cured.

SATURDAY, JULY 25TH

(31st apparition, according to Vicka's diary). (DV.1,2).

After the usual questions on the subject of the ill, the Gospa responded:

God, help us all!

MONDAY, JULY 27TH

(33rd apparition, at 6:30, according to Vicka's diary). (DV.1,3).

Only four of us came because they put pressure on Ivica, Ivanka and Mirjana to go to Sarajevo. At 6:30 exactly, the Gospa appeared.

Vicka asked her about certain sick people, took some objects which had been given to her by some people, and approached Our Lady so that she could bless them. The Gospa made the Sign of the Cross and said:

In the name of the Father, and of the Son, and of the Holy Spirit.

Then we questioned her on the subject of the sign, and the Gospa answered:

Await, it will not be for long. If I will leave you a sign, I will still appear to you.

Vicka asked if we would be able to see her again one more time this evening on the hill. The Gospa agreed and said:

I will come at 11:15 p.m. Go in the peace of God.

Saying this, she began to disappear and we saw in the heavens the heart and the cross. Mary said:

My angels, I send you my Son, Jesus, Who was tortured for His faith, and yet He endured everything. You also, my angels, will endure everything.

Jesus had long hair, brown eyes, and a beard. We only saw His head. (We transpose this phrase which came before the word of Mary.) She said that we prayed and sang beautifully:

It is beautiful to listen to you. Continue in this manner.

In conclusion she said:

Don't be afraid for Jozo. (The pastor who had been threatened by the police).

WEDNESDAY, JULY 29TH
(35th apparition, 6:30, according to Vicka's diary). (DV.1,3).

Today we waited for the Blessed Virgin in Vicka's room. At exactly 6:30, the Gospa came and greeted us.

Praised be Jesus!

Jakov was the first to question her on the subject of a person who was ill. The Blessed Virgin said:

She will be cured. She must believe firmly.

Vicka asked why she had not come yesterday. The Blessed Mother said something, smiled, but no one heard it. Then Maria and Jakov asked her about certain sick people. We then took some articles and all four approached the Gospa so that she would bless them. When we were doing this, our hands became very cold.

Jakov asked if we could embrace her. The Blessed Virgin said that we should approach and embrace her. Then we asked her to leave us the sign. She said:

Yes.

Then:

Go in the peace of God.

And she began to disappear. On the ceiling the Cross and the Heart were visible.

The cross, the heart and the sun are mentioned by Vicka in her diary, in later apparitions. (Aug. 22, 27, 30 and 31, Sept. 1 and Nov. 22, 1981, as well as on Feb. 6 and Mar. 12, 1982).

In church we saw the Blessed Virgin a second time toward eight o'clock in the choir loft. While we were praying, the Blessed Virgin prayed with us. (DV.1, 3).

THURSDAY, JULY 30TH

We did not go to the hill. (DV.1, 4). (Vicka's diary contains no more observations until August 22nd.)

JULY

Carry out well your responsibilities and what the Church asks you to do. (BL.307).

SUNDAY, AUGUST 2ND

Maria sees the Virgin in her room:

All of you together go to the meadow at Gumno. A great battle is about to take place. A battle between my Son and Satan. Human souls are at stake.

The seers, accompanied by some 40 people, went to the praire of Gumno, 200 meters from Vicka's house.

Everyone here may touch me. (D).

After many people had touched her, a black stain appeared on the dress of the Virgin. Maria cried. Marinko invited the people who were present to go to Confession.

THE BEGINNING OF AUGUST

"What do you wish that we do later?"

I would like for you to become priests and religious, but only if you, yourselves, would want it. It is up to you to decide. (L.2, 83).

THURSDAY, AUGUST 6TH (FEAST OF THE TRANSFIGURATION)

I am the Queen of Peace. (L.1, 75).

FRIDAY, AUGUST 7TH

On Mt. Krizevac, at two o'clock in the morning:
That one do penance for sins. (L.2, 76).

SATURDAY, AUGUST 8TH

Do penance! Strengthen your faith through prayer and the sacraments. (D.).

MONDAY, AUGUST 17TH

Do not be afraid. I wish that you would be filled with joy and that the joy could be seen on your faces. I will protect Father Jozo. (The latter was the pastor of the parish at Medjugorje who was imprisoned). (BL.338).

SATURDAY, AUGUST 22ND

Father Jozo has nothing to fear. All that will pass. (DV.1, 3).

SUNDAY, AUGUST 23RD

Praised be Jesus! I have been with Ivica until now.[1] *Pray, my angels, for this people.*
My children, I give you strength. I will give you some of it always.
When you need me, call me. (DV.1, 4).

MONDAY, AUGUST 24TH

In her diary, for the date of August 25th, Vicka writes: "Yesterday, Monday the 24th at 10:45, Mirjana and I were at Ivan's house. We heard an uproar and we went out running. Outside, everybody was looking at the cross on Krizevac. At the spot of the cross, Mirjana, Jakov, Ivan and I saw the Blessed Virgin, and the people saw something like her statue which began then to disappear, and the cross appeared again.

Over the entire sky one saw, written in letters of gold, MIR: "PEACE."

Vicka's diary then reports the apparition on August 25th. (DV.1, 4).

---

1. This diminutive refers sometimes to Ivan, sometimes to Ivanka. Here, the context does not permit one to be more specific.

A little after the Virgin prayed for peace, a large inscription appeared on top of Krizevac. The word "Peace" (MIR in Croatian). The inscription was seen by the pastor and many persons of the village. There is written testimony by those who saw the inscription. The seers affirmed that the Blessed Virgin Mary promised that there would still be many other signs as forerunners at Medjugorje, and in other parts of the world, before the great sign. (K58, which observes the event one evening in July 1981).

TUESDAY, AUGUST 25TH

Some persons who were present said...to request of the Blessed Virgin the permission to touch her. The Gospa said:

It is not necessary to touch me. Many are those who do not feel anything when they touch me. (DV.1, 4).

She also said that, among those present, there was a spy (no other clarification was given on this point).

On the matter of the sign, you do not have to become impatient for the day will come. (DV.1, 4).

WEDNESDAY, AUGUST 26TH

Today, for the first time, we waited for the Blessed Virgin at the home of Zdenka Ivankovic. There were five of us, because Ivanka had not yet returned. The Blessed Virgin appeared and said:

Praised be Jesus.

She said that tomorrow the people did not have to come, and thus we would be by ourselves. Then also:

Do not give advice to anyone. I know what you feel and that will pass, also. (DV.1,4).

THURSDAY, AUGUST 27TH

Maria and I came to Jakov's house today about six o'clock. We helped Jakov's mother to prepare supper. At six o'clock the Blessed Virgin came toward us. I was outside when the Blessed Virgin Mary came. She said that they should not have to make one suffer so.

We asked her with respect to the sign, and she said:

Very soon, I promise you.

We commended certain sick people to the Holy Virgin. She stayed with us for 15 minutes. Then we left for the home of Marinko Ivankovic in order to wait for the Blessed Virgin there. She came at 6:30. She told Ivan (Dragicevic):

Be strong and courageous.

She left, and the cross, the heart and the sun appeared. (DV.1, 5).

FRIDAY, AUGUST 28TH

At the hour of the apparitions, the seers wait in the room of Father Jozo, who is in prison. The Virgin does not appear. It is the second time that this has happened. They go to church and pray. She appears to them:

I was with Father Jozo. That is why I did not come. Do not trouble yourselves if I do not come. It suffices then to pray. (DV.1, 5).

Today, Ivan entered the seminary of Visoko:

You are very tired. Rest, so that you can find strength. Go in the peace of God. Goodbye. (Adieu: Ivan's Journal).

SATURDAY, AUGUST 29TH

Jakov: "Are you also appearing to Ivan in the seminary?"

Yes, just like to you.

"How is Ivan in prison?"[2]

He is well. He is enduring everything. All that will pass. Father Jozo sends you greetings. (DV.1).

"What is the news from our village?"

My angels, you are doing your penance well.

"Will you help us in our studies?"

God's help manifests itself everywhere.

Go in the peace of God with the blessing of Jesus and mine. Goodbye. (Ivan's Journal: C76).

Ivanka: "Will you leave us a sign soon?"

Again, a little patience. (DV.1).

---

2. Ivan Ivankovic, son of Pero, and cousin of Vicka, one of the four men at Bijakovici who bear this name. He had been arrested by the police August 12th, on the hill of the apparitions, and imprisoned.

SUNDAY, AUGUST 30TH

At 6:20, we began to pray at the home of Marinko Ivankovic. The Virgin arrived and said:

Praised be Jesus!

Vicka asked the Virgin:

"People say that since they locked up Father Jozo in his cell, the doors unlocked by themselves. Is that true?"

It is true, but no one believes it.

Ivanka: "How is Mirjana? What are her feelings?"

Mirjana is sad because she is all alone. I will show her to you.

Suddenly, we saw Mirjana's face. She was crying.

"Dear Gospa, there are some young people who betray our faith."

Yes, there are many.

She mentions some names.

Vicka asks the Virgin concerning a woman who wanted to leave her husband because he was making her suffer.

Let her remain close to him and accept her suffering. Jesus, Himself, also suffered.

On the matter of a sick young boy:

He is suffering from a very grave illness. Let his parents firmly believe, do penance, then the little boy will be cured.

Jakov asks her about the sign:

Again, a little patience. (DV.1, 6).

Ivan, who had been several days without an apparition: "How will I do in this seminary?"

Be without fear. I am close to you everywhere and at all times. (L.2, 84).

Ivan's diary: "Are the people pious in our village?"

Your village has become the most fervent parish in Hercegovina. A large number of people distinguish themselves through their piety and their faith. (c.77).

END OF AUGUST:

"Which is the best fasting?"

A fasting on bread and water.

I am the Queen of Peace. (L.1, 98 and 187; MM6).

TUESDAY, SEPTEMBER 1ST

"Will there be a Mass on Mt. Krizevac?"
Yes, my angels.

Jakov: "Are the police setting up a trap around the church?"
There's nothing at all. Have the people pray and remain in church as long as possible.
Go in the peace of God.
The cross, the heart, and the sun appeared. (DV.1, 6).

Ivan's diary: "I prayed with her so that Jesus might help me in my vocation. Then we recited the rosary. The Gospa smiled with kindness."
Do not be afraid. I am close to you and I watch over you. (c.77).

WEDNESDAY, SEPTEMBER 2ND

Concerning the young man who hanged himself:
Vicka: "Why did he do that?"
Satan took hold of him. This young man should not have done that. The Devil tries to reign over the people. He takes everything into his hands, but the force of God is more powerful, and God will conquer. (DV.1, 6).

Ivan's diary: "How will things go for Anton, Dario, Miljenko, my friends in the seminary, and for me?"
You are, and you will always be my children. You have followed the path of Jesus. No one will stop you from propagating the faith in Jesus. One must believe strongly. (C.78).

THURSDAY, SEPTEMBER 3RD

Jakov: "When will the sign which was announced come?"
Again, a little patience. (DV.1, 6).

FRIDAY, SEPTEMBER 4TH

Ivanka and *Maria:* "We will not be at home except on Saturdays and Sundays. The other days we will be far away in school. What must we do?"
It is enough for you to pray. Come here Saturdays and Sundays. I will appear to all of you. (DV.1, 6).

To Ivan in the seminary:
The sign will be given at the end of the apparitions.
Ivan: "When will that be?"
You are impatient, my angel. Go in the peace of God. (L.2, 84).

SATURDAY, SEPTEMBER 5TH

Ivan's diary: "I was praying in the chapel. The Gospa came when I was reciting the Our Father."
Praise be Jesus and Mary.
(The Virgin was using a salutation of pious people in Croatia, probably with the desire to revive it.)
Go in the peace of God, my angel. May the blessing of God accompany you. Amen. Goodbye. (C.79).

SUNDAY, SEPTEMBER 6TH

Ivan's diary: "I was praying in the chapel. Suddenly there was a great light."
Pray especially on Sunday, so that the great sign, the gift of God may come. Pray with fervor and a constancy so that God may have mercy on His great children.
Go in peace, my angel. May the blessing of God accompany you. Amen. Goodbye. (C.79).

MONDAY, SEPTEMBER 7TH

Ivan's diary:
Be converted all of you who are still there. The sign will come when you will be converted. (C.79).

TUESDAY, SEPTEMBER 8TH
(FEAST OF THE NATIVITY OF THE VIRGIN)

Ivan's diary:
I ask you only to pray with fervor. Prayer must become a part of your daily life, to permit the true faith to take roots. (C.79).
Jakov wishes the Blessed Virgin a happy birthday.
She answers:
It is for me a beautiful day. With respect to you, persevere in the faith and in prayer. (CP.7).

Do not be afraid. Remain in joy. It is my desire. Let joy appear on your faces. I will continue to protect Father Jozo. (CP.8).

THURSDAY, SEPTEMBER 10TH

Ivan's diary: "We prayed a lot. Prayers filled with joy and love, prayers of the heart." Then she says:
Go in the peace of God, my angel. Amen. Goodbye. (C.80).

SUNDAY, SEPTEMBER 13TH

Ivan's diary: "The students in the seminary prayed the rosary after they had gone to Confession." The Virgin came near the image of Jesus and said:
There is your Father, my angel.
Go in the peace of God, my angels. (C.80).
Christ is our Brother, but in a sense, our Father: Formula used by some of the most reknown mystics.
In an apparition to Gemma Galgani, Jesus said, *I am your Father. Your Mother, here she is.* And He pointed out to her the Blessed Virgin. (J.F. Villepelée, "Vie de G. Galgani.").

MONDAY, SEPTEMBER 14TH

To Vicka: *Stay here so that Jakov will not be alone. Persevere (both of you) with patience. You will be rewarded.*
She also told her that she had scolded Mirjana and Ivanka for a behavior which was not detailed. (CP.10).

TUESDAY, SEPTEMBER 15TH

If this people is not converted very soon, bad things will happen to them. (CP.10).

WEDNESDAY, SEPTEMBER 16TH

The militia will not stay here a long time. I will leave the sign. Be patient still. Don't pray for yourselves. You have been rewarded. Pray for others. (CP.11).

THURSDAY, SEPTEMBER 17TH

Concerning a sick person:
He will die very soon.

Then the Blessed Virgin encouraged the children:
Persevere and you will be rewarded. (CP.11)

SUNDAY, SEPTEMBER 20TH

To Vicka and Jakov:
*Do not relax in your prayers. I ask both of you to fast for
a week on bread and water.* (Bl. 190).

WEDNESDAY, SEPTEMBER 30TH

*Don't ask useless questions dictated by curiosity. The most
important thing is to pray, my angels.* (CP.12)

THURSDAY, OCTOBER 1ST

Written questions asked of the seers: "Are all religions good?"
*All religions are similar before God. God rules over them
just like a sovereign over his kingdom. In the world, all religions
are not the same because people have not complied with the
commandments of God. They reject and disparage them.*[3]
"Are all churches the same?"
*In some, one prays to God more. In others, less. That de-
pends on the priests who motivate others to pray. That also
depends on the power which they have.*
"Why are there so many apparitions which repeat themselves so many times? Why does the Blessed Virgin appear
to children who do not follow the way of God?"
*I appear to you often and in every place. To others, I ap-
pear from time to time and briefly. They do not follow yet,
completely the way of God. They are not aware of the gift
which He has made them. That, no one deserves. With time,
they also will come to follow the right way.* (CP.14).

TUESDAY, OCTOBER 6TH

*The evening Mass must definitely be kept. The Mass of the
sick must be celebrated on a specific day at a time which
is most convenient. Father Tomislav must begin with the prayer
group. It is very necessary. Have Father Tomislav pray with
fervor.* (CP.16).

---

3. On this ambiguous response see annex 2, pages 344 to 347.

WEDNESDAY, OCTOBER 7TH

The seers: "Is there, outside of Jesus, other intermediaries between God and man, and what is their role?"

There is only one mediator between God and man, and it is Jesus Christ.

On the request from Father Tomislav:

"Should we found here a community just like that of Saint Francis of Assisi?"

God has chosen Saint Francis as His elected one. It would be good to imitate his life. In the meantime, we must realize what God orders us to do. (CP.16).

THURSDAY, OCTOBER 8TH

Maria humbly reports that the Gospa had scolded her for having stayed (during Mass) with her school mates of religious instruction, who asked her about the apparitions:

You would have done better to attend Mass rather than to satisfy human curiosity. (CP.17).

SATURDAY, OCTOBER 10TH

It is up to you to pray and to persevere. I have made promises to you; also be without anxiety. (DV.2).

Faith will not know how to be alive without prayer. (Bl.137).

Pray more. (CP.17).

SUNDAY, OCTOBER 11TH

The Virgin answers, as usual, questions on the subject of people who are sick or who have disappeared:

Tomo Lovic (an old man) *is dead.* (CP.17).

MONDAY, OCTOBER 12TH

"Where are the Kingdom of God and of paradise?"

In Heaven.

"Are you the Mother of God?"

I am the Mother of God and the Queen of Peace.

"Did you go to Heaven before or after death?"

I went to Heaven before death.

"When will you leave us the sign?"

I will not yet leave the sign. I shall continue to appear. Father Jozo sends you greetings. He is experiencing difficulties, but he will resist, because he knows why he is suffering. (CP. 18: DV.2, 10).

SATURDAY, OCTOBER 17TH

Questioned on the subject of the visible sign, Our Lady responds:

It is mine to realize the promise. With respect to the faithful, have them pray and believe firmly.

MONDAY, OCTOBER 19TH

Pray for Fr. Jozo and fast tomorrow on bread and water. Then you will fast for a whole week on bread and water. Pray, my angels. Now I will show you Fr. Jozo. (CP 20).

The seers have a vision of Fr. Jozo in prison. He tells them not to be afraid for him, that everything was well.

With respect to Marinko who protected the visionaries:

There are a few similar faithful. He is made a sufficient number of sacrifices for Jozo. He underwent many torments and sufferings. Continue, and do not let anyone take the faith away from you.

TUESDAY, OCTOBER 20TH

Vicka: "Dear Gospa, have mercy on Fr. Jozo tomorrow during the trial. Paralyze someone; strike someone on the head. I know it is a sin to speak so, but what can we do?"

The Gospa smiles at my words, then she sings:

"Jesus Christ, in Your Name. When we finished the song, (with the Gospa) she tells us:"

Go in the peace of God.

Then she leaves. (DV.2, 13; CP. 20).

WEDNESDAY, OCTOBER 21ST

With respect to Fr. Jozo who is awaiting sentence from the court:

Vicka: "Dear Gospa, I know that you do not have the spirit of vengeance, but try nevertheless to bring certain people to reason, so that they might judge impartially."

*Jozo looks well and he greets you warmly. Do not fear for
Jozo. He is a saint, I have already told you.* (CP. 21).

"Will Jozo be condemned?"

*Sentence will not be pronounced this evening. Do not be
afraid, he will not be condemned to a severe punishment. Pray
only, because Jozo asks from you prayer and perseverance.
Do not be afraid because I am with you.* (DV. 2, 14).

THURSDAY, OCTOBER 22ND

Jozo has been sentenced. Let us go to church to pray.

"We were sad because of Jozo."

You should rejoice! (DV. 2, 14; CP. 21).

"Is the whiteness of the cross a supernatural phenomenon?"

Yes, I confirm it. (DV. 2, 15; CP. 21).

After many people saw the cross on Mt. Krizevac transform
itself into a light, then into a silhouette of the Virgin:

*All of these signs are designed to strengthen your faith until
I leave you the visible and permanent sign.* (F2, 155).

SUNDAY, OCTOBER 25TH

Three girls from Citluk, returning home after Mass, suddenly see a great light from which fifteen silhouettes, dressed
in Franciscan frock, are apparent. They go down on their
knees, pray and cry. The Blessed Virgin was questioned on
this subject:

It was a supernatural phenomenon. I was among the saints.
(CP. 23).

MONDAY, OCTOBER 26TH

The Blessed Virgin appeared smiling:

*Praise be Jesus. You are not to ask me any more questions
on the subject of the sign. Do not be afraid, it will surely
appear. I carry out my promises. As far as you are concerned,
pray, persevere in prayer.* (DV. 2, 16: CP. 23-24).

WEDNESDAY, OCTOBER 28TH

"Were you there at Krizevac yesterday for half an hour?"

Yes, didn't you see me? (DV. 1, 17; CP. 251).

Several hundred people saw, at the site of the first apparition, a fire which burned without burning up anything. In the evening, the Virgin tells the seers:

The fire seen by the faithful was of a supernatural character. It is one of the signs; a forerunner of the great sign. (CP. 25).

THURSDAY, OCTOBER 29TH

You, my angels, be on your guard. There is enough mendacious news which people are spreading. Of course, I will show you my mercy. Be a little patient. Pray! (DV. 2, 17).

FRIDAY, OCTOBER 30TH

Praise be Jesus!

Jakov and **Vicka:** "What was there in the sealed envelope which they showed us at city hall?" (Someone had told them that he would believe in the apparitions, if they would read what was in the sealed envelope.)

Do not respond anything. It is a bad trick which they are playing on you. They have already given so much false news. Do not believe them. Continue to pray and to suffer! I will make the power of love appear. (CP. 25-26; DV. 2, 18).

"Should one celebrate Christmas Mass in the evening or at Midnight?"

Have them celebrate it at midnight. (CP. 25).

To the seers:

Pray! Go in the peace of God! (DV2, 17).

To Ivanka:

Pray more. The others are praying and suffering more than you.

To the seers:

Tell the young people not to allow themselves to be distracted from the true way. Let them remain faithful to their religion. (CP. 26).

SATURDAY, OCTOBER 31ST—Two versions:

1. Vicka's diary: (D. 1, 17).

Mirjana arrives from Sarajevo, where she is studying at a professional school, and where she has had daily apparitions.

Vicka reports: "The Gospa advises as an attentive mother would. She tells Mirjana twice that she must distrust, which persons to avoid, how to conduct herself with those who reproach her and insult God."

"She also tells her to break a relationship with a girl who wanted to get her into drugs (. . .), and; not to quarrel with anyone, to answer a point when it is useful, or to remain silent and go on her way when that is better. She tells her also that Father Jozo will not spend more than four years in prison. She was happy because all five of us were together. On the question of Danny Ljolje, the Gospa said:"

There is a lot of deception and erroneous information.

"Then she shows us a part of paradise; indescribable beauty; many people, particularly children. We were afraid. The Blessed Virgin tells us not to be afraid."

All those who are faithful to God will have that. (DV. 2, 17).

2. Parish Chronicle:

T. Vlasic summarizes the advice given to Mirjana in this manner:

"The Blessed Virgin advises her, as an attentive and good mother. She also shows her what she should pay attention to, which persons to avoid, how to handle those who provoke and offend God. The Blessed Virgin advised her to sever all types of relationships with a young girl who intended to get her into drugs. Then she put her on guard against other dangers. She told her not to argue with people and to answer calmly, and when she sees that serves no purpose, to keep quiet and continue on her way."

"Often she would motivate her to prayer and to perseverance."

"She also tells her that Father Jozo would not have more than four years in prison. The Blessed Mother shows a great joy, because the five seers were together again. To a question which was brought up again concerning Danny Ljolje, the Blessed Virgin said:"

There is enough trickery and false information.

"She asks the children to separate from such persons. And then the Gospa shows the children a part of paradise, indescribable beauty, many people, especially children. The seers were surprised and shocked. The Gospa told them not to fear:"

It will be like this for all those who are faithful to God.

"Ivanka saw her mother in paradise as well as another person who was of her acquaintance." (CP. 26-27).

OCTOBER

Regarding the conflict between the Franciscans and the Bishop of Mostar in Hercegovina:

It is going to find a solution. We must have patience and pray.

In response to a question posed by the seers: "What will become of Poland?"

There will be great conflicts but in the end, the just will take over.

With respect to Russia:

It is the people where God will be most glorified. The West has made civilization progress, but without God, as if they were their own creators. (K. 60).

SUNDAY, NOVEMBER 1ST

Be persevering! Pray! Many people are beginning to convert. (CP. 27; DV. 2,18).

THE BEGINNING OF NOVEMBER

The Virgin appears with a picture of John Paul II in her hand. She embraces the picture:

He is our father, and the father of all. It is necessary to pray for him.

MONDAY, NOVEMBER 2ND

"Why did you show us paradise the day before yesterday?"

I did it so that you could see the happiness which awaits those who love God.

Jesus appears to them crowned with thorns and with injuries all over His body. The children are afraid.

Do not be afraid. It is my Son. See how He has been martyred. In spite of all, He was joyful and He endured all with patience.

Jesus tells them:

Look at me. How I have been injured and martyred. In spite of all, I have gained the victory. You also, my angels, be persevering in your faith and pray so that you may over-come. (CP. 28, DV. 2,18).

TUESDAY, NOVEMBER 3RD

"The Virgin begins the song, 'Come, Come to Us Lord' and we continued it with her."

I am often at Krizevac, at the foot of the cross, to pray there. Now I pray to my Son to forgive the world its sins. The world has begun to convert.

She smiles, then leaves. (CP. 28, DV.2, 18).

FRIDAY, NOVEMBER 6TH

"After twenty minutes, the Gospa disappears and before us Hell appears. Later she tells us:"

Do not be afraid! I have shown you Hell so that you may know the state of those who are there. (DV. 2, 19).

SUNDAY, NOVEMBER 8TH

The Blessed Virgin kisses an image of the Pope and says:
It is your father, the spiritual father of all. (L2, 90).

The seers have a vision of Fr. Jozo in prison. The Blessed Virgin tells them:

Have you seen how our Fr. Jozo struggles for God? (dv. 2, 20).

MONDAY, NOVEMBER 9TH

"Jakov and I were alone in the room. We were speaking of the militia which passed by. The Virgin arrived:"

Do not be afraid of the militia. Do not provoke anybody. Be polite with everybody. (DV. 2, 20).

TUESDAY, NOVEMBER 10TH

Do not give in. Keep your faith. I will accompany you at every step. (DV. 2, 20).

FRIDAY, NOVEMBER 13TH

Praise be Jesus!
The seers: "Always Jesus and Mary."
"Then the Blessed Virgin shows us beautiful landscapes.

The Baby Jesus was walking there. We were not able to recognize Him. She said:"

It is Jesus. On my arrival and when I depart always sing the song, 'Come, Come to us O Lord.'

"Then she blessed us." (DV. 2, 21: CP. 29).

SUNDAY, NOVEMBER 15TH

"We were in Fr. Jozo's room. The Gospa did not come. She appeared to us in the church after the prayers of 7 Our Father's, Hail Mary's, and Glory Be's. We asked her why she had not appeared. She answered that she had not appeared because someone had installed something there."

The world is on the point of receiving great favors from me and from my Son. May the world keep a strong confidence. (CP. 29; DV. 2,22).

MONDAY, NOVEMBER 16TH

The Devil is trying to conquer us. Do not permit him. Keep the faith, fast and pray. I will be with you at every step. (CP. 31).

To Jakov* and *Vicka:
Persevere with confidence in prayer and in faith. (DV. 2, 22).

SUNDAY, NOVEMBER 22ND

"We asked the Blessed Virgin what the cross, the heart and the sun, seen during the apparition, meant:"

These are the signs of salvation: The cross is a sign of mercy, just like the heart. The sun is the source of light, which enlightens us. (DV. 12,24; cf. 29XI; DV. 12, 19; CP. 33).

A shining silhouette takes the place of the cross again on Krizevac. The seers ask the Virgin if it was she.

Why do you ask me my angels? Have you not seen me? (L21, 92).

The world must find salvation while there is time. Let it pray with fervor. May it have the spirit of faith. (CP. 33).

MONDAY, NOVEMBER 23RD

"The Gospa was all dressed in gold. Around her veil, on her dress, everything shined and sparkled. It was indescribable. She was very, very beautiful."

The people have begun to convert. Keep a solid faith. I need your prayers.

THURSDAY, NOVEMBER 26TH

"This evening, the Blessed Virgin was smiling. We prayed and sang with her. We asked her questions about the sick."

Have a strong faith, pray and fast and they will be cured. Be confident and rest in joy. Go in the peace of God. Be patient and pray for the cure. Goodbye, my dear angels. (CP. 34; DV. 2, 25).

SATURDAY, NOVEMBER 28TH

"We were five, Ivan was absent. Profound harmony reigned over us. The Virgin came at the moment when we began to say the Our Father. We conversed with her. Then she blessed the objects. She looked at us with sweetness and said,"

Ah, it is so beautiful to see all of you together! Go in the peace of God, my angels. Goodbye. (DV. 2, 26).

SUNDAY, NOVEMBER 29TH

It is necessary for the world to be saved while there is still time; for it to pray strongly and to have the spirit of faith. (CP. 34).

NOVEMBER:

The Devil tries to impose his power on you. But you must remain strong and persevere in your faith. You must pray and fast. I will be always close to you.

Vicka: "This warning concerns everybody." (C 100).

WEDNESDAY, DECEMBER 2ND

Maria, Vicka and **Jakov:** "We asked the Blessed Virgin on the matter of a young man who had suddenly lost his memory and stopped learning. She said,"

It is necessary to hospitalize him.

"We still questioned her. She did not respond to some of the questions."

It is not necessary to ask questions on every subject.

"She greeted us then, as usual." (CP. 35; DV. 2, 28).

THURSDAY, DECEMBER 3RD

Pray, and persevere through prayer. (CP. 35; DV. 2,29).

SUNDAY, DECEMBER 6TH

Be strong and persevering.
My dear angels, go in the peace of God. (DV. 2,30).

MONDAY, DECEMBER 7TH

The people are converting. It is true, but not yet all.
She spoke while looking at the crowd which was present at the different sites of the apparitions. (C53).
Apparition at Jakov's home: "The blessed Virgin prayed all the time with us. She then said:"
Pray and persist in prayers. (DV. 2, 30 and CP. 36).
On the walls there was written in letters of gold "MIR LJUDIMA" (Peace to the people). (CP. 36).

TUESDAY, DECEMBER 8TH
(Feast of the Immaculate Conception).

Responding to a question from the seers with respect to their future:
I would like for all of you to become priests and religious, but only if you desire it. You are free. It is up to you to choose. (L1, 136).
If you are experiencing difficulties or if you need something, come to me. (K.72).
If you do not have the strength to fast on bread and water, you can give up a number of things. It would be a good thing to give up television, because after seeing some programs, you are distracted and unable to pray. You can give up alcohol, cigarettes and other pleasures. You yourselves know what you have to do. (T. 55).
On this day of the Feast of the Immaculate Conception, the Gospa was serious; she knelt down with arms extended while praying:
My beloved Son, I beseech you to be willing to forgive the world its great sin through which it offends you. (C 53).

WEDNESDAY, DECEMBER 9TH

"While we were saying our prayers, the Blessed Virgin intervened:"

Oh, My Son Jesus, forgive these sins, there are so many of them!

"Then we were all silent."

Continue to pray, because that is the salvation of this people. (CP. 37; DV.2, 31).

FRIDAY, DECEMBER 11TH

Vicka: "I recommend to the Gospa my parents who are in Germany."

I promise to protect them. Everything will go well. (DV. 2, 32; CP. 37).

SATURDAY, DECEMBER 12TH

As vacation approached, which permitted the seers to be back, the Blessed Virgin was happy:

Very soon you will all be united. You will be able to have a good time together. (CP. 38, DV. 2,32).

WEDNESDAY, DECEMBER 16TH

Kneel down, my children, and pray. Persevere in prayer. (CP. 38).

Jakov and *Vicka:* "Every word of the Blessed Virgin invited us to be joyful." (CP. 39).

FRIDAY, DECEMBER 18TH

"The Blessed Virgin did not respond to our questions. She sang: 'Jesus Christ, in Your Name.' After the first verse, she said:"

Come on, sing more joyfully. Why are you so pensive?

"After the prayer, she began, 'Queen of the Holy Rosary' and she departed." (CP. 39).

SATURDAY, DECEMBER 19TH

It is the date of the first ambiguous oracle on the Bishop. Complete text, which is questionable and disputed, has been referred to Annex 1, below pages 325 to 343.

MONDAY, DECEMBER 21ST

Be on your guard, my children. Prepare yourselves for difficult days. All kinds of people will come here. (CP. 40).

THURSDAY, DECEMBER 24TH

Celebrate the days which are coming. Rejoice with my Son. Love your neighbor. May harmony reign among you. (CP. 41).

FRIDAY, DECEMBER 25TH

Love one another, my children. You are brothers and sisters. Don't argue among yourselves.
Then she blesses them and leaves. (CP. 41).
After having had a vision of Jesus:
Give glory to God, glorify Him and sing, my angels. (Bl. 53).

WEDNESDAY, DECEMBER 30TH

In response to some questions concerning the sick, she began prayer with the "Our Father," then the song "The Queen of the Holy Rosary," and she departed. (CP. 42).

THURSDAY, DECEMBER 31ST

Ivan: "How can one put priests, who do not believe in the apparitions, on the right track?"
It is necessary to tell them that, from the very beginning, I have been conveying the message of God to the world. It is a great pity not to believe in it. Faith is a vital element, but one cannot compel a person to believe. Faith is the foundation from which everything flows.
"Is it really you who appears at the foot of the cross?"
Yes, it is true. Almost every day I am at the foot of the cross. My Son carried the cross. He has suffered on the cross, and by it, He saved the world. Every day I pray to my Son to forgive the sins of the world. (CP 42; cf. L2, 126).

CHAPTER 3

Apparitions in the "Chapel"

OPPOSITE THE SACRISTY

(January-February 1982 until April 11, 1985)

The apparitions, since July 1981, often taking place in the church, where they occurred spontaneously toward the end of the rosary, are transferred to the room serving as a store-room. It is opposite the sacristy and provided privacy from the curiosity of the pilgrims and every provocation on part of the police. This room was cleaned and decorated. Subsequently, it has since been called "chapel of the apparitions." Before the end of February this transfer was definitive, except for rare occasions (apparitions in the sacristy, when the chapel was found overrun or certain days for medical exams).

MONDAY, JANUARY 11TH

I invite you very specially to participate at mass. Wait for me at church, that is the agreeable place. (CP. 43).

THURSDAY, JANUARY 14TH

After the prayers, the songs and the questions, The Gospa reprimanded two seers because of their behavior, and recommended to them not to behave in this manner again. In case of observation, the other seers did not understand what the Gospa told those she reprimanded, and observed only her expression and guessed what it was all about. Those whom she reprimanded say that at that moment, she was gentle and attentive in respect for them. (CP. 44).

MONDAY, JANUARY 18TH

On the matter of a sick person with heart problems:
There is little hope for her. I will pray for her.
After her departure, the children see the cross, the heart and the sun, signs which they perceive from time to time. (CP. 46).

WEDNESDAY, JANUARY 20TH

Must the children from Izbicno meet us tomorrow? They say that you told them of this meeting.
It is not necessary for you to meet them.
They want to transfer Fr. Tomislav from here. What must he do?
If it is in God's design, that he depart, as has been the case with Fr. Jozo, have him abandon himself to the will of God. He must think very much, and you must pray for him. (CP. 47).

THURSDAY, JANUARY 21ST

The seers: Why don't you leave a concrete sign, so that the priests are convinced and that they be converted, in order to be able to convert the others?
The sign will appear at the desired time.
Why are there apparitions in different places in Hercegovina?
My children, don't you see that the faith begins to extinguish itself, and that it is necessary to awaken the faith among men?
What must we do so that peace may reign among the priests?
Fast and pray! (CP. 46).

FRIDAY, JANUARY 22ND

Is the apparition at Izbicno coming from God or from the devil?
It is coming from God. (CP. 47).

TUESDAY, FEBRUARY 2ND

When must one celebrate the feast of The Queen of Peace?
The Blessed Virgin smiled as she answered:

*I would prefer that it take place June 25th. The faithful
have come for the first time on that day, on the hill.* (CP. 48).

MONDAY, FEBRUARY 8TH

Jakov and I were in the sacristy. When we began to pray
the "Our Father," the Gospa arrived. It was five minutes after
six. We questioned her on the matter of a person who was
sick, emotionally:

*He must pray. I will help him within the limitation of my
power.*

To the Slovenes who were praying while she was with us:

Persevere in prayer.

Then she blessed some articles. (DV3, 3).

TUESDAY, FEBRUARY 9TH

At the fourth "Our Father," the Blessed Virgin arrived. We
always ask questions with respect to the sick:

*Pray for all the sick. Believe firmly. I will come to help,
according to that which is in my power. I will ask my Son,
Jesus, to help them. The most important thing, in the meantime, is a strong faith. Numerous sick persons think that it
is sufficient to come here in order to be quickly healed. Some
of them do not even believe in God, and even less, in the
apparitions, and then they ask for help from the Gospa!* (Dv3, 3).

WEDNESDAY, FEBRUARY 10

Jakov and I were alone. Just as every evening, we prayed,
conversed with the Blessed Virgin, and asked many questions.
To them she responded:

*Pray, Pray! It is necessary to believe firmly, to go to confes-
sion regularly, and likewise receive Holy Communion. It is
the only salvation.*

Her preferred prayer is the "Creed." When we recite it,
the Blessed Virgin does not cease to smile. I think that no
one has seen her happier than during this prayer. (DV3, 4).

THURSDAY, FEBRUARY 11TH

Just like every evening, except on Fridays, Saturdays, and
Sundays, Jakov and I are alone. The Blessed Virgin begins

first of all to pray the "Our Father," then the "Glory Be." We recommend the sick and then present her questions:

Pray my angels, persevere! Do not let the enemy take possession of you in anything. Be courageous. Go in the peace of God, my angels. Goodbye. (DV3,4).

FRIDAY, FEBRUARY 12TH

Be more calm, more poised. Do not take sides with other children. Be agreeable, well mannered, pious!

When the Gospa prays, she joins her hands. When she speaks she opens them and raises them toward Heaven, her palms turned upwards. (DV3,5).

SATURDAY, FEBRUARY 13TH

To the seminarians who were present:
Through prayer, one obtains everything. (C.52).

SUNDAY, FEBRUARY 14TH

We are four seers today. When we are in a group, I feel a little happier and joyful in the presence of the Holy Virgin. Likewise, the other four:

Be together like brothers and sisters. Do not argue.

Satan exists! He seeks only to destroy. With regards to you, pray, and persevere in prayer. No one will be able to do anything against you. (DV3, 6).

TUESDAY, FEBRUARY 16TH

The Blessed Virgin began "Jesus in Your Name." Since she has appeared to us she hasn't been sad. Whatever she says, her countenance is smiling and filled with serenity. Her joy attracts us. She wants us to be joyful, we also, wanting nothing to deceive us, any intrigue, or inventive story.

> *Satan only says what he wants. He interferes in everything. You, my angels, be ready to endure everything. Here, many things will take place. Do not allow yourselves to be surprised by him.* (DV3, 7).

FRIDAY, FEBRUARY 19TH

We asked if we could pray the "Hail Mary." She said yes. And while we prayed, she looked at us with a smile, but without praying with us. Truly, her beauty is indescribable. Since I have seen the Blessed Virgin, I have been filled with joy. Whatever her words may be, what she has told me, I have always done it. I have obeyed. She makes attentive remarks, as a mother.

Listen attentively at holy Mass. Be well mannered. Do not chatter during holy Mass. (DV3, 8).

SUNDAY, FEBRUARY 21ST

Be together, and do not argue, do not be disorderly. My angels, I will make you attentive. I will guide you on a sure way. (DV3, 9).

TUESDAY, FEBRUARY 23RD

When we asked the Gospa, she did not answer, but began immediately to pray. When we asked her if such a person were alive, she says:

Do not ask me any more questions! I know what there is in each sick person, or what there is in my power to help him. I will pray to my Son to put out His mercy on each one. (DV3, 10).

THURSDAY, FEBRUARY 25TH

Be persevering and courageous. Do not fear anything. Pray, and do not pay attention to others.

We asked for news about Fr. Jozo:

Do not fear for him. (DV3, 12).

SUNDAY, FEBRUARY 28TH

Thank Tomislav very much, for he is guiding you very well.

Then she smiles, and begins to say the "Glory Be."

Go in the peace of God, my angels! (DV3, 15).

END OF FEBRUARY AND BEGINNING OF MARCH, 1982.

Messages received by Jelena:

Dear children, if you would know how much I love you, your heart would weep over it.

If there is someone there who asks you for something, give it to him.

I also present myself to many hearts, and they do not open up. Pray so that the world may welcome my love.

Dear children, I would like for the whole world to be my child, but it does not want it. I wish to give everything for it. For that, Pray! (L2, 131).

MONDAY, MARCH 1

All of you be happy, and may my blessing accompany you at each step.

She blessed many articles; she touched them with her hands. (DV3, 16). Since the Yugoslavian authorities demanded that they put an end to the prayer meetings for the young people, the Blessed Virgin was questioned and responded:

It is better to temporarily suspend prayer meetings and those of meditation because of the authorities. Take them up later, when it will be possible. (CP. 49).

TUESDAY, MARCH 2ND

A woman, who had come from Osijek, brought two large pictures of the Pope. The Blessed Virgin came at six o'clock with her smile. I believed she was smiling at us; but it was because of the pictures on the table. She said:

He is your father, my angels.

Then she began the "Our Father." On leaving she said:

Open the door well, follow the Mass well!

Go in the peace of God, my angels! If you suffer for a just cause, blessings will be still more abundant for you. (DV3, 17).

THURSDAY, MARCH 4TH

I asked questions with respect to a woman who had no children. She is not of our faith. The Blessed Virgin said:

Let her believe firmly. God, who comes to help everyone, will likewise help her. Be patient, my angels, do not be afraid of anything. I am at your side and guard you. If you have any problems, whatever it be, call me. I will come immediately and help you in advising you on best resolving the difficulty. (DV3, 19).

Go in peace, my angels. Goodbye.

FRIDAY, MARCH 5TH

I questioned the Blessed Virgin on the matter of an Italian, who was very sick, and about another man who acquired cancer. She responded:

Tell them to pray and to put themselves in the hands of God. I too, will call on the mercy of my Son. I will do everything in my power to help them. But it will be necessary to believe completely. Without a strong faith, nothing is possible. Goodbye my angels. (DV3, 19).

SUNDAY, MARCH 7TH

The Blessed Virgin said that she has been with Ivan (at the Seminary at Visoko):

He prays well; he is obedient. He follows my instructions. (DV3, 20).

MONDAY, MARCH 8TH

Concerning a boy named Bora, (age 16), from Metkovic, who disappeared for a week:

He left because of many troubles. He himself, created some of the problems. (DV3, 21).

TUESDAY, MARCH 9TH

On the matter of a young man from Hadromilje, named Mladen, who disappeared from his home:

He has serious problems. It is necessary to pray for him very much, my angels. The people are beginning to be converted. Prayer has been taken up again, in the homes, where people had no longer prayed. (DV3, 21).

THE BEGINNING OF APRIL:

Mirjana: Do you wish the establishment of a special feast in your honor?

I wish a feast for the Queen of Peace, on the 25th of June, anniversary of the first apparition. (L2, 127).

HOLY WEEK: APRIL 4TH - APRIL 10TH

Jelena sees Mary holding Jesus by the hand, and in the palm of Jesus' hand, the inscription "Glory." Asked about the meaning, the Blessed Virgin responded:

These are the names of all those who have been inscribed in the heart of Jesus. (L2, 132).

EASTER SUNDAY, APRIL 11TH

Is it necessary to establish prayer groups, formed by Priests, Sisters and laity in the parish?

It is necessary, but not only here. Communities of prayer are necessary in all parishes. (CP.54).[1]

WEDNESDAY, APRIL 21ST

Father Vlasic questioned the seers. They say that the Blessed Virgin continues to appear to them everyday. The messages can be summarized thusly:

Be patient! Everything is developing according to God's plan. His promises will be realized. May one continue to pray, to do penance, and to be converted. (CP 55).

THURSDAY, APRIL 22ND

Are the luminous signs at the cross on Krizevac natural, or do they come from God? What does the letter "S" and the letter "T," which appear on the cross mean?

They are signs of God, and not of natural phenomena. "S" and "T" are signs of salvation. (B1.55; CP.55).

SATURDAY, APRIL 24TH

What must one do in order to have more cures?

Pray! Pray and believe firmly. Say the prayers which have already been requested. (Seven "Our Father's," "Hail Mary's," "Glory Be's" and the "Creed.")

Do more penance. (CP.55).

---

1. It does not mean just "Charismatic Groups," as the polemists, adversaries of this movement, have indicated.

SUNDAY, MAY 2ND

I have come to call the world to conversion for the last time. Later, I will not appear any more on this earth. (L2, 128).

THURSDAY, MAY 6TH

May we write on a piece of paper, the date of the great sign, describe it, seal it, and put it in the archives? (as requested by the commission).

> *No! I have entrusted that only to you. You will unveil it when I will tell you. Many persons will not believe you, I know, and you will suffer very much for it. But you will endure everything, and you will finally be the happiest.* (CP.56).

THURSDAY, MAY 13

After the attempt on the life of John Paul II:
His enemies have wanted to kill him, but I protected him. (Bu. 151).

SPRING, 1982

Question asked at the request of the pastor at Izbicno, alleged place of other apparitions:
Why are there so many signs in Hercegovina?
It is God who gives them. My children, have you not observed that faith began to extinguish itself? There are many who do not come to church except through habit. It is necessary to awaken the faith. It is a gift from God.
People are surprised that you are appearing in so many places:
If it is necessary, I will appear in each home. (C.92-93).
With respect to the little seers from Izbicno:[2]
Did I not tell you not to come together with those children? I am your mother, you must obey me. (C93).

---

2. Izbicno, 60 kilometers from Medjugorje. In 1982-83, 18 persons mostly females, said they had apparitions. The seers from Medjugorje were said to have received kind words for those from Izbicno, but the Blessed Virgin reminded them strongly, that they must not have any contact with these persons, nor invite them to Medjugorje.

For Jakov, who was crying to see Vicka ill:
The cross is necessary because of the sins of the world.
(L2, 128).

WEDNESDAY, JUNE 23RD (Possibly a few days preceeding)

Just before the anniversary of June 24th, Vicka answered some quesitons asked by Fr. Tomislav Vlasic, who reported them in the parish Chronicle, on June 27th, regarding responses of Our Lady:

1. *The most important thing is that you, the seers, remain united. Let peace be among you. Pay very close attention to that. Obey, and do what the priests and your parents tell you. Go often to holy Mass and receive Communion. Be very attentive these days. Some dishonest people will come to you, in numbers, in order to tempt you. Be careful of your statements. These days, I am expecting of you, a very special discipline. Do not move around anywhere, or often, and do not separate from one another.* (Some of the seers understood that these words were directed specifically to them, and they began to cry).

2. *A number of those who have been very enthusiastic will cool off. But you, persist, and be proud of each of my words. Have the people pray very much. Have them pray more for salvation, and only for salvation, because it is in prayer. And let the people be converted so long as it is possible. There are many sins, vexations, curse words, lies and other bad things. Let them be converted, go to confession and receive Holy Communion.*

3. *Let them not print books on the apparitions before the anniversary has passed, because that could have some undesirable consequences.* (Repression by the authorities?).

4. *You have asked me to keep in this parish good and faithful priests who will continue the work. Do not be afraid of anything. This grace will be given to you. From priests, I do not demand anything other*

than prayer, with perseverance, and preaching. May they be patient and wait for the promises of God.

5. With respect to the two Franciscans who had been suspended, see the Annex 1, page 334.

6. With respect to a question from a theologian: Does the Holy Spirit have two natures?

He has only one; the Divine nature.

7. **The seers:** They have said that these would be the last apparitions on earth? Is it true?

These apparitions are the last in the world.

"As far as I have understood," observes Tomislav Vlasic, "her answer is not only given in Medjugorje, but also in other parts of the world."

THURSDAY, JUNE 24TH OR FRIDAY, JUNE 25TH

Before the evening Mass, during the apparition, the Virgin told the priests, through the intermediary of the seers:

Thank the people in my name for the prayers, the sacrifices and the penance. Have them persevere in prayer, fasting and conversion, and have them wait with patience the realization of my promise. Everything is unfolding according to God's plan. (C 98; CP 60 and 64).

MONDAY, JULY 12TH

Will there be a third world war?

The third world war will not take place. (CP 68).

WEDNESDAY, JULY 21ST

To the response conveyed by Father T. Vlasic on Purgatory:

There are many souls in Purgatory. There are also persons who have been consecrated to God: some priests, some religious. Pray for their intentions, at least seven Our Father's, Hail Mary's and Glory Be's and the Creed. I recommend it to you. There is a large number of souls who have been in Purgatory for a long time because no one prays for them.

A response to a question on fasting:

The best fast is on bread and water. Through fasting and prayer, one can stop wars, one can suspend the laws of nature.

Charity cannot replace fasting. Those who are not able to fast can sometime replace it with prayer, charity and a confession; but everyone, except the sick, must fast. (CP 69).

SATURDAY, JULY 24TH

Answer to some questions which were asked:

We go to Heaven in full conscience: that which we have now. At the moment of death, we are conscious of the separation of the body and the soul. It is false to teach people that we are re-born many times and that we pass to different bodies. One is born only once. The body, drawn from the earth, decomposes after death. It never comes back to life again. Man receives a transfigured body. Whoever has done very much evil during his life can go straight to Heaven if he confesses, is sorry for what he has done, and received Communion at the end of his life. (CP 70).

SUNDAY, JULY 25TH

A response to questions asked regarding Hell:

Today many persons go to Hell. God permits his children to suffer in Hell due to the fact that they have committed grave unpardonable sins. Those who are in Hell, no longer have a chance to know a better lot. (CP 71).

Response to questions regarding cures:

For the cure of the sick, it is important to say the following prayers: the Creed, seven Our Father's, Hail Mary's and Glory Be's, and to fast on bread and water. It is good to impose one's hands on the sick and to pray. It is good to anoint the sick with holy oil. All priests do not have the gift of healing. In order to revive this gift, the priest must pray with perseverance and believe firmly. (CP 71).

FRIDAY, AUGUST 6TH (Feast of the Transfiguration)

A response to questions which were asked concerning Confession:

One must invite people to go to Confession each month, especially the first Saturday. Here I have not spoken about it yet. I have invited people to frequent Confession. I will give you yet some concrete messages for our time. Be patient

because the time has not yet come. Do what I have told you.
They are numerous who do not observe it. Monthly Confes-
sion will be a remedy for the Church in the West. One must
convey this message to the West. (CP 72).

That night the Gospa gave a sign to a group of young people who prayed with Ivan Dragicevic: two luminary signs
descended on Krizevac and the church. This phenomenon was
observed by Father Tomislav Vlasic near the church. Ivan commented on this phenomenon to all those who were there and
added, "The Blessed Virgin told me that she would appear
to you now in Heaven." (CP 72).

TUESDAY, AUGUST 10TH

No special message, but the visionaries only said—the
Blessed Virgin told us that now we can give some information
in writing to people according to the plan which we had already worked out. (CP 73).

WEDNESDAY, AUGUST 11TH

No special message. The Blessed Virgin only scolded the
seers for their lack of seriousness during the evening Mass.

SUNDAY, AUGUST 15TH

The vision lasted about seven minutes. The Gospa entrusted
a new secret to Vicka and Ivanka—only to them. The others
saw that it was about a secret, but they did not understand
anything. (CP 74).

MONDAY, AUGUST 16TH

No special message. The Gospa only corrected "the very
resonant and very rapid prayer of the seers and the people
in church."

Mirjana says that, at the time of the apparition, she sees
heavenly persons: Jesus, Mary, angels, in three-dimensions,
and earthly persons in two-dimension, at the same time she
sees Father Jozo, or Ivan Ivankovic imprisoned because of
their faith. (CP 74).

WEDNESDAY, AUGUST 18TH

Mirjana reports to Fr. Tomislav Vlasic what the Gospa has told her concerning the sick:

Have them believe and pray; I cannot help him who does not pray and does not sacrifice. The sick, just like those who are in good health, must pray and fast for the sick. The more you believe firmly, the more you pray and fast for the same intention, the greater is the grace and the mercy of God. (CP 76).

Asked with respect to a plan of marriage between a Catholic and an Orthodox:

In my eyes and in the sight of God, everything is equal. But for you, it is not the same thing because you are divided. If it is possible, it is better if she were not to marry this man because she will suffer and her children also. She will be able to live and follow only with difficulty, the way of her faith. (CP77).

(On this ambiguous message, see Annex 2, page 347.)

SUNDAY, AUGUST 29TH

With reference to the critiques according to which the apparitions have divided the priests in Hercegovina:

I have not desired your division. On the contrary, I desire that you be united. Do not ignore the fact that I am the Queen of Peace. If you desire a practical advise: I am the Mother who has come from the people; I cannot do anything without the help of God. I, too, must pray like you. It is because of that, that I can only say to you: Pray, fast, do penance and help the weak. I am sorry if my preceding answer was not agreeable to you. Perhaps you do not want to understand it. (CP 79).

TUESDAY, AUGUST 31ST

I do not dispose all graces. I receive from God what I obtain through prayer. God has placed His complete trust in me. I protect particularly, those who have been consecrated to me. The great sign has been granted. It will appear independently of the conversion of the people. (CP 79).

THE END OF AUGUST 1982

Ivan is on the hill of Bijakovici with his friends. The Virgin appears to him.

Now, I am going to give you a sign in order to strengthen your faith.

They see two rays of light, one on the church, the other on the cross at Krizevac. (L2, 129).

SATURDAY, SEPTEMBER 4TH

Jesus prefers that you address yourselves directly to Him rather than through an intermediary. In the meantime, if you wish to give yourselves completely to God and if you wish that I be your protector, then confide to me all your intentions, your fasts, and your sacrifices so that I can dispose of them according to the will of God. (CP 80).

SUNDAY, SEPTEMBER 26TH

For a religious who had come from Rome:
Have her strengthen the faith of those who have been entrusted to her.

For Father Faricy and Forrest:
They are on the good path, have them persist.

For the Pope:
Have him consider himself the father of all mankind, and not only of Christians. Have him spread untiringly and with courage the message of peace and love among all mankind. (CP 82).

FRIDAY, OCTOBER 1ST

I am happy because you have begun to prepare the monthly feast of the sacrament of Reconciliation. That will be good for the whole world. Persevere in prayer. It is the true way which leads you toward my Son. (CP. 83).

THURSDAY, NOVEMBER 4TH

Questioned with respect to a vision of Andja, from Mostar, who had seen one evening during prayer, 13 persons coming from the East; another evening six persons:
It is about a true vision. They were some souls of her close

family from Purgatory. It is necessary to pray for them. (CP 85).

SATURDAY, NOVEMBER 6TH

Frightened by the eighth secret, Mirjana prayed to the Blessed Virgin to preserve humanity from this calamity:

> *I have prayed; the punishment has been softened. Repeated prayers and fasting reduce punishments from God, but it is not possible to avoid entirely the chastisement. Go on the streets of the city, count those who glorify God and those who offend Him. God can no longer endure that.* (CP 86).

MONDAY, NOVEMBER 8TH

Father Tomislav has the seers ask the Virgin if it is necessary to write to the Bishop and to priests so that they can call the faithful to intensify their prayers, or if it is better to wait for other events:

It is better to wait than to precipitate that. (CP 86).

MONDAY, NOVEMBER 15TH

Jakov: "Must Vicka take the prescribed medicines, or must she have herself admitted to a hospital in Zagreb?"

It is necessary to send Vicka to Zagreb.

Vicka refused to question the Blessed Mother on this subject. She said that she wanted to accept what God would send her. (CP 87).

SATURDAY, DECEMBER 18TH

With respect to the article of the Bishop of Mostar in the journal, "Vijesnik," on the events of Medjugorje, Fr. Tomislav Vlasic had the seers ask:

Must we respond to the Bishop in writing?

Yes, respond! (CP. 91).

MONDAY, DECEMBER 20TH

With respect to the same article (Dec. 18, 1982), the visionaries ask: Is it necessary to give the faithful of Mostar objective information concerning the case in Hercegovina?

No! (CP 95).

Is it better for the seers to pray with you, and for the pilgrims to ask their questions to the priests instead?

Yes, it is better that the children pray with me, and that the pilgrims ask the priests and look for solutions with them. In the meanwhile I will continue to answer the questions which they ask me. (CP. 95).

THURSDAY, DECEMBER 23RD

To Mirjana:
On Christmas I will appear to you for the last time. (F. 11,74).

SATURDAY, DECEMBER 25TH

To Mirjana after she had received the tenth secret:

> *Now you will have to turn to God in the faith like any other person. I will appear to you on the day of your birthday and when you will experience difficulties in life.* (F2, 149-150).
>
> *Mirjana, I have chosen you, I have confided in you everything that is essential. I have also shown you many terrible things. You must now bear it all with courage. Think of Me, and think of the tears I must shed for that. You must remain courageous. You have quickly grasped the messages. You must also understand now that I have to go away. Be courageous.* (G. 1, 22).

MONDAY, DECEMBER 27TH

Today the statue of the Queen of Peace was finished. It was sculptured by Vipotnik, a sculptor from Slovenia, and painted by Luka Stojaknac and Florijan Mickovic, who wanted to maintain anonymity. This statue has been a source of grace for Luka, who is Orthodox; he put his marriage in order.

The Seers: "May we put the statue in church?"

Yes, you may! (CP. 96).

It is this statue which had been venerated for a long time in the nave. It was removed from there on orders from the bishop on March 25th, 1985. It then found itself consigned to the small chapel of the apparitions.

WEDNESDAY, DECEMBER 29TH

Jelena: "May I know the ten secrets?"

I did not appear to you as to the other six because my plan is different. To them I entrusted messages and secrets. Forgive me if I cannot tell you the secrets which I have entrusted to them; it concerns a grace which is for them, but not for you. I appeared to you for the purpose of helping you to progress in spiritual life and through your intermediary I want to lead people to holiness. (Bo. 37).

FRIDAY, DECEMBER 31ST

On Vicka's request, the Blessed Virgin gives this message for the new year:

Pray as much as possible and fast!

In the evening, to the seers:

You must persevere in prayer and fasting. (C. 140).

I wish that the new year will be spent in prayer and penance. Persevere in prayer and in sacrifice, and I will protect you and will hear your prayers. (CP. 98).

1983

SATURDAY, JANUARY 1ST (The Feast of Holy Mary, Mother of God.)

Ivanka: "Are you still appearing to Mirjana?"

After Christmas, I am no longer appearing to her for the present. (CP. 99).

BEGINNING OF 1983

Jelena asks the Blessed Virgin on the authenticity of the apparitions of the six seers, and on the sign which has been promised:

Pardon me, but you cannot know it; it is a special gift for them. You will have to believe it like all the others. In the meantime, everything that they say corresponds to truth. (Bo.38).

WEDNESDAY, JANUARY 5TH

Tomislav receives, from the four seers present (Ivan, Jakov,

Maria and Vicka), the following information: Maria has received 7 secrets, Vicka 8, Jakov, Ivanka and Ivan 9, and Mirjana 10. We do not know how long the apparitions will last, nor why she no longer appears to Mirjana after Christmas. The Gospa invites us constantly to prayer, to fasting, to conversion. She confirms her promises.

Ivan thinks that the apparitions have ceased for Mirjana because she did not pray enough outside of the apparitions. The Gospa probably did it so that Mirjana would learn to pray in the faith, he volunteers. (According to other interpretations, the end of the apparitions would be, on the contrary, a sign of achievement and maturity.)

Questioned with respect to the time of the sign: "Which month? Which year?"
Ivan says: "It is forecast." (CP. 103-104).

FRIDAY, JANUARY 7TH

Mary begins to tell her life to the visionaries. They are invited to write down her testimony. They will not be able to make it public until they have received her authorization. (CP. 105).

This transmission will last:
    for Jakov until April,
    for Ivanka, until May 22nd,
    for Maria, until July 17th.

Maria, who was still attending the school for hairdressers in Mostar, received only an abridged account, the days when she was in Medjugorje.

For Vicka, it lasted until April 10th, 1985: a long account which filled three notebooks. Up to this day, the seers have not received authorization to reveal these contents.

MONDAY, JANUARY 10TH

Confidences from Mirjana to Father Tomislav Vlasic:
"During the 18 months that I saw the Gospa, a great intimacy was established between us. I felt her maternal love. I could ask her all kinds of questions. Thus I asked her why God was so merciless in sending sinners to Hell for eternity?"
Men who go to Hell no longer want to receive any benefit

from God. They do not repent nor do they cease to swear and to blaspheme. They make up their mind to live in Hell and do not at all contemplate leaving it. (C.103).

(Man's refusal is an irreversible choice.)

Questioned on the subject of Purgatory, the Blessed Virgin says:

There is there, different levels of which the lowest are close to Hell and the highest gradually draw near to Heaven. It is not on all souls day, but at Christmas, that the greatest number of souls leave Purgatory. There are in Purgatory, souls who pray ardently to God, but for whom no relative or friend prays for them on earth. God makes them benefit from the prayers of other people. It happens that God permits them to manifest themselves in different ways, close to their relatives on earth, in order to remind men of the existence of Purgatory, and to solicit their prayers close to God who is just, but good. The majority go to Purgatory. Many go to Hell. A small number go directly to Heaven. (C. 103).

WEDNESDAY, JANUARY 12TH

Regarding an American television team:

"Will they be able to finish without difficulties?

There will be some difficulties, but it will be for the glory of God. (CP. 108).

TUESDAY, MARCH 1ST

To Jelena:

Transcribe all the lessons which I give you for the spiritual life; later you will deliver them to the authorities of the Church. (T. 64).

APRIL 4TH (Easter Monday)

A message addressed by Jelena to Tomislav, who had written on Good Friday, April 1st, a letter of protest on the subject of the problems suffered in the parish.

"I was expecting the corrections from a Canonist and no one knew anything except the Pastor" he observes in detail. Monday, Jelena appeared without knowing anything, and tells me:

"Do not have recourse to anyone. When you have a problem,

you must remain smiling and praying. When God begins a work, no one will stop it."

Father Vlasic judges this fundamental message as per (VB. 4, p. 100), "the Madonna does not stop telling us":

Pray, fast, and allow Got to act.

Jelena transmits the message from the Blessed Virgin:

Do not pity anyone. If the police cause you some anxiety, continue on your way joyful and calm. Pray for them. When God begins His work, no one can stop it. (CP.127-bis).

Father Vlasic notes in the "Parish Chronicle" the internal locutions which have been received by Jelena after December 15, 1982. The Madonna's message:

Hurry to be converted. Do not wait for the great sign. For the unbelievers, it will then be too late to be converted. For you who have the faith, this time constitutes a great opportunity for you to be converted, and to deepen your faith. Fast on bread and water before every feast, and prepare yourselves through prayer.

Fast once a week on bread and water in honor of the Holy Spirit outside of Friday.

Have the largest possible number of persons pray and fast during the novena of the Holy Spirit, so that it may spread over the church. Fast and pray for the Bishop. (CP. 127 bis).

WEDNESDAY, APRIL 20TH

To Jelena, the Blessed Virgin, in tears:

I give all the graces to those who commit grave sins, but they do not convert. Pray! Pray for them! Do not wait for Friday. Pray now. Today your prayers and your penance are necessary to me. (CP. 130).

THURSDAY, APRIL 21ST

You (the visionaries), *must behave well; be pious and set a good example for the faithful.*

Jakov admits that the Blessed Virgin has made remarks to him several times, concerning his conduct. She has taught him how to participate at Mass, to pray, and to behave around others. (CP. 130).

SUNDAY, APRIL 24TH

Message for an Italian doctor who is present:
I bless him just as those who work with him at the hospital in Milan, for everything they are doing. Have them continue, and pray. I bless the sick of this hospital, just like the sick for whom you have prayed this evening, and those for whom you will pray. (Bo. 11).

MONDAY, APRIL 25TH

Message received by Jelena, these last days:
Be converted! It will be too late when the sign comes. Beforehand, several warnings will be given to the world. Have people hurry to be converted. I need your prayers and your penance. (CP. 131).

My heart is burning with love for you. It suffices for you to be converted. To ask questions is unimportant. Be converted. Hurry to proclaim it. Tell everyone that it is my wish, and that I do not cease repeating it. Be converted, be converted. It is not difficult for me to suffer for you. I beg you, be converted.

I will pray to my Son to spare you the punishment. Be converted without delay. You do not know the plans of God; you will not be able to know them. You will not know what God will send, not what He will do. I ask you only to be converted. That is what I wish. Be converted! Be ready for everything, but, be converted. That is all I wish to say to you. Renounce everything. All that is part of conversion. Goodbye, and may peace be with you. (CP. 132).

FRIDAY, APRIL 29TH

Marijana, (aged 11) sees the Blessed Virgin at the same time as Jelena, but she does not hear her words.
Jelena: "Why doesn't Marijana hear?"
I do not want to separate you. (CP. 133).
(Does the Gospa wish to mean that these two adolescents compliment each other?)

THURSDAY, MAY 5TH

With respect to a sick person from Vienna: The doctor has

diagnosed schizophrenic. Some priests think it is a question of diabolical possession.

It is a diabolic possession. One can succeed only through prayer. (CP. 135).

WEDNESDAY, MAY 25TH

To Jelena:

Assemble about twenty young people who are ready to follow Jesus, without reservation. Bring them together within a months notice. I will initiate them into the spiritual life. They can likewise be more than twenty. Even some adults and children can participate, all those who will accept the rule.

I will ask these people to do penance for certain intentions. They will fast and pray for the Bishop. They will give up what they cherish the most, drink, coffee, pleasures, television. It is necessary to have persons who wish to consecrate themselves more specifically to prayer, and to fast. I will give them the rules to follow. (see June 16, 1983)

The persons who will follow these rules, will be consecrated whatever their state in life may be. (CP 136).

SATURDAY, MAY 28TH

To Jelena:

It is very beautiful to remain Thursdays, for the adoration of my Son in the Blessed Sacrament of the altar. It is likewise beautiful to venerate the cross each Friday. I wish that every Saturday, which is the day that the Church had dedicated to me, you will consecrate to me at least a quarter of an hour. Meditate during this time, on my life, my messages, and pray. (CP. 141).

WEDNESDAY, JUNE 1ST

Dear Children: I hoped that the world would begin to be converted on its own. Do now, everything you can, so that the world can be converted. (CP. 137).

THURSDAY, JUNE 2ND

Read what has been written about Jesus. Meditate on it, and convey it to others. (CP. 137).

FRIDAY, JUNE 3RD

Father Vlasic has begun to form a prayer group requested by the Virgin on May 25th. (Jakov, Vicka, Ivanka).

"What do you expect of Fr. Tomislav? Has he begun well?"

Yes, it is good. Have him continue.

"What should one do so that people will not drive from here, the priests who work with faith and love?"

Pray and fast for this intention. I will tell you when the moment comes, what you must do.

"Father Tomislav wants to call the parish to prayer and fasting, so that the church recognizes that the events here are supernatural. It is a good way?"

Yes, it is a good way. Have the parish pray for this gift. Have them pray also for the gift of the Holy Spirit so that all those who come here will feel the presence of God. (CP. 138).

FRIDAY, JUNE 10TH

Jelena, Marijana and Anita, (age 11), are arguing. The first two make peace, but Anita refuses. The other two enter the church. Anita follows them, and suddenly extends to them, her hand. An indescribable joy penetrates their hearts.

I had been waiting for quite a while for your success. Continue in this manner, says the Gospa. (CP. 142-143).

SUNDAY, JUNE 12TH

Ivan: May the priests begin new work around the church or must they request authorization from the authorities?

Do not begin the work until receiving permission from the authorities. Otherwise, someone will inform the latter and the works would be forbidden. Go, and kindly request the authorization. It will be given to you. (CP. 145).

TUESDAY, JUNE 14TH

Ivan: What do you wish that the priests preach during the ten anniversary days of the first apparitions?

Have them do what they think is best. It would be good to remind the faithful of the events which have been revealed here in relation to my coming. Have them remind them the reasons for my coming here. (CP.145).

THURSDAY, JUNE 16TH

On May 25, 1983, the Blessed Virgin has repeated her desire that a prayer group, totally abandoned to Jesus, be formed. On June 16th she dictated to Jelena the rules for this group:

1. *Renounce all passions and inordinate desires. Avoid television, particularly evil programs, excessive sports, the unreasonable enjoyment of food and drink, alcohol, tobacco, etc.*

2. *Abandon yourselves to God without any restrictions.*

3. *Definitely eliminate all anguish. Whoever abandons himself to God does not have room in his heart for anguish. Difficulties will persist, but they will serve for spiritual growth and will render glory to God.*

4. *Love your enemies. Banish from your heart, hatred, bitterness, preconceived judgments. Pray for your enemies and call the Divine blessing over them.*

5. *Fast twice a week on bread and water. Reunite the group at least once a week.*

6. *Devote at least three hours to prayer daily, of which at least, half an hour in the morning and half an hour in the evening. Holy Mass and the prayer of the Rosary are included in this time of prayer. Set aside moments of prayer in the course of the day, and each time that circumstances permit it, receive Holy Communion. Pray with great meditation. Do not look at your watch all the time, but allow yourself to be led by the grace of God. Do not concern yourself too much with the things of this world, but entrust all that in prayer to Our Heavenly Father. If one is very preoccupied, he will not be able to pray well because internal serenity is lacking. God will contribute to lead to a successful end, the things of here below, if one strives to do his utmost in working on his own.*

Those who attend school or go to work must pray half an hour in the morning and in the evening, and, if possible, participate in the Eucharist. It is neces- sary to extend the spirit of prayer to daily work (that is to say, to accompany work with prayer.)

7. Be prudent because the Devil tempts all those who have made a resolution to consecrate themselves to God, most particularly, those people. He will sug- gest to them that they are praying very much, they are fasting too much, that they must be like other young people and go in search of pleasures. Have them not listen to him, nor obey him. It is to the voice of the Blessed Virgin that they should pay attention. When they will be strengthened in their faith, the Devil will no longer be able to seduce them.

8. Pray very much for the Bishop and for those who are responsible for the church. No less than half of their prayers and sacrifices must be devoted to this intention.

To Jelena:
I have come to tell the world that God is truth; He exists. True happiness and the fullness of life are in Him. I have come here as Queen of Peace to tell the world that peace is neces- sary for the salvation of the world. In God, one finds true joy from which true peace if derived. (Ll, 100).

SPRING 1983

Hasten your conversion. Do not await the sign, which has been announced, for those who do not believe. It will be too late. You who believe, be converted and deepen your faith. (Ll, 99).

To Jelena, concerning Anita, to whom the Blessed Virgin appeared after Good Friday, and who only seldom gets together with Jelena and Marijana, because of her many obligations:
If she cannot come because of her responsibilities, have her pray for a quarter of an hour at least, and I will appear to her and bless her.

WEDNESDAY, JUNE 22ND

To Jelena:

Love your enemies and bless them! (L1. 100).

FRIDAY, JUNE 24TH

The sign will come, you must not worry about it. The only thing that I would want to tell you is to be converted. Make that known to all my children as quickly as possible. No pain, no suffering is too great to me in order to save you. I will pray to my Son not to punish the world; but I beseech you, be converted.

You cannot imagine what is going to happen nor what the Eternal Father will send to earth. That is why you must be converted! Renounce everything. Do penance. Express my acknowledgement to all my children who have prayed and fasted. I carry all this to my Divine Son in order to obtain an alleviation of His justice against the sins of mankind. (C. 145 - 146).

I thank the people who have prayed and fasted. Persevere and help me to convert the world. (CP. 151).

SUNDAY, JUNE 26TH

Love your enemies. Pray for them and bless them. (MM. 24).

TUESDAY, JUNE 28TH

To Jelena:

Pray for three hours a day. You pray very little. Pray at least a half hour in the morning and in the evening. (L2. 133).

FRIDAY, JULY 1ST (toward 11 o'clock at night on Krizevac)

I thank all those who have responded to my call. I bless all of you. I bless each of you. In these days, I ask you to pray for my intentions. Go in the peace of God. (Bl. 81).

THE BEGINNING OF JULY

Concerning the tensions which involved the diocese:
Fast two days a week for the intentions of the Bishop, who bears a heavy responsibility. If there is a need to, I will ask for a third day. Pray each day for the Bishop. (L2. 134).

SATURDAY, JULY 2ND

To Jelena:
Devote five minutes to the Sacred Heart. Each family is an image of it. (Ll. 100).

MONDAY, JULY 4TH

To Jelena:
You have begun to pray three hours a day, but you look at your watch, preoccupied with your work. Be concerned with only the essential. Let yourself be guided by the Holy Spirit in depth, then your work will go well. Do not hurry. Let yourself be guided and you will see that everything will be accomplished well. (Ll. 100).

TUESDAY, JULY 26TH

To Jelena:
Be on your guard. This period is dangerous for you. The Devil is trying to lead you astray from your way. Those who give themselves to God will be the object of attacks. (L. 2. 134).

To Maria:
Dear children, today I would like to invite you to constant prayer and penance. Particularly, have the young people of this parish become more active in their prayer. (F2, 113).

TUESDAY, AUGUST 2ND

To Jelena:
Consecrate yourself to the Immaculate Heart. Abandon yourselves completely. I will protect you. I will pray to the Holy Spirit. Pray to Him also. (L2, 134).

SATURDAY, AUGUST 6TH

On orders form the Bishop, Father Pervan, the parish priest put an end to the custom which calls for the seers beginning the prayers of the Rosary and the seven Our Father's, Hail Mary's and Glory Be's. Jakov questioned the Blessed Virgin on this subject:
If it is so, then do not go against it so as not to provoke any quarrels. If it is possible, talk about it tomorrow among

yourselves. All of you come to an agreement beforehand. (CP. 165).

FRIDAY, AUGUST 12TH

This was an exceptionally long apparition (38 minutes). The Blessed Virgin gives the seers instructions to guide their lives which only concerned them:

Pray more for your spiritual life. Do your utmost in this sense. Pray for your Bishop. (CP. 158).

MONDAY, AUGUST 15TH

To Jelena:

See how I am happy here! There are many who have come to honor me. In the meanwhile, do not forget that in other places there are still more persons who hurt me and offend me. (CP 160).

Do not be in anxiety. May peace unite your hearts. Every disorder comes from Satan.

To the young people who are returning to school:

Be careful not to diminish the spirit of prayer. (Ll. 101).

Satan is enraged against those who fast and those who are converted. (Ll. 101).

TUESDAY, AUGUST 23RD

With respect to Father Emilien Tardif, the Canadian priest of the charismatic renewal:

Have him announce my messages to the whole world. Let Jesus, only Jesus, be at the center of his efforts. (Bl. 368; CP. 162).

THURSDAY, AUGUST 25TH

Father Tardif, Father Raucourt and Dr. Phillippe Madre have been arrested and expelled by the Yugoslavian authorities:

Do not worry for them. Everything is in God's plan. (CP. 163).

MONDAY, AUGUST 29TH

For the intention of a group of young people before their departure on their pilgrimage to Brijeg:

I wish that you pray throughout your trip, and that you glorify God. There, you will be able to meet other young people. Convey the messages which I have given you. Do not hesitate to speak to them about it. (CP. 159).

Some begin to pray and to fast just as they have been told, but they get tired very quickly, and thus loose the graces which they have acquired. (CP. 159).

MONDAY, SEPTEMBER 5TH

The mother of Jakov (12 years old) dies. The Blessed Virgin consoles him and reveals to him:
Your mother is with me in Heaven. (CP. 163).

MONDAY, SEPTEMBER 12TH

Pray. When I give you this message, do not be content to just listen to it. Increase your prayer and see how it makes you happy. All graces are at your disposal. All you have to do is to gain them. In order to do that, I tell you again—Pray! (BN 5, 7).

FRIDAY, SEPTEMBER 16TH

Pray, pray, pray! Do not be discouraged. Be in peace because God gives you the grace to defeat Satan. (Bl. 288).

In my messages, I recommend to everyone, and to the Holy Father in particular to spread the message which I have received from my Son here at Medjugorje. I wish to entrust to the Pope, the word with which I came here: 'MIR, (peace),' which he must spread everywhere. And here is a message which is especially for him: That he bring together the Christian people, through his words and his preaching; that he spread particularly among the young people, the messages which he has received from the Father in his prayers, when God inspires him. (CP. 169).

MONDAY, SEPTEMBER 26TH

My Son suffers very much because the world is not converting. May the world be converted and make peace. (CP. 171).

THURSDAY, SEPTEMBER 29TH

To Jelena:

I desire for a great peace and a great love to grow in you. Consequently, Pray!

For three priests from Liverpool:

Preach my messages. Speak about the events at Medjugorje. Continue to increase your prayers. (Bl. 368).

SATURDAY, OCTOBER 15TH

To Jakov:

My Son suffers very much because men do not want to be reconciled. They have not listened to me. Be converted, be reconciled. (CP, not paged).

THURSDAY, OCTOBER 20TH

To Jelena, for the prayer group:

I ask you for a commitment of four years. It is not yet the time to choose your vocation. The important thing is first of all, to enter into prayer. Later, you will make the right choice.

For the parish:

Have all the families consecrate themselves to the Sacred Heart each day. I am very happy when the entire family meets to pray each morning, for half an hour. (Ll. 101).

FRIDAY, OCTOBER 21ST

The important thing is to pray to the Holy Spirit, so that He may descend on you. When one has Him, one has everything. People make a mistake when they turn only to the saints to request something. (Ll. 101).

MONDAY, OCTOBER 24TH

To Jelena, for the prayer group:

If you pray, a source of life will flow from your hearts. If you pray with strength, if you pray with faith, you will receive graces from this source, and your group will be strengthened. (Ba. 45).

TUESDAY, OCTOBER 25TH

To Jelena:
Pray! Pray! Prayer will give you everything. It is with prayer that you can obtain everything. (Ba. 45).

WEDNESDAY, OCTOBER 26TH

To Jelena:
I pour out my blessing over you, and my heart wishes to be with you. (Ba. 45).

THURSDAY, OCTOBER 27TH

To Jelena:
Pray, pray, pray. You do not learn anything from chatter, but only from prayer. If someone asks you about me, and about what I say, answer: 'That doesn't explain anything. It is in praying that we will understand better.' (Ba. 45).

FRIDAY, OCTOBER 28TH

To Jelena:
I see that you are tired. I wish to support you in your effort, to take you in my arms so that you may be close to me. All those who wish to ask me questions, I will answer: 'There is only one response, prayer, a strong faith, an intense prayer, and fasting.' (Ba. 46).

SATURDAY, OCTOBER 29TH

To Jelena:
I give you my heart; receive it! I would not want to distress you, nor to stop talking to you, but I cannot stay always with you. You have to get used to it. In the meantime, I wish to be constantly with you, from the bottom of my heart. It is necessary to pray very much, not to say: 'If today we have not prayed, it is nothing serious.'
You must strive to pray. Prayer is the only road which leads to peace. If you pray and fast, you will obtain everything that you ask for. (Ba. 46).

SUNDAY, OCTOBER 30TH

To Jelena:

Why do you not put your trust in me? I know that you have been praying for a long time, but really, surrender yourself. Abandon your concerns to Jesus. Listen to what He says in the Gospel: 'And who among you, through his anxiety, is able to add a single cubit, to the length of his life.' (Mt. 6:27).

Pray also, in the evening when you have finished your day. Sit down in your room, and say to Jesus: 'Thank you.'

If in the evening you fall asleep in peace, and in prayer, in the morning you will walk up thinking of Jesus. You will then be able to pray for peace, but if you fall asleep in distraction, the day after will be misty, and you will forget even to pray that day. (Ba. 46).

MONDAY, OCTOBER 31ST

To Jelena:

I know that you prayed today, and that you did all your work while praying. Still, I have a particular intention for which I am asking you to say each day, seven Our Father's, seven Hail Mary's, and the Creed. (Ba. 47).

FRIDAY, NOVEMBER 4TH

To Jelena:

I wish that you tell them, that tomorrow is a day of fasting, in order to sanctify yourselves in the Holy Spirit. And pray! Let this message be conveyed to the group. (Ba. 47).

SATURDAY, NOVEMBER 5TH

Jelena: "Our Lady looked at us tenderly and said:"
I know my children, that you have worked and prayed today. But, I beseech you, be generous, persevere, continue to pray. (Ba 47).

SUNDAY, NOVEMBER 6TH

To Jelena:

Where are the prayers which you addressed to me? My clothes were sparkling. Behold them soaked with tears. Oh, if you would know how the world today is plunged into sin. It seems to you that the world sins no longer, because here, you live in a peaceful world where there is no confusion or perversity.

If you know how lukewarm they are in their faith, how many do not listen to Jesus. Oh, if you knew how much I suffer, you would sin no more. Oh, how I need your prayers. Pray! (Ba. 47).

MONDAY, NOVEMBER 7TH

To Jelena:

Do not go to confession through habit, to remain the same after it. No, it is not good. Confession should give an impulse to your faith. It should stimulate you and bring you closer to Jesus. If confession does not mean anything for you, really, you will be converted with great difficulty. (Ba. 47).

TUESDAY, NOVEMBER 8TH

To Jelena:

Pray and fast! All that you can do for me is to pray and fast. (Ba. 48).

WEDNESDAY, NOVEMBER 9TH

To Jelena:

Pray! I have such a great need for your prayers. Give me your hearts. (Ba. 48).

THURSDAY, NOVEMBER 10TH

To Jelena:

I ask you to pray. That is all that I expect of you. Do not forget to pray to the Lord, morning and evening. Pray, Pray. (Ba. 48).

FRIDAY, NOVEMBER 11TH

To Jelena:

Pray! You can do everything, yes, you can do it through prayer. Place an image of the hearts of Jesus and Mary in your homes.

SATURDAY, NOVEMBER 12TH

To Jelena:
Give me your hearts, open them to me.
"How do we do that?"
You must redouble your efforts. Day after day, increase your fervor. (Ba. 48).

SUNDAY, NOVEMBER 13TH

To Jelena:
Pray, and do it with fervor. Include the whole world in your prayer. Pray, because prayer makes one live.
In response to a question, the Gospa only says:
Pray and you will understand that, some day. (Ba. 49).

MONDAY, NOVEMBER 14

To Jelena:
Pray, because prayer is life. Through it and in it, you live in prayer. (Ba. 49).

TUESDAY, NOVEMBER 15TH

To Jelena:
Pray and fast!
For the intention of the group:
I have often reproached you. Pray with me. Begin right now. (Ba. 49).

WEDNESDAY, NOVEMBER 16TH

To Jelena:
Pray and fast. Have all the members of your group come on Tuesday as often as possible. Speak to them about fasting. Fast three days a week for the Bishop. If that cannot be done by everyone the same day, have each one do it whenever he is able. (Ba. 49).

THURSDAY, NOVEMBER 17TH

To Jelena:
Pray! If I always ask you to pray, do not think that your prayers are not good. But I invite you to prolong your personal

prayer, to pray more intensely for the others. (Ba. 49).

FRIDAY, NOVEMBER 18TH

To Jelena:
At Medjugorje, many have begun well, but they have turned toward material goods, and they forget the only good. (Ba. 49).

SATURDAY, NOVEMBER 19TH

To Jelena:
My children, pray only! (Ba. 50).

SUNDAY, NOVEMBER 20TH

To Jelena:
My children, do not believe everything that people tell you. One must not, because of that, weaken in his faith. (Ba. 50).

MONDAY, NOVEMBER 21ST

To Jelena:
Tuesday, that is tomorrow, the whole group will find peace in prayer. All its members will be invigorated in prayer, as it is the wish of Jesus. He entrusts something to each one, and wishes something from each one. It is necessary to make them come back to their promises, which were made at the beginning, and to pray. (Ba. 50).

TUESDAY, NOVEMBER 22ND

To Jelena:
Pray, pray, pray. . .Pray, my children. Pray, because only prayer can save you. (Ba. 50).

WEDNESDAY, NOVEMBER 23RD

To Jelena:
Oh my sweet children, pray! I ask you only to pray. You yourselves can see that only prayer can save. (Ba. 50).

THURSDAY, NOVEMBER 24TH

To Jelena:
Pray and fast! (Ba. 50).

FRIDAY, NOVEMBER 25TH

Jelena: "The Blessed virgin stayed just a little time. She only said:"
Pray and fast. (Ba 51).

ADVENT

Begin by calling on the Holy Spirit each day. The most important thing is to pray to the Holy Spirit. When the Holy Spirit descends on earth, then everything becomes clear and everything is transformed. (Bl. 125).

SATURDAY, NOVEMBER 26TH

She only said:
Prayer and fasting. (Ba. 51).

SUNDAY, NOVEMBER 27TH

To Jelena:
My children, pray and keep your soul pure. I wish to be constantly with you. (Ba. 51).

MONDAY, NOVEMBER 28TH

To Jelena:
Pray, pray! Have the parish pray each day to the hearts of Jesus and Mary during the Novena of the Immaculate Conception. (Ba. 51).

This same day, some prayers were dictated or inspired by her. (Ba. 65).

CONSECRATION TO THE HEART OF JESUS

O Jesus, we know that You are sweet (*Mt.* 11:29).
That you have given Your heart for us.
It was crowned with thorns by our sins.
We know that today You still pray for us
    so that we will not be lost.
Jesus, remember us if we fall into sin.
Through Your most Sacred Heart,
    make us all love one another.
Cause hatred to disappear among men.

Show us Your love.

All of us love You.

And we desire that you protect us with Your
　　Heart of the Good Shepherd.

Enter into each heart, Jesus!

Knock on the door of our hearts.

Be patient and tenacious with us.

We are still locked up in ourselves, because we
　　have not understood Your will.

Knock continuously, Oh Jesus.

Make our hearts open up to you,
　　at least in reminding us of the passion
　　which you suffered for us. Amen

CONSECRATION TO THE
IMMACULATE HEART OF MARY

O Immaculate Heart of Mary, overflowing
　　with goodness, Show us your love for us.

May the flame of your heart, Oh Mary,
　　Descend upon all peoples.

We love you immensely.

Impress in our hearts a true love.

May our hearts yearn for you.

Oh Mary, sweet and humble of heart,
　　Remember us when we sin.

You know that all mankind are sinners.

Through your most sacred and maternal heart,
　　Cure us from every spiritual illness.

Make us capable of looking at the beauty
　　of your maternal heart,

And that, thus, we may be converted
　　to the flame of your heart. Amen

TUESDAY, NOVEMBER 29TH

To Jelena:

Pray!

For the intention of the group:

*I am your mother full of goodness, and Jesus is your great
friend. Do not fear anything in His presence. Give Him your*

heart, from the bottom of your heart. Tell Him your suffer-ings, thus you will be invigorated in prayer, with a free heart, in a peace without fear. (Ba. 51).

WEDNESDAY, NOVEMBER 30TH

To Maria, for a priest:
You must warn the Bishop very soon, and the Pope, with respect to the urgent and the great importance of the message for all humanity.
This message, which was given in September was:
I have already said many times that the peace of the world is in a state of crisis. Become brothers among you, increase prayer and fasting in order to be saved. (T. Vlasic, Apr. 22, 1984, VB. 1, 13).
To Jelena:
Pray, pray, pray! (Ba. 51).

NOVEMBER

Before the novena to the Immaculate Conception, the Blessed Virgin tells Jelena:
Before Mass it is necessary to pray to the Holy Spirit.
"We followed this message during the novena, praying be-fore Mass and asking the faithful to respond, 'O come Holy Spirit.' After Communion, we sang the hymn to the Holy Spirit, then we stopped doing it." In January, 1983, Jelena says that the Blessed Virgin requested that these prayers be resumed. "We should not have stopped it. The prayers to the Holy Spirit should always accompany the Mass." (Ba. 51).

THURSDAY, DECEMBER 1ST

Thanks to all of you who have come here, so numerous during this year, in spite of snow, ice and bad weather, to pray to Jesus. Continue, hold on in your suffering. You know well that when a friend asks you for something, you give it to him. It is thus with Jesus. When you pray without ceasing, and you come in spite of your fatigue, He will give you all that you ask from Him. For that, pray. (Ba. 51).

FRIDAY, DECEMBER 2ND

To Jelena:
Thank you, thanks to everyone!
That evening, it was particularly cold:
You are very good to come to mass without looking for an excuse. Show me that you have a generous heart. (Ba. 52).

SUNDAY, DECEMBER 4TH

To Jelena:
Pray, pray, pray only. Prayer should be for you, not only a habit, but also a source of goodness. You should live by prayer. (Ba. 52).

TUESDAY, DECEMBER 6TH

To Jelena:
Pray, pray! If you pray, I will keep you and I will be with you. (Ba. 52).

WEDNESDAY, DECEMBER 7TH

The vigil of the Immaculate Conception, To Jelena:
Tomorrow will really be a blessed day for you, if every moment is consecrated to my Immaculate Heart. Abandon yourselves to me. Strive to make your joy grow; to live in the faith, to change your hearts. (Ba. 52).

THURSDAY, DECEMBER 8TH

To Jelena:
Thank you my children for having come so often. Thank you. Continue your efforts and be persevering and tenacious. Pray without ceasing. (Ba. 52).

SUNDAY, DECEMBER 11TH

To Jelena:
Pray and fast! I wish that prayer be renewed in your heart every day. Pray more, yes, more each day. (Ba. 52).

MONDAY, DECEMBER 12TH

To Jelena:
Pray, pray, thus I will protect you. Pray and abandon your

hearts to me, because I wish to be with you. (Ba. 52).

TUESDAY, DECEMBER 13TH

To Jelena:
Pray and fast! I do not wish to say anything else to you.
(Ba. 52).

WEDNESDAY, DECEMBER 14TH

Pray and fast! I am asking you for prayer. (Ba. 52).

THURSDAY, DECEMBER 15TH

Fast on Thursday and Friday for the Bishop.
To Jelena on the subject of catstrophic predictions:
That comes from false prophets. They say: 'Such a day, on such a date, there will be a catastrophe.' I have always said that evil will come if the world does not convert itself. Call the world to conversion. Everything depends on your conversion. (Ba. 53).

FRIDAY, DECEMBER 16TH

Pray and fast only! (Ba. 53).

SATURDAY, DECEMBER 17TH

To Jelena:
Pray and fast! (Ba. 53).

SUNDAY, DECEMBER 18TH

To Jelena:
In this novena for Christmas, pray as much as you can. I ask you. (Ba. 53).

MONDAY, DECEMBER 19TH

To Jelena:
Pray! (Ba. 53).

TUESDAY, DECEMBER 20TH

To Jelena:
Pray!
For the intention of the group:
Fast on Wednesday, Thursday, and Friday. (Ba 53).

WEDNESDAY, DECEMBER 21ST

To Jelena:
My children, I say to you again, pray and fast. (Ba. 54).

THURSDAY, DECEMBER 22ND

To Jelena:
Pray! What is most important for your body is prayer. (Ba. 54).

FRIDAY, DECEMBER 23RD

To Jelena:
Pray, pray, especially tomorrow. I desire your prayers. (Ba. 54).

SATURDAY, DECEMBER 24TH

To Jelena:
Pray, pray my children. I wish that this night be spent in prayer. (Ba. 54).

SUNDAY, DECEMBER 25TH

To Jelena:
My children, pray! I cannot tell you anything else than pray. Know that in your life, there is nothing more important than prayer. (Ba. 54).

MONDAY, DECEMBER 26TH

To Jelena:
My children, pray, pray more. It is not necessary to Say: 'Our Lady only repeats, pray.' I cannot tell you anything else than to pray. You would need to live this Christmas in prayer. You have rejoiced very much this Christmas, but your hearts have not attained and lived what you have desired. No one withdrew to his room to thank Jesus. (Ba. 54).

To a question from Father Laurentin, Ivan conveys this answer from the Virgin:
Our Lady prays for that. May he who undertakes it, do it in prayer. It is there that he will find his inspiration. (Bl. 367).

TUESDAY, DECEMBER 27TH

To Jelena:

My children, pray, pray, pray. Remember that the most important thing in our lives is prayer. (Ba. 54).

WEDNESDAY, DECEMBER 28TH

My children, understand that the most important thing in our lives is prayer. (Ba 54).

THURSDAY, DECEMBER 29TH

To Jelena:

I wish that one love, one peace, flourish in you. Pray then. (Ba 55).

FRIDAY, DECEMBER 30TH

To Jelena:

My children, pray and fast. I wish to strengthen you, but prayer alone is your strength. (Ba. 55).

DECEMBER

There are many Christians who are no longer faithful, because they do not pray anymore. Have them began again to recite each day, at least, seven Our Father's, seven Hail Mary's, seven Glory Be's, and the Creed, once. (Bl. 137).

Above all, abstain from television programs. They represent a great peril for your families. After you have seen them, you cannot pray any more. Give up likewise, alcohol, cigarettes, and pleasure of this kind. (Bl. 214; a variant of the message of Dec. 8, 1981).

The fasting which you are doing in eating fish, instead of meat, is not fasting but abstinence. The true fast consists in giving up all our sins, but one must also renounce himself, and make the body participate in it. (Bl. 191).

Monthly confession will be a remedy for the Church in the west. Whole sections of the Church could be cured, if the believers would go to confession once a month. (Bl. 224).

SATURDAY, DECEMBER 31ST

To Jelena:
For you, I only wish that this new year will really be a holy one. On this day, go then, to confession, and purify yourself in this new year. (Ba. 55).

She asks the group to continue to pray for the Bishop. (Ba 55)

1984

SUNDAY, JANUARY 1ST

My children, pray! I say again, pray, because prayer is indispensable to life. (Ba. 55).

THE BEGINNING OF 1984

For the intention of the pilgrims:
When you are in the room of the apparitions or at the church, you should not preoccupy yourself with taking pictures. You should rather use the time to pray to Jesus, especially in those moments of particular grace during the apparitions. (T.58).

MONDAY, JANUARY 2ND

Why have you stopped saying the prayer to the Holy Spirit. I have asked you to pray always and at all times so that the Holy Spirit may descend over all of you. Begin again to pray for that.
"We had stopped saying the prayer to the Holy Spirit thinking that it was said only until Christmas." (Ba.55).

TUESDAY, JANUARY 3RD

My children, pray; I say it again, pray! Know that in your life the most important thing is prayer. (J).

WEDNESDAY, JANUARY 4TH

Before all, pray! That, I do not cease to ask you for. (J).

SUNDAY, JANUARY 8TH (Feast of the Epiphany)

My children, pray! I say it again, pray! I will say it to you again. Do not think that Jesus is going to manifest Himself again in the manger; friends, He is born again in your hearts. (DN 1, 30).

SUNDAY, JANUARY 15TH

I know that I speak to you very often about prayer, but know that there are many people in the world who do not pray; who do not even know what to say, in prayer. (J).

TUESDAY, JANUARY 17TH

Pray and fast! I wish that in your hearts prayer and fasting flourish. (J).

WEDNESDAY, JANUARY 18TH

I wish to engrave in every heart the sign of love. If you love all mankind, then there is peace in you. If you are at peace with all men, it is the kingdom of love. (DN 1, 30).
To Jelena:
Pray and fast!
For the intention of the group:
Have everyone get up early, some to go to school, others to go to work, still others to help the poor like themselves, also those who need help. (J).

THURSDAY, JANUARY 19TH

Pray and fast, because without prayer you cannot do anything. (Ba55).

SATURDAY, JANUARY 21ST

Pray and fast. Do not give up on meditation. At home meditate at least half an hour. (Ba55).

SUNDAY, JANUARY 22ND

Pray and fast. I permit all those who mortify themselves, to do it at the most three times a week. May they not prolong it. (Ba56).

MONDAY, JANUARY 23RD

Pray and fast. You have not understood well, what it means to pray: If you can understand that, I desire it very much. (Ba56).

TUESDAY, JANUARY 24TH

Pray very much. I desire to permeate you with prayer. (Ba56)

WEDNESDAY, JANUARY 25TH

Pray and fast. You need enthusiasm in your prayer. May you pray in meditation for a long time and fervently. (Ba56).

THURSDAY, JANUARY 26TH

Thank you for adoring my Son in the Sacred Host. That touches me very much. With respect to you, pray! I desire to see you happy. (Ba56).

FRIDAY, JANUARY 27TH

Pray and fast. I wish that you deepen and continue your life in prayer. Every morning say the prayer of consecration to the Heart of Mary. Do it in the family. Recite each morning the Angelus, five Our Father's, Hail Mary's, and Glory Be's in honor of the holy Passion and a sixth one for our Holy Father, the Pope. Then say the Creed and the prayer to the Holy Spirit. And, if it is possible, it would be well to pray a rosary. (Ba56).

SATURDAY, JANUARY 28TH

I wish that all of you pray, and that my heart extend to the whole world. I wish to be with you. (Ba57).

SUNDAY, JANUARY 29TH

Pray and fast! I wish for you to purify your hearts. Purify them and open them to me. (Ba57).

MONDAY, JANUARY 30TH

Pray! I desire to purify your hearts. Pray. It is indispensable, because God gives you the greatest graces when you pray. (Ba57).

TUESDAY, JANUARY 31ST

To Jelena:

Pray! Do not think of anything, pray. Do not think of anything else except of those for whom you pray. Then prayer will be better and you will be faithful to it.

To the group:

Continue to help the poor, the sick, and to pray for the dead. You should not feel any fear. Let all free themselves completely and let them abandon their hearts to me so that I can be with them. Have them listen to me and discover me in the poor, and in every person. (Ba57).

WEDNESDAY, FEBRUARY 1ST

It is raining at this time, and you say: 'It is not reasonable to go to church in this slush. Why is it raining so much? Why doesn't the rain stop?' Do not ever speak like that. You have not ceased to pray so that God may send you rain which makes the earth rich. Then, do not turn against the blessing from God. Above all, thank him through prayer and fasting. (Ba 57).

THURSDAY, FEBRUARY 2ND

Pray, because I need many prayers. Be reconciled, because I desire reconciliation among you and more love for each other, like brothers. I wish that prayer, peace, and love bloom in you. (Ba57).

FRIDAY, FEBRUARY 3RD

To Jelena:

It is up to you to pray and I will take care of the rest. You can not even imagine how powerful God is. That is why you pray. Pray because he wants to be with you and wants to cleanse you from all sin.

Our Lady gave this message on the request that we address her on the arrival of a document from the Bishop. (Jan. 13, 1984) Reference 54-84: "The matter of the diary of Vicka Ivankovic on the apparitions," asking Mary, consequently, what we should do.

SATURDAY, FEBRUARY 4TH

Pray, because prayer is very necessary to you. With prayer, your body and soul will find peace. There are some young people who have consecrated themselves to me. But there are in the parish, some persons, who have not entirely given themselves.

As soon as mass has ended, they are in a hurry to leave the church. That is not good. That way they will never be able to give themselves completely. It is not good for them to linger about the church. One must be pious and set a good example for others, in order to awaken in them the faith. It is necessary to pray as much as possible while offering your heart. They should consecrate themselves in order to become truly better. (Ba58).

SUNDAY, FEBRUARY 5TH

Pray and fast. I desire to live in your hearts.
And especially for the prayer group:
Some of them still have a week of rest. They do not fast ...others have come here and fast on Wednesday, Thursday, and Friday; others help the poor and the sick; others love everybody and want to discover Jesus in each one. Some are not convinced, others are. They are mine. See how they honor me. Lead them to me so that I may bless them. (Ba59).

MONDAY, FEBRUARY 6TH

Pray, pray, I ask of you. (Ba59).

WEDNESDAY, FEBRUARY 8TH

To Jelena:
From you, I expect only prayer. Thus, pray. (Ba59).

THURSDAY, FEBRUARY 9TH

Pray, pray! How many persons have followed other beliefs or sects and have abandoned Jesus Christ. They create their own gods; they adore idols. How that hurts me! If they could be converted. Like the unbelievers, they are many. That will change only if you help me with your prayers. (Ba59).

FRIDAY, FEBRUARY 10TH

Pray and fast! I desire humility from you. But you can become humble only through prayer and fasting. (Ba59).

SATURDAY, FEBRUARY 11TH

Open your hearts to me, I desire to bless them fully. (Ba59).

SUNDAY, FEBRUARY 12TH

Pray and fast! I ask of you. Pray for the peace and humility of your hearts. (Ba59).

MONDAY, FEBRUARY 13TH

To Jelena:
Fast and pray! Give me your hearts. I desire to change them completely. I desire for them to be pure. (Ba60).

TUESDAY, FEBRUARY 14TH

Pray and fast! I desire to purify your hearts completely. I wish to make you happy. (Ba60).

WEDNESDAY, FEBRUARY 15TH

In very cold weather and an icy wind:
The wind is my sign. I will come in the wind. When the wind blows, know that I am with you. You have learned that the cross represents Christ; it is a sign of him. It is the same for the crucifix you have in your home. For me, it is not the same. When it is cold, you come to church, you want to offer everything to God. I am, then, with you. I am with you in the wind. Do not be afraid. (Ba60).

FRIDAY, FEBRUARY 17TH

My children, pray! The world has been drawn into a great whirlpool. It does not know what it is doing. It does not realize in what sense it is sinking. It needs your prayers so that I can pull it out of this danger. (Ba60).

MONDAY, FEBRUARY 20TH

Pray and fast! I desire to purify you and to save you. For that, help me with your prayers. (Ba60).

TUESDAY, FEBRUARY 21ST

Pray and fast! I expect generosity and prayers from your hearts. (Ba60).

THURSDAY, FEBRUARY 23RD

I hold all of you in my arms. You are mine. I need your prayers so that you may be mine. I desire to be all yours and for you to be all mine. I receive all your prayers. I receive them with joy. (Ba61).

FRIDAY, FEBRUARY 24TH

Pray and fast! I desire to be with you always. I desire to stay in your hearts always and for you to stay in mine. (Ba61).

SATURDAY, FEBRUARY 25TH

Know that I love all of you. Know that you are all mine. To no one do I desire to give more than to you. Come to me all of you. Stay with me. I want to be your Mother. Come, I desire all of you. (J).

SUNDAY, FEBRUARY 26TH

Pray and fast! Know that I love you. I hold all of you on my knees. (J).

MONDAY, FEBRUARY 27TH

Do not be tired. I desire to be with you. (J).

TUESDAY, FEBRUARY 28TH

Pray and fast! Love everyone on earth, just as you love yourselves.
For the intention of the group:
Have each one decide alone. In the meantime, it would be good, that this week they fast on Thursday. Have them read the Bible and meditate on it. (J).

WEDNESDAY, FEBRUARY 29TH

Pray! It may seem strange to you that I always speak of prayer. And yet I say: pray! Why do you hesitate? In Holy Scripture, you have heard say: 'Do not worry about tomorrow, each day will have its own worries.' (Mt. 6:34). Then do not worry about the other days. Be content with prayer, I your Mother, will take care of the rest. (Ba61-62).

THURSDAY, MARCH 1ST

Message to Marijana:
Pray and fast. When I tell you to pray, do not think that you have to pray more, but pray. Let prayer and faith awaken in your hearts. (Ba62).

To Maria, the first message of Thursday, addressed to the parish:

> *Dear children, I have chosen particularly this parish because I wish to guide it; I watch over it with love, I would like for all of you to be mine. I thank you for having responded this evening to my call. I would like for you to be always with me and my Son. Every Thursday I will give a special message for you.*

(NB. These messages of Thursday have been widely disseminated, and have been edited by MM, and in our translation, in Medjugorje, Paris, DDB, 1987, p.26-90 L3)

Dear children, today I ask you to read the Bible in your homes, every day. Put it in a very visible place in your home, that way it will encourage all to prayer. (M53).

Thursday (day of the Eucharist), may each one find his way to fast; he who smokes, may abstain from smoking; he who drinks alcohol, have him not drink. Have each one give up something which is dear to him. May these recommendations be conveyed to the parish. (DN 1, 31).

To Jelena:
Each Thursday, read again the passage of Matthew 6, 24-34, before the most Blessed Sacrament, or if it is not possible to come to church, do it with your family. (F2, 104).

MONDAY, MARCH 5TH

To Jelena:
Pray and fast! Ask the Holy Spirit to renew your souls, to renew the entire world. (DN 1 31).

THURSDAY, MARCH 8TH

Message to the parish:
Dear children, be converted in the parish. It is my second wish. Thus all those who will come here will be able to be converted. Thank you for having responded to my call.

LENT (March 7 - April 22)

Do not be afraid for yourselves, you are already saved. Pray rather for those who are in sin and who do not believe. (T.57).

WEDNESDAY, MARCH 14TH

Pray and fast so that the kingdom of God may come among you. Let my Son set you aglow with His fire. (DN 1,31).

THURSDAY, MARCH 15TH

To Maria, for the parish:
This evening, dear children, I am particularly grateful to you for your presence. Adore continuously, the Most Blessed Sacrament. I am always present when Christians are in adoration. They then receive some particular graces. (DN 5, 75).
Dear children, pray! All agitation comes from Satan. Your prayer should lead to peace. (BN 18,22).

SATURDAY, MARCH 17TH

To Jelena, during the novena in preparation for the Annunciation:
Pray and fast, so that during this novena, God will fill you with His power. (DN 1,31).

MONDAY, MARCH 19TH

Dear children, sympathize with me! Pray, pray, pray! (B. 358).

WEDNESDAY, MARCH 21ST

To Jelena:
Today I rejoice with all my angels. The first part of my program has been achieved.

Then, while crying:
There are so many men who live in sin. Here there are likewise among you some people who have offended my heart. Pray and fast for them. (BN 18,22).

THURSDAY, MARCH 22ND

Message for the parish:
Dear children, this evening I ask you in a special way during this Lenten season, to honor the wounds which my Son has received from this parish. Unite yourselves to my prayers for the intention of this parish, so that its sufferings become tolerable. Thank you for responding to my call. (F2, 123).

Pray each day the 'Veni Creator Spiritus' (Come Holy Ghost) and the 'Angelus.' God has given each one the will to decide for himself. My wish is for all to be converted, but I do not want to force anyone. (BN 18,22).

To Jelena:
Yesterday evening I said that the first wish of my plan, was realized. (DN 1,31).

SUNDAY, MARCH 25TH (Annunciation)

The 1,000th apparition at Medjugorje.
Rejoice with me and with my angels because a part of my plan has already been realized. Many have been converted, but many do not want to be converted. Práy.

After these words, the Blessed Virgin began to cry. (C.148).

TUESDAY, MARCH 27TH

To Jelena:
In the group, some have given themselves up to God so that He may guide them. Let the will of God be realized in you. (DN 1,31).

WEDNESDAY, MARCH 28TH

Many persons come here out of curiousity and not as pilgrims. (BN 18,23).

THURSDAY, MARCH 29TH

A message for the parish:
Dear children, this evening I would like to invite you to persevere in your trials. Even today the All Powerful suffers because of your sins. When sufferings occur, offer them as a sacrifice to God. (DN 5,76).

FRIDAY, MARCH 30TH

I wish that your hearts would be united to mine, like my heart is united to that of my Son. (DN 1,32).

To Jelena:
My children, I wish that the holy mass be for you the gift of the day. Attend it, wish for it to begin. Jesus gives Himself to you during the mass. Thus, look forward to that moment when you are cleansed. Pray very much so that the Holy Spirit will renew your parish. If people attend mass with lukewarmness, they will return to their homes cold, and with an empty heart. (DN 1,31-32).

TUESDAY, APRIL 3RD

To Jelena:
I ask for you to pray for the conversion of all men. For that, I need your prayers. (DN 1,32).

THURSDAY, APRIL 5TH

To Maria, for the parish:
Dear children, this evening I ask you very specially, to venerate the heart of my Son, Jesus. Make reparation for the injury inflicted on the Heart of my Son. This heart has been wounded through all kinds of sin.
If you would be strong in the faith, Satan would not be able to do anything against you. Begin to walk the path of my messages. Be converted, be converted, be converted. (BN 18,23).

SUNDAY, APRIL 8TH

I ask you to pray for the conversion of everyone. For that, I need your prayers. (M 29).

THURSDAY, APRIL 12TH

A message for the parish:

Dear children, this evening I ask you to stop your slandering and to pray for unity, because my Son and I have a special project for this parish.

Prepare yourselves in a special way for Holy Saturday. (BN 18,24).

SATURDAY, APRIL 14TH

To Jelena:

How can you not be happy? Jesus gives Himself to you. I wish to inundate souls. If I am sad this evening, the reason is that many have not prepared themselves for Easter. They do not permit Jesus on that day, to unite Himself to their souls. (L 2, 138).

HOLY WEEK APRIL 15TH-22ND

To Jelena:

Raise your hands and open your hearts. Now, at the time of the Resurrection, Jesus wishes to give you a special gift. This gift of my Son is my gift. Here it is. You will be subjected to trials and you will endure them with great ease. We will be ready to show you how to escape from them if you accept us. Do not say that the Holy Year has ended and that there is no need to pray. On the contrary, double your prayers, because the Holy Year is just another step ahead.

At this time, the risen Jesus appeared. Rays of light came forth from His wounds. He said:

> *Receive my graces and tell the whole world that there is no happiness except through Me.* (M 29).

HOLY THURSDAY, APRIL 19TH

Message for the parish:

Dear children, share my compassion; pray, pray, pray!

To Jelena:

I'm going to reveal a spiritual secret to you: if you want to be stronger than evil, make yourself a plan of personal prayer. Take a certain time in the morning, read a text from Holy Scripture, anchor the Divine word in your heart, and strive to live it during the day, particularly during the moment of trials. In this way, you will be stronger than evil. (Bl. 186).

That same day, the Blessed Virgin had "dictated" to Jelena the following prayer:

HOW TO GIVE ONESELF TO MARY
MOTHER OF GOODNESS, OF LOVE AND OF MERCY

Oh my Mother!
Mother of goodness, love and mercy!
I love you immensely, and I offer myself to you.
Through your goodness, your love,
And your mercy, save me!
I wish to be yours.
I love you immensely
And I wish that you protect me.
In my heart, oh mother of goodness,
Give me your goodness,
So that I go to Heaven.
I ask you for your immense love
That you may give me the grace
That I will be able to love each one
Just like you loved Jesus Christ.
I ask you in grace
That I be able to be merciful[1] to you.
I offer myself completely to you
And I wish that you will be with me at each step,
Because you are full of grace.
I wish never to forget your grace,
And if I should lose it,
I will ask, make me find it again. Amen.

---

1. It is an ambiguous and confusing expression on which one has commented in different ways. According to Fr. Slavko, it means: "That I know how to love your will when it differs from mine."

To T. Vlasic' question, asked by Jelena:
"How could Jesus pray all night?" "With what method?"

> *He had a great longing for God and for the sal-*
> *vation of souls.* (T. Vlasic, June 1, 1984, VB 1, 39, often
> taken up subsequently).

If you want to be stronger against evil, have an active con-
science. For that, pray very much in the morning and read a
passage from the Gospel. Plant the Divine Word in your heart
and live it during the day, in this special way, in trials and
in the evening, you will be very strong. (T. Vlasic, Aug. 3, 1984).

GOOD FRIDAY, APRIL 20TH

To Jelena:
You should be filled with joy. Today, Jesus died for your
salvation. He descends into Hell and opens the gates of para-
dise. Let joy reign in your hearts!
When you pray, seek the advantage of prayer. Prayer is a
conversation with God. To pray means to listen to the Lord.
Prayer is for me a service, because after it all things become
clear. Prayer leads to knowing happiness.

HOLY SATURDAY, APRIL 21ST

To Jelena:
Raise your hands, yearn for Jesus because in his Resurrec-
tion, he wants to fill you with graces. Be enthusiastic about
the Resurrection. All of us in Heaven are happy, but we seek
the joy of your hearts. My Son's gift and mine, at this moment
is this: you will be comforted in your trials, they will be easier
for you because we will be close to you. If you listen to us,
we will show you how to overcome them.
Pray very much tomorrow. May Jesus truly rise in your
families, that peace be established there, where there are wars.
I wish that someone is born again in your hearts. My chil-
dren, I thank you. Continue to bring about the Resurrection
of Jesus in all men. The Holy Year has ended, but it represents
only a step in our life. Continue to pray. (BN 18,24).

EASTER SUNDAY, APRIL 22ND

We all rejoice in Heaven. Rejoice with us. (DN 1,27).

MONDAY, APRIL 23RD

There is no need to give more information to the people, they already know what they are supposed to do. (T. Vlasic, Aug. 12, 1984 VB 1, 861).

TUESDAY, APRIL 24TH

With sadness and with tears:

So many people, after they have begun here to pray, to be converted, to fast, and do penitence, quickly forget when they return home, and return to their bad habits. (DN 1,27).

The information suffices. People already know enough. Tell them this place is a place of prayer. Pray as much as you can, pray however you can, but pray more always. Each of you could pray even four hours a day. But I know that many do not understand because they think only of living for their work.

T. Vlasic then had this conveyed to Our Lady: "If I tell this to the people, then they will go away completely."

Even you do not understand. It is hardly a sixth of your day. (T. Vlasic, May 26, 1984, VB 1, 30).

To Jelena:

Many times, confronting justice and confronting your sins, many times I returned from your home in tears. I could not say a single word. I am your Mother and I do not want to oppose you. But on you, will depend what I wish to do, in you.

We must rejoice in Jesus, to make Him happy. (Tk. Vlasic, Nov. 10, 1984, VB 1, 128).

THURSDAY, APRIL 26TH

No message.

MONDAY, APRIL 30TH

Maria asks the reason for there not being a message last Thursday:

I had a special message for the parish so as to awaken the faith of all the believers. In the meantime, I do not want

*to force anyone to whatever it may be which would not be
felt or desired. Not all have accepted the Thursday messages.
At the beginning there were more.*

*But now it seems that all that has become common place
to them. And recently, some have asked for the message, only
out of curiosity, and not with faith and piety to my Son and
me.* (F 2,110).

THURSDAY, MAY 3RD

No message.

THURSDAY, MAY 10TH

The absence of a message, the 26th of April, and again
the 3rd of May, had been reported in the same way as the
explanation of April 30th. The response was quick in coming:

*I address you the words, and I will continue to do so. But
listen to these instructions.*

THURSDAY, MAY 17TH

To Maria for the parish:
*I am happy today because many of you have desired to con-
secrate yourselves to me. I thank you for it. You have not
been mistaken. My Son Jesus Christ wants, through my intercession, to extend the graces of predilection over you. He
rejoices that you are consecrating yourselves to Him.*

SATURDAY, MAY 19TH

To Jelena:
*Dear children, at this time it is especially necessary for
you to consecrate yourselves to me and to my heart. Love,
pray and fast.*

MONDAY, MAY 21ST

To Jelena:
*O dear children, how I wish that you would turn to me.
Imagine my little children that it is the end of the school year
and you have reached halfway. That is why now you must
become a little more serious.* (Ba 62).

WEDNESDAY, MAY 23RD

To Jelena:

I wish that the parish prepare itself through a novena, to receive the sacrament of Confirmation on the day of the feast of the Ascension. (which will take place May 31). (M. 30).

THURSDAY, MAY 24TH

To Maria, for the parish:

Dear children, I have already said it to you; I have chosen you in a special way, just as you are. I am your mother; I love all of you. At every moment, when you have difficulties, do not be afraid because I love you, even when you are far from me and my Son.

I ask you not to permit my heart to cry with tears of blood, because of souls who are lost through sin. That is why dear children, pray, pray, pray!

FRIDAY, MAY 25TH

To Jelena:

I truly wish that you would be pure on the day of Pentecost. Pray, pray that your spirit be changed on that day. (Ba 62).

SATURDAY, MAY 26TH

To Jelena:

Dear children, thank you for every prayer. Try to pray continously, and do not forget that I love you and wish that all of you would love one another.

To Jelena, who is requested to ask questions of the Blessed Mother:

For all of these questions, there is an answer: pray to the Holy Spirit so that He may enlighten you, and you will come to know all that you wish. (Ba 63).

MONDAY, MAY 28TH

To Jelena:

Love is a gift from God. Pray then, that God may give you the gift to love. (Ba 62).

WEDNESDAY, MAY 30TH

To Jelena:

The priests should visit families, more particularly those who do not practice anymore, and who have forgotten God. Priests should carry the Gospel of Jesus to the people, and teach them the way of prayer. And the priests themselves, should pray more and even fast. They should give to the poor, what they don't need. (T 64).

THURSDAY, MAY 31ST (Feast of the Ascension)

To Maria, for the parish:

I will give you the message for the parish, Saturday, June 2nd. It should be announced on Sunday.

MAY

To Jelena, after inquiring about August 5th, 1984, if they would be celebrating her two thousandth birthday:

Throughout the centuries, I have given myself completely to you. Is it too much to give me, three days? Do not work on those days. Take your rosaries and pray. Fasting has been forgotten during the last quarter of the century, within the Catholic Church. (T. 57).

Jelena: "I know that all families can pray four hours a day. But, if I tell that to people, they will back out."

Don't you understand, that it is only one-sixth of the day? (F2, 113).

FRIDAY, JUNE 1ST

To Jelena:

May the love of God be always in you, because without it, you cannot be fully converted. Let the rosary in your hands make you think of Jesus.

Dear children, strive to be absorbed in mass, just as you should. (J).

SATURDAY, JUNE 2ND

To Maria, for the parish (a message which had been anticipated: it will not be given Thursday, June 7th)

Dear children, this evening I recommend to you the novena (of Pentecost). Pray for the outpouring of the Holy Spirit on all your families, and on your parish. Pray and you will not be sorry for it. God will bestow His gifts on you, thanks to the fact that you will be glorifying Him until the end of your life. (F2, 124).

To Jelena:

Thank you for every prayer. Continue to pray, but pray with the heart. Dear children, again it is necessary for you to pray to the Holy Spirit and it would be good for you to pray seven 'Our Father's,' in the church, as one does it for Pentecost. (J).

During the novena, in preparation for Pentecost, the priest who leads the prayer, makes a brief introduction before each "Our Father" to ask for the seven gifts of the Holy Spirit.

MONDAY, JUNE 4TH

Dear children, I am happy that you have begun to pray as I requested of you. Continue. (Ba 63).

FRIDAY, JUNE 8TH

To Jelena:

Dear children, you need love. I have said it to you many times, and I remind you. Continue only to pray and be happy because I am with you. (J).

SATURDAY, JUNE 9TH (Vigil of Penticost)

Tomorrow evening, pray to receive the spirit of truth. More particularly, you, members of this parish. The spirit of truth is indispensible to you in order to convey the messages, such as I give them to you, without adding or deleting whatever it may be. Pray, so that the Holy Spirit inspires you, a spirit of prayer, so that you may pray more. I your mother, find that you pray too little.

MONDAY, JUNE 11TH

To Jelena:

I wish that you continue to pray and to fast.

To the group:

I wish that you would become like a flower in the spring. The love which I give you is great, but sometimes you reject it, and thus, it becomes less. Always accept immediately, the gifts which I give you, so that you can profit from them. (J).

WEDNESDAY, JUNE 13TH

Dear children, I invite you to pray more, you and the entire parish, until the day of the anniversary. Let your prayer become a sign of offering to God. Dear children, I know that you are all tired. You do not know how to offer yourselves to me. Offer yourselves completely to me these days. (Bl. 141).

THURSDAY, JUNE 14TH

No "Thursday message" to the parish. (BN 18, 26 indicated one, though with some confusion).
Pray, Pray!

MIDDLE OF JUNE, 1984

To Jelena:
Prepare yourselves through prayer, for the third anniversary of the beginning of the apparitions. June 25th should be celebrated as the Feast of Mary, 'Queen of Peace.' (M30).

THURSDAY, JUNE 21ST

To Maria, for the parish:
Pray, pray, pray! Thank you for having responded to my call.
To Jelena:
If you knew how much I love you, you would cry with joy. When anyone is before you, and asks you something, you will give it to him. I am before so many hearts, but they remain closed. Pray so that the world receives my love. (BN 18,24).

Each member of the group is like a flower; and if someone tries to crush you, you will grow and will try to grow even more. If someone crushes you a little, you will recover. And if someone pulls a petal, continue to grow as though you were complete.
To Marijana:
My only wish is that you become as joyful and enthusiastic as you were during the first days of my apparitions. (Ba 64).

SATURDAY, JUNE 23RD

Dear children, I am very happy that there are so many people here this evening. Thank God alone. (Ba).

After Easter, Our Lady does not speak to Jelena or Marijana every day, but specially on Tuesday, Wednesday, Saturday and Sunday.

SUNDAY, JUNE 24TH (Feast of Corpus Christi)

Third anniversary of the apparitions.

My Children, I thank you for each sacrifice that you have made during these days. Be converted, forgive each other, fast, pray, pray, pray! (C. 149).

MONDAY JUNE 25TH

Thank you for all your sacrifices. (DN 1,27).

TUESDAY, JUNE 26TH

When I say pray, pray, pray, I do not want to say to only increase the number of hours of prayer, but also to reinforce the desire for prayer, and to be in contact with God. Place yourself permanently in a state of spirit bathed in prayer. (F2, 112).

THURSDAY, JUNE 28TH

No Thursday message to the parish.

THURSDAY, JULY 5TH

Message to the parish:

Always pray before your work and end it with prayer. If you do that, God will bless you and your work. These last days, you have prayed little and worked very much. Pray more. In prayer, you will find repose.

THURSDAY, JULY 12TH

Message for the Parish:

Dear children, in these days, Satan wants to destroy all my plans. Pray with me so that his design will not be realized. I will pray to my Son, Jesus, so that He may give you the grace to experience His victory over Satan's temptations.

MONDAY, JULY 16TH

I pray for the priests and the parishoners, that no one may be troubled. I know the changes which will take place soon, (in the parish clergy). *At the time of the changes, I will be there. Also, do not be afraid, there will be in the future, signs concerning sinners, unbelievers, alcoholics and young people. They will accept me again.* (T 42).

THURSDAY, JULY 19TH

Message for the parish:
Dear children, these last days, you have experienced the work of Satan. I am with you always. Do not be afraid of these temptations. God watches over you always. I am with you in the least of trials.

FRIDAY, JULY 20TH

Late in the evening, on the hill of the apparitions:
Open your hearts to me, come close. Say in a loud voice, your intentions, and your prayers.

The Blessed Virgin paid close attention to the prayers of the seers. When they prayed for the Bishop of Mostar, her eyes were filled with tears. While crying, she tells them:
You are my little flowers. Continue to pray, my task is lighter because of it.

She disappeared into Heaven, as she continued to cry, after she had blessed everyone with a crucifix. (T. 43).

THURSDAY, JULY 26TH

A message to the parish:
Dear children! Today also I would like to call you to persistent prayer and penance. Especially, let the young people of this parish be more active in their prayers.

AT THE BEGINNING OF AUGUST

To Jelena:
This message is dedicated to the Pope and to all Christians. Prepare the second millennium of my birth which will take place August 5th, 1984. Throughout the centuries, I consecrated my entire life to you. Is it too much for you to consecrate three days for me? Do not work, on that day, but take up the rosary and pray. (M. 30).

THURSDAY, AUGUST 2ND

A message to the parish:
Dear children! Today I am happy and I thank you for your prayers. Pray more these days for the conversion of sinners.
For the presentation of Mary's second millennium.
Dear children! Pray as much as possible. Pray at least the entire rosary every day. Fast on bread and water on Wednesdays and Fridays. (BN 18, 27).
To Jelena:
I am happy for your participation at Mass. Continue as you did this evening. Thank you for having resisted the temptation of Satan. (DN 1,33).

SUNDAY, AUGUST 5TH

The celebration of the second millennium of Mary's birthday was preceded by three days of fasting and continuous prayer. Seventy priests heard confessions without respite; there were conversions in great numbers.
Never in my life have I cried with sorrow, as I have cried this evening with joy. Thank you! (BN 18,27).
In anticipation of this day the Gospa had said:
The priest who will hear confession will have great joy on that day.
During these 3 days of fasting and continuous prayer *the seers* say the Blessed Virgin was "very joyful," and she repeated:
I am very happy, continue, continue. Continue to pray and to fast.
Her joy seemed to have reached a peak Sunday, August 5th. Like a flower when it blooms, and full of joy, she said:
Continue, continue, open your hearts, ask God and I will ask for you. (T. Vlasic, Aug. 6, 1984, VB. 1,761).

MONDAY, AUGUST 6TH

Continue and make me happy each day. (T. Vlasic, Aug. 7, 1984, VB 1,79).

THURSDAY, AUGUST 9TH

A message for the parish:

Dear children, Satan continues to hinder my plans. Pray, pray, pray! In prayer, abandon yourselves to God. Pray with the heart. Thank you for your response to my call.

SATURDAY, AUGUST 11TH

Dear children!

Pray, because Satan is continually trying to thwart my plans. Pray with your heart and in prayer give yourselves up to Jesus. (F2, 118).

TUESDAY, AUGUST 14TH

To Ivan, at the time of an unexpected apparition, at his home:

I ask the people to pray with me these days, as much as they can. Fast strictly on Wednesdays and Fridays. Every day, at least one rosary, Joyful, Sorrowful and Glorious mysteries. (C.150).

THURSDAY, AUGUST 16TH

A message to the parish:

Dear children! I beg all of you, especially the members of this parish, to live my messages and to tell them to whomever you meet.

THURSDAY, AUGUST 23RD

To Maria, for the parish:

Pray, pray, pray!

Besides, Maria said, she asks that everyone, and especially the young people, behave in a worthy manner during holy mass.

SATURDAY, AUGUST 25TH

To Mirjana:

Wait for me September 13th, I will speak to you about the future. (DN 3,12).

THURSDAY, AUGUST 30TH

Message to the parish, with respect to the cross erected

on Mount Krizevac in 1933, for the 1,950th anniversary of the death and resurrection of Jesus:

Dear children! The cross was in God's plan when you built it. These days especially, go up on the mountain and pray at the foot of the cross. I need your prayers.

FRIDAY, AUGUST 31ST

I love very specially the cross which you have providentially erected on Mount Krizevac. Go there more often and pray. (Bl.34).

THURSDAY, SEPTEMBER 6TH

Message to the parish:
Dear children! Without prayer there is no peace. For that reason, I say to you; dear children, pray at the foot of the cross for peace.

MONDAY, SEPTEMBER 10TH

To Jelena:
Dear children, you must understand that one has to pray. Prayer is no joke, prayer is a conversation with God. In every prayer you must listen to the voice of God. Without prayer one can not live. Prayer is life. (T. Vlasic, November 10, 1984; VB. 1, 130).

THURSDAY, SEPTEMBER 13TH

Message for the parish:
Dear children! I continually need your prayers. You wonder what all these prayers are for. Look around, dear children, and you will see how much ground sin has gained in this world. Because of that, pray that Jesus conquers.

THURSDAY, SEPTEMBER 20TH

Message for the parish:
Dear children! Today I ask you to start fasting, putting your heart in it. There are many people who fast only because everyone else is fasting. It has become a custom which no one wants to stop. I ask the parish to fast out of gratitude to God for allowing me to remain so long in this parish. Dear children, fast and pray with your heart.

THURSDAY, SEPTEMBER 27TH

Message for the parish:
Dear children! Your prayer has helped my plans to be ful-filled. Pray continually for their complete fulfillment. I beg the families of the parish to pray the family rosary.

THURSDAY, OCTOBER 4TH

Message for the parish:
Dear children! Today I would like to tell you that your prayers delight me, but there are some people in the parish who do not pray and for that my heart is sad. Pray, there-fore, that I may bring all your sacrifices and prayers to the Lord.

FRIDAY, OCTOBER 5TH

To Jelena:
I love you. Love me, love one another. (DN 1,33).

MONDAY, OCTOBER 8TH

Let all the prayers that you say in the evening in your homes, be for the conversion of sinners, because the world is truly in sin. Recite the rosary every evening. (F.2, 106).

Jakov was sick that day and received this message at his home:
Dear children! All the prayers which you recite in the eve-ning in your homes, dedicate them to the conversion of sin-ners because the world is immersed in a great moral decay. Recite the rosary each evening. (M.36).

THURSDAY, OCTOBER 11TH

Message for the parish:
Dear children! Thank you for offering all your afflictions to God, even at this time when He is trying your patience as you reap your crops. (Our Lady is alluding to prolonged rain which came in the middle of the harvesting and caused great damage.) *Be aware, dear children, that He loves you and that it is for that reason that He tests you. Always present your burdens to God and do not worry.*

SATURDAY, OCTOBER 13TH

For the priests of the Marian Movement of Priests:
A message to you and to all those who love me. Dear children, pray unceasingly and ask the Holy Spirit to inspire you always. In everything that you ask, in everything that you do, look only for the will of God. (BN 18,27).

Live according to your convictions and respect others. (Bl. 221).

THURSDAY, OCTOBER 18TH

Dear children! Today I ask you to read the Bible in your homes every day. Place it in a visible place there, where it will always remind you to read it and to pray.

SATURDAY, OCTOBER 20TH

When you pray, you must feel more. Prayer is a conversation with God. To pray means to listen to God. Prayer is useful for you because after prayer everything is clear. Prayer makes one know happiness. Prayer can teach you how to cry. Prayer can teach how to blossom. Prayer is not a joke. Prayer is a dialogue with God. (T. Vlasic, November 10, 1984; VB 1, 125-126).

WEDNESDAY, OCTOBER 24TH

At 10:00 in the evening at Krizevac:
My dear children, I am so happy to see you pray. Pray with me so that God's plan may be realized, thanks to your prayers and to mine. Pray more, and more intensely. (T.45).

THURSDAY, OCTOBER 25TH

Message for the parish:
Dear children! Pray during this month. God has allowed me to help you every day with graces, in order to protect you from evil. This month is mine. I would like to give it to you. Pray and God will give you the graces that you ask for. I will support your requests.

OCTOBER

I would like to guide you spiritually, but I would not know how to help you, if you are not open. It suffices for you to think, for example, where you were with your thoughts yesterday during mass. When you go to mass, your trip from home to church should be a time of preparation for mass. You should also receive Holy Communion with an open and pure heart; purity of heart and openness. Do not leave the church without an appropriate act of thanksgiving. I can help you only if you are accessible to my suggestions; I can not help you if you are not open. (T-59).

The most important in spiritual life is to ask for the gift of the Holy Spirit. When the Holy Spirit comes, then peace will be established. When that occurs, everything changes around you. Things will change. (T. 59).

THURSDAY, NOVEMBER 1ST

Message for the parish:
Dear children! Today I call you to renew family prayer in your homes. The field work is over. Now, may all of you devote yourselves to prayer. Let prayer have first place in your families. Thank you for your response to my call.

THURSDAY, NOVEMBER 8TH

Message for the parish:
Dear children! You are not aware of the importance of the messages which God is sending you through me. He is giving you great graces and you do not realize it. Pray to the Holy Spirit for enlightenment. If only you knew how many graces God is giving you, you would pray without ceasing.

THURSDAY, NOVEMBER 15TH

Message for the parish:
Dear children! You are a chosen people and God has given you great graces. You do not realize the importance of every message I am giving you. Now I only wish to say: Pray, pray, pray! I do not know what else to tell you because I love you and wish that in prayer you come to know my love and the love of God.

SATURDAY, NOVEMBER 17TH

To Jelena:
Pray. Do not ask yourself about the reason why I constantly

invite you to prayer. Intensify your personal prayer so that it will become a channel for the others. (BN 18, 30).

THURSDAY, NOVEMBER 22ND

To Maria, for the parish:
Dear children! These days, live all of my messages and continue to root them in your hearts this week.

THURSDAY, NOVEMBER 29TH

Message for the parish:
Dear children! You do not yet know how to love, nor do you listen with love to the words I am giving you. Be assured, my beloved ones, that I am your Mother, and that I have come on earth to teach you how to listen with love, how to pray with love, and not be compelled by the cross you are carrying. Through the cross, God is glorified in every person.

THURSDAY, DECEMBER 6TH

Message for the parish:
Dear children! These days, I am calling you to family prayer. Many times, I have given you messages in God's name, but you have not listened. This Christmas will be an unforgettable day for you, provided you accept the messages I am giving you. Dear children, do not allow that day of joy, to be a day of deepest sorrow for me.

THURSDAY, DECEMBER 13TH

To Maria, for the parish:
Dear children! You know that the day of joy is coming near, but without love you will obtain nothing. Therefore, first of all start loving your family and everyone in the parish. Then you will be able to love and accept all those who will come here. Let this week be the week of learning how to love.

This Christmas will be unforgettable if you follow me. Disconnect your television sets and your radios, and begin God's programs; meditation, prayer, reading of the Gospel. Prepare yourselves with faith; then you will have understood love, your life will be filled with happiness. (BN 18, 31).

MONDAY, DECEMBER 17TH

Message conveyed by the seers to Monsignor Franic, Archbishop of Split, during a retreat which he is making at Medjugorje:

You will have to suffer more. (DN 3, 18).

THURSDAY, DECEMBER 20TH

To Jelena:

Today I am asking you to do something concrete for Jesus Christ. On the day of joy, I would like every family of the parish to bring a flower as a sign of self-offering to Jesus. I would like every member of the family to have a flower next to the crib, so that Jesus can come and see your offering of self to Him. (VB 2,16).

To Maria, for the parish:

Today I invite you to show a concrete gesture for Jesus Christ, I wish that each family in the parish bring each day a flower, as a sign of surrender to Jesus until Christmas which is approaching. Have each member of the family place a flower near the manger; and Jesus, at the time of his arrival, will see your love for Him there.

On December 24th the parishoners carried their flowers near the manger. The whole sanctuary was converted into a flower bed in blossom.

FRIDAY, DECEMBER 21ST

Dear children! I would like for all of you to be like a flower, which is going to open at Christmas for Jesus; a flower which does not cease to blossom after Christmas. Be the good shepherds of Jesus. (Bl. 298).

TUESDAY, DECEMBER 25TH

The Virgin did not give a message, but she appeared holding the Child Jesus in her arms. (DN 5,77).

THURSDAY, DECEMBER 27TH

Message for the parish:

Dear children! This Christmas, Satan wanted in a special

way to thwart God's plans. You, dear children, witnessed Satan even on Christmas day. But God conquered in your hearts. Let your hearts continue to rejoice.

SATURDAY, DECEMBER 29TH

To Jelena, the anniversary day of her first apparition.
Today is the feast of the Mother of goodness, of mercy, and of love.
"And she gave us her blessing saying:"
Up until now I have not given it to you.
"And the group felt strongly changed because of it."
She motivated them to receive this blessing:
Receive it, do not neglect it as before. I can give you my blessing, but I cannot give it to you if you do not want it.
(T. Vlasic, Mar. 2, 1985, VB 2,381).

To Jelena:
I wish that a great love, a great peace would flourish in you. Thus, pray. (Bl. 257).

1985

WEDNESDAY, JANUARY 2ND

At 11:30 at night at Krizevac, the Virgin appeared surrounded by five angels:
I am very happy to have been able to come here for three years, thanks to the prayers of believers. Continue to pray thusly. A part of my plan has been realized. God blesses in a special way, all those who are here. You can return happily to your homes. You do not immediately understand the reasons. Offer your prayers of thanksgiving for next week.
(T, 47).

THURSDAY, JANUARY 3RD

To Maria, for the parish:
Dear children! These days, the Lord granted you many graces. Let this week be a week of thanksgiving for all the graces God has granted you. Thank you for having responded to my call.

WEDNESDAY, JANUARY 9TH

I thank the faithful for having come to church in very bad and cold weather. (T. 48).

THURSDAY, JANUARY 10TH

To Maria, for the parish:
Dear children! Today I want to thank you for all your sacrifices. I thank especially those who come here gladly, and have become dear to my heart. There are parishoners who do not listen to my messages; but because of those who are especially close to my heart, I give messages to the parish. And I will continue giving them, for I love you and want you to spread them with love.

THURSDAY, JANUARY 17TH

To Maria, for the parish:
In these days, Satan is fighting deviously against this parish, and you, dear children, have fallen asleep in (regard to) prayer. Only some of you are going to Mass. Persevere in these days of temptation.

THURSDAY, JANUARY 24TH

To Maria, for the parish:
Dear children! These days you have savored the sweetness of God through the renewal in your parish. Satan plans to work even more energetically to take the joy away from each of you. Through prayer, you can totally disarm him and ensure your happiness.

THURSDAY, JANUARY 31ST

To Maria, for the parish:
Dear children! Today I want to ask you to open your hearts to God, just like the flowers in the spring that yearn for the sun. I am your Mother and I would like you to be ever closer to the Father, so that he pour gifts into your hearts abundantly.

JANUARY - FEBRUARY

To Vicka, at the time of a prayer meeting on the mountain:

My dear children, Satan is strong. He wishes, with all his strength, to destroy my plans. Pray only, and do not stop doing it. I will also pray to my Son, so that all the plans that I have begun will be realized.

Be patient and persevere in prayer. Do not permit Satan to take away your courage. He works very hard in the world. Be on your guard. (DN 3,26).

SUNDAY, FEBRUARY 3RD

I wish for Father Slavko to stay here, for him to guide the life and to assemble all the news, so that when I leave there will be a complete image of everything that has happened here. I am also praying now for Slavko and for all those who work in this parish. (DN3, 25-26).

THURSDAY, FEBRUARY 7TH

To Maria, for the parish:
Dear children! Satan is manifesting himself in this parish in a particular way these days. Pray, dear children, that God's plan be carried out, and that every work of Satan be turned to the glory of God. I have remained this long to help you in your great trials.

THURSDAY, FEBRUARY 14TH

To Maria, for the parish:
Dear children! Today is the day when I give you the message for the parish, but not everyone in the parish accepts my messages and lives them. I am sad and I want you, dear children, to listen to me and to live my messages. Every family must pray and read the Bible.

SUNDAY, FEBRUARY 17TH

Pray, dear children, so that God's plan may be accomplished, and all the works of Satan be changed in favor of the glory of God. (F 2, 158).

WEDNESDAY, FEBRUARY 20TH (Ash Wednesday)

To Jelena:
I give you an advice; I would like for you to try to conquer

*some fault each day. If your fault is to get angry at every-
thing, try each day, to get angry less. If your fault is not
to be able to study, try to study. If your fault is not to be
able to obey, or if you cannot stand those who do not please
you, try on a given day, to speak with them. If your fault
is not to be able to stand a proud person, you should try
to approach that person. If you desire that person to be humble, be humble yourselves. Show that humility is worth more
than pride.*

*Thus, each day, try to go beyond, and to reject every vice
from your heart. Find out which are the vices that you most
need to reject. During this Lent, you should try and truly desire to spend it in love. Strive as much as possible.* (DN 4bis, 68).

THURSDAY, FEBRUARY 21ST

A message to the parish:

*Day after day I have been appealing to you for renewal
and prayer in the parish. But you are not responding. Today
I am appealing to you for the last time. This is the season
of Lent, and you, as a parish in Lent, should be moved through
love of my appeal to take the first step. If you do not take
this step, I do not want to give you any more messages. God
will allow me not to give you any more.*

MONDAY, FEBRUARY 25TH

To Jelena:

*Know that I love you. Know that you are mine. I do not
wish to do anything more for anyone, that I do not wish to
do for you. Come all of you to me. Remain with me and I
will be your Mother always. Come, because I wish to have
all of you.* (Bl. 261).

To Maria:

*For next week, I invite you to say these words: 'I love God
in everything.' With love, one obtains everything. You can receive many things, even the most impossible. The Lord wishes
for all the parishes to surrender to Him, and I too, in Him.
I desire it. Each evening, make your examination of conscience,
but only to give thanks in acknowledgment for everything that
His love offers us at Medjugorje.* (DN 3, 301).

THURSDAY, FEBRUARY 28TH

Message to the parish:
Today I call you to live these words during this week: 'I love God.' Dear children, with love, you can achieve everything, even what appears impossible. God wants this parish to belong to Him completely. And I wish that too.

FEBRUARY - MARCH

Dear children! You have always prayed that I not abandon you. Now I ask of you, in turn, not to abandon me. Satan wants especially during these days to disperse you. For that, pray very much these days.

Dear children, I came again to thank you. You have not yet understood what that means. To give joy to my heart. It is a very great thing. I ask you only to persevere in prayer. As long as you pray I will have words for you. Good-bye, I thank you dear children. My love for you is unlimited; be happy with me, because I am happy with you. (DN 4 bis, 68).

THURSDAY, MARCH 7TH

Message for the parish:
Dear children! Today I invite you to renew prayer in your families. Dear children, encourage the very young to pray and to go to holy Mass. (BN 19, 30).

SATURDAY, MARCH 9TH

You can receive a grace immediately, or in a month, or in ten years. I do not need a hundred or two hundred 'Our Fathers.' It is better to pray only one, but with a desire to encounter God. You should do everything out of love. Accept all annoyances, all difficulties, everything, with love. Dedicate yourselves to love. (BN 19, 30).

WEDNESDAY, MARCH 13TH

Message addressed to Vicka, at a time when a mistake by Ivan, who was frightened, caused a stir. (Described in detail in DN 4, p. 17-23).

Pray, pray, pray! It is only with prayer that you will be

able to avoid Ivan's error. He should not have written. And after that had to clearly acknowledge it, so as not to plant any doubts.

THURSDAY, MARCH 14TH

To Maria, for the parish:

Dear children! In your life, you have all experienced light and darkness. God gives every person the power to recognize good and evil. I am calling you to light, which you must carry to all those who are in darkness. From day to day, people who are in darkness come into your houses. You, dear children, give them light.

MONDAY, MARCH 18TH

To Mirjana:

The rosary is not an ornament for the home, as one often times limits himself to using it. Tell everyone to pray it. (DN 4 bis, 421).

Right now, many are greatly seeking money, not only in the parish, but in the whole world. Woe to those who seek to take everything from those who come, and blessed are those from whom they take everything. (This relates to the exploitation of some pilgrims.) (DN 4 bis, 26).

May the priests help you because I have entrusted to you a heavy burden, and I suffer from your difficulties. Ivan did not make a big mistake. I have sufficiently reprimanded him for the error. It is not necessary to scold him anymore. (BI 111).

THURSDAY, MARCH 21ST

To Maria, for the parish:

Dear children! I want to give you the messages. Therefore I ask you to accept these messages. Dear children, I love you. In a special way I have chosen this parish which is more dear to me than any of the others to which I gladly came when the Almighty sent me. Therefore, dear children, I ask you to accept me for your well-being. Live the messages.

SUNDAY, MARCH 24TH (vigil of the Annunciation)

Today I invite all of you to Confession, even if you have

already gone to Confession during the last days. I wish that you would live my feast in your hearts. You are not able to, if you do not abandon yourselves completely to the Lord. It is for this reason that I call all of you to reconciliation with the Lord. (DN. 4 bis, 64).

LENT 1985 (February 20-April 6)

To Jelena:
Fast on bread and water during the first week of the Passion and on Holy Wednesday, Holy Thursday, and Good Friday. (Bl. 209).

MONDAY, MARCH 25TH (Feast of the Annunciation)

Through my joy and the joy of this people, I say to all of you this evening, I love you, and I wish you well. (DN. 4 bis, 64).
Jelena: "Why are you so beautiful?"
I am beautiful because I love. If you want to be beautiful, love. There is no one in the world who does not desire beauty. (Bl. 263).

THURSDAY, MARCH 28TH

Message to the parish:
Dear children! Today, I am asking you to pray, pray, pray. In prayer you will experience great joy and the solution to every hopeless situation. Thank you for making progress in prayer. Each one of you belongs to my heart. I am grateful to all of you who have begun praying in your families.
To Jelena:
You all know the flowers. A flower must blossom and each part of the flower is very important. But there is a moment when the flower must wilt so that the seed can ripen, and after, when the seed is ripe, other flowers will come.
Jelena did not know how to explain this parable. But Tomislav Vlasic explained: One finds in it the whole liturgy of this evening (Saturday, vigil of Palm Sunday); one must die in order to be able to rise again. We say sometimes that it is sad that a flower must wilt. But, if it does not wilt, it is not able to ripen the seed from where the other flowers come. If it does not die, life can not multiply itself. (S. Barbaric, April 6, 1985, VB. 2, 801).

THURSDAY, APRIL 4TH (Holy Thursday)

Message to the parish:

Dear children! I am thankful that you have begun to reassure more highly in your hearts the glory of God. Today is the day that I wanted to stop giving messages because certain people do not accept them. The parish has responded and I wish to continue to give messages to a degree, such as has never before been witnessed in the world, since the beginning of history. Try to remain in my heart. Do not remain on the side. (T. Vlasic, April 29, 1985; VB 2, 135).

FRIDAY, APRIL 5TH

You, the members of this parish, have a large and heavy cross to bear. But do not be afraid to carry it. My Son is here to help you. (DN 4 bis, 65).

CHAPTER 4

Apparitions at the Rectory

April 11, 1985–September 1987

On orders from the Bishop (letter of March 25th), the apparitions, forbidden in every room contiguous to the Church itself, were transferred to the rectory.

THURSDAY, APRIL 11TH

To Maria, for the parish:
I would like to tell everyone in the parish: pray especially to be enlightened by the Holy Spirit. Beginning today, the Lord wants to try the parish in a special way, in order to strengthen it in faith.

MONDAY, APRIL 15TH

You must begin to work in your hearts as you work in the field. Work and change your hearts so that the new spirit of God can dwell there. (C 207)

THURSDAY, APRIL 18TH

To Maria, for the parish:
Dear children! Today I thank you for the opening up of your hearts. Joy overwhelms me for every heart that opens to God, especially in the parish. Rejoice with me. Pray all the prayers for the opening of sinful hearts. I desire this. God desires this through me.

THURSDAY, APRIL 25TH

Message for the parish:

Dear children! Today, I invite you to pray with your heart and not only through habit. Some come here but do not pray with their hearts. Therefore, as your mother, I beg you to pray that prayer may prevail in your hearts at every moment.

THURSDAY, MAY 2ND

Dear children! Today, I invite you to pray with your heart and not only through habit. Some come here but do not pray with their hearts. Therefore, as your mother, I beg you to pray that prayer may prevail in your hearts at every moment.

FRIDAY, MAY 3RD

To Jelena:

Sometimes prayers said in a loud voice keep Jesus at a distance, because when men want to conquer with their own power there is no place for God. Prayers said in a loud voice are good when they come from the heart. (BN. 19, 33)

TUESDAY, MAY 7TH

Ivanka has a vision at home, which lasts about an hour: "the Blessed Virgin was more beautiful than ever and was accompanied by two angels. She asks me what I wished. I prayed to her to let me see my mother. The Blessed Virgin smiled and approved with a nod. My mother appeared to me very soon. She was smiling. Our Lady told me to stand up. My mother embraced me then as she said 'My child, I am so proud of you.' She embraced me again and disappeared. Our Lady said to me then:"

> *My dear child, today is our last meeting, do not be sad. I will return to see you at each anniversary of the first apparition (June 25), beginning next year. Dear child, do not think that you have done anything bad, and that this would be the reason why I'm not returning near to you. No, it is not that. With all your heart you have accepted the plans which my Son and I formulated, and you have*

accomplished everything. No one in the world has had the grace which you, your brothers and sisters have received. Be happy because I am your Mother and I love you from the bottom of my heart. Ivanka, thank you for the response to the call of my Son, thank you for persevering and remaining always with Him as long as He will ask you. Dear child, tell all your friends that my Son and I are always with them when they call on us. What I have told you during these years on the secrets, do not speak to anyone about them.

"Dear Gospa, may I embrace you?"
"The blessed Virgin gives an affirmative sign with her head. I then embraced her. I asked her to bless me. She did it with a smile and added:"
Go in the peace of God.
Then she left slowly with the two angels. (F 2, 150-152 and VB 3, 149)

THURSDAY, MAY 9TH

To Maria, for the parish:
Dear children! You do not know how many graces God is bestowing upon you. You are not willing to get moving in these days when the Holy Spirit is working in a special way; you do not want to advance. Your hearts are turned to earthly things and you are preoccupied by them. Turn your hearts to prayer and ask that the Holy Spirit be poured upon you.

THURSDAY, MAY 16TH

To Maria, for the parish:
Dear children! I am calling you to more attentive prayer and to greater participation in the Mass. I want you to experience God within yourselves at Mass. I want to tell young people especially, to be open to the Holy Spirit, because God desires to draw you to Himself, during these days when Satan is active.

SUNDAY, MAY 19TH

To Jelena:

Dear children, at this time I ask you particularly to conse-crate yourselves to me and to my Immaculate Heart. Love, pray, and fast. (Bl 304).

THURSDAY, MAY 23RD (day before Pentecost)

Message to the parish:

Dear children, I invite you especially these days, open your hearts to the Holy Spirit. The Holy Spirit acts now through you. Open your hearts and offer your life to Jesus, so that he will act in your hearts and strengthen you in the faith. Thank you for your response to my call.

TUESDAY, MAY 28TH

Love is a gift from God. Pray so that God may grant you the gift to be able to love. (Bl 255)

THURSDAY, MAY 30TH

To Maria, for the parish:

Dear children, I am calling you again to prayer of the heart. Let prayer, dear children, be your everyday food, especially when work in the fields is exhausting you, and you cannot pray with your heart. Pray, and then you will overcome every tiredness. Prayer will be your happiness and rest.

SATURDAY, JUNE 1

To Jelena:

Always have the love of God in you, because without this love, you are not able to convert yourselves completely. Let the rosary be in your hands in memory of Jesus. Dear chil-dren, strive to deepen your knowledge of the mass as you should. (J).

SUNDAY, JUNE 2ND

Dear children, this evening I would like to tell you to pray more during the novena for an out pouring of the Holy Spirit, on your families and your parish. Pray, you will not be sorry for it. God will present you with gifts for which you are going to glorify Him all your earthly life.

THURSDAY, JUNE 6TH

To Maria, for the parish:
Dear children! Many people of all nationalities will come to the parish and now I am calling you to love. Love first of all the members of your own family and then you might be able to accept and love all those who are coming.

THURSDAY, JUNE 13TH

To Maria, for the parish:
Dear children: I am begging you, the people of this parish, to pray more until the anniversary of the apparitions. (June 25th). May your prayer be an act of devotion and commitment to God. I know about your tiredness, dear children, but you do not know how to give yourselves to me. These days, I beg you, make an act of total dedication to me.

THURSDAY, JUNE 20TH

To Maria, for the parish:
Dear children! For the coming feast I want to say to you: Open your hearts to the Lord of all hearts! Give me all your feelings and all your problems. I want to console you in all your trials. My wish is to fill you completely with God's peace, joy, and love.

SATURDAY, JUNE 22ND

Jelena: The Gospa dictated to me (perhaps, it would be better to say, inspired) this prayer and advised me to recite it in our prayer group:

PETITION TO GOD

Oh God, our heart is in deep obscurity,
in spite of our union to Your Heart.
Our heart is struggling between You and Satan;
do not permit it to be in this manner!

Every time that the heart is divided
between good and evil,
let it be enlightened by Your light
and let it be unified.

Never permit,
for there to be able to exist in us two loves,
that there can never co-exist in us two faiths,
and that there can never co-exist in us;
lying and sincerity,
love and hatred,
honesty and dishonesty,
humility and pride.

Help us on the contrary,
so that our hearts may be elevated toward You
just like that of a child.
May our heart be ravished with peace
and continue to always have the nostalgia of it.

May Your Holy will and Your love
find a permanent place in us, that at least
sometimes we would really wish to be Your
children and when, Oh Lord,
we will desire to be Your children,
remember our past desires
and help us to receive You again.

We open our hearts to you
so that Your holy love will remain in us.
We open our souls to you,
so that they may be touched by Your holy mercy
which will help us to see clearly all our sins,
and will make us realize,
that which makes us impure is sin.

God, we want to be Your children,
humble and devout,
to the point of becoming your cherished and
sincere children,
such as only the Father

would be able to desire that we be.
Help us, Jesus our brother,
to obtain the goodness of the Father in our regard,
and to be good to Him.

Help us Jesus,
to understand well what God gives us,
although sometimes we fail to perform a good act,
as though it were for us an evil.
(VB 3, 218-219).

PRAYER FOR A SICK PERSON

Likewise dictated (inspired) to Jelena, with this clause: "Here is the most beautiful prayer that you could recite for a sick person."

O my God
behold this sick person before You.
He has come to ask You
what he wishes
and what he considers as the most important thing
for him.
You, oh my God,
make these words enter into his heart:
(What is important, is the health of his soul)

Lord, may Your will in everything
take place in his regard, if You want for him to
be cured,
let health be given to him;
but if Your will is something else,
let him continue to bear his cross.

I also pray to You for us,
who intercedes for him;
purify our hearts,
to make us worthy to convey
Your holy Mercy.

Protect him and relieve his pain,
that Your holy will be done in him,
that Your holy name be revealed through him,
help him to bear his cross with courage.
(VB 3, 220-221).

Before this prayer and the preceeding one, recite three times
the "Glory Be."

TUESDAY, JUNE 25TH

On this anniversary day of the first apparition on the hill,
Maria asks:
"What do you wish from the priests?"
*I urge you to ask everyone to pray the rosary. With the
rosary you will overcome all the troubles which Satan is try-
ing to inflict on the Catholic Church. Let all priests pray the
rosary. Give time to the rosary.* (F 2, 118).
To Jelena:
*A heart which belongs to the Lord is splendid, even if it
is flooded with difficulties and trials. But if the heart engaged
in difficulties, strays away from God, it loses its splendor.*
(BN 19,34).

THURSDAY, JUNE 27TH

To Maria, for the parish:
*Today I invite you to humility. These days all of you have
felt a great joy because of all the people who came here,
and to whom you spoke with love about your experience. With
humility and an opening of the heart, continue to speak with
all those who come.*

JUNE—1985

To Jelena:
*Dear children, if there is someone and he asks you for some-
thing, give it to him. I too, ask before many hearts, and they
do not open up. Pray so that the world may receive my love.*
(Bl. 258).

MONDAY, JULY 1ST

On the hill of the apparitions:
I thank all those who have responded to my call. I bless all of you, I bless each of you. These days I ask you to pray for my intentions. Go in the peace of God. (Bl. 183).

THURSDAY, JULY 4TH

Message for the parish:
Dear children, I thank you for each sacrifice you have made. Now I urge you to offer all your sacrifices with love.
I want you who are troubled to begin to help pilgrims with confidence and the Lord will give to you in the same manner.

THURSDAY, JULY 11TH

Message to the parish:
Dear children! I love your parish and I protect it under my mantle against every satanic enterprise. Pray that Satan will flee from your parish and from everyone who comes to your parish. In that way you will be able to hear each appeal from God and to respond to it with your life. Thank you for your response to my call.

THURSDAY, JULY 18TH

Message to the parish:
Dear children! Today I invite you to put more blessed objects in your home and may every person carry blessed objects on himself. Let everything be blessed. Then, because you are armored against Satan, he will tempt you less.

THURSDAY, JULY 25TH

To Maria, for the parish:
Dear children! I want to shepherd you but you do not want to obey my messages. Today I call you to obey my messages and then you will be able to live everything that God tells me to relate to you. Open yourselves to God, and God will work through you, and give you everything you need.

THURSDAY, AUGUST 1ST

To Maria, for the parish:
Dear children! I wish to tell you that I have chosen this parish. I guard it in my hands like a little flower that does not want to die. I beg you to give yourselves to me so that I can offer you as a gift to God, fresh and without sin. Satan has undertaken one part of my plan and wants to possess it. Pray that he does not succeed because I desire to have you for myself so that I can offer you to God.

MONDAY, AUGUST 5TH

Message to Ivan, during an apparition in the evening, on the mountain of Krizevac, where she came "with vestments of gold."
Praise be Jesus Christ. My children, I'm happy to be with you this evening, and to see you so numerous. I bless you with a special blessing.

After having prayed for a long time and listened to Ivan who recommended the persons present, she concluded:
Make progress in holiness through the messages, I will help you. Give your utmost and we will go together, sensitive to the sweetness of life, light, and joy.

After having blessed them, she left in the sign of the radiant cross while saying:
Go in the peace of God, my children, my little children.

THURSDAY, AUGUST 8TH

Message for the parish:
Dear children! Today I am calling you to begin your struggle against Satan with prayer. Satan wants to work more now that you know he is active. Dress up, dear children, in clothes of armor against Satan; with rosaries in your hands, you will conquer.

WEDNESDAY, AUGUST 14TH

To Ivan:
Observe the complete fasts, Wednesdays and Fridays. Pray at least an entire Rosary: Joyous, Sorrowful, and Glorious mysteries. (BN. 19, 351).

THURSDAY, AUGUST 15TH (Feast of the Assumption)

Message to the parish:

Dear children! Today I bless you and I wish to tell you that I love you. I appeal to you at this moment to live my messages. Today I bless you all with the solemn blessing which the Almighty has granted me.

To Mirjana:

My angel, pray for unbelievers. People will tear their hair, brother will plead with brother, he will curse his past life, lived without God. They will repent, but it will be too late. Now is the time for conversion. I have been exhorting you for the past four years. Pray for them. (BN 19, 35).

Invite everyone to pray the Rosary. (Bl. 154).

THURSDAY, AUGUST 22ND

To Maria, for the parish:

Dear children! Today I wish to tell you that the Lord wants to put you to the test, which you can overcome by prayer. God puts you to the test in your daily activities. Pray now that you pass every test peacefully. Come through every test from God more open to Him and approach Him with greater love.

THURSDAY AUGUST, 29TH

To Maria, for the parish:

Dear children! I invite you especially to prayer because Satan wants to help himself with the harvests of your vineyards. Pray so that he will not succeed. (Placed on guard against the materialism which surrounded them, still, certain persons began to sell grapes to the pilgrims more expensively.)

THURSDAY, SEPTEMBER 5TH

To Maria, for the parish:

Dear children! I thank you today for all your prayers. Pray continually and pray more so that Satan will go far away from this place. Dear children, the plan of Satan has failed. Pray that every plan of God be realized in this parish. I especially thank young people for the sacrifices they have offered.

THURSDAY, SEPTEMBER 12TH

To Maria, for the parish, before the celebration of the feast of the Holy Cross, day of the largest pilgrimage of the year, at Krizevac:

Dear children! I wish to tell you these days to put the Cross at the center of your life. Pray especially before the Cross which is the origin of great graces. In your homes make a special consecration to the Cross of the Lord. Promise that you will not offend Jesus and that you will not insult Him, nor the Cross.

FRIDAY, SEPTEMBER 20TH (instead of Thursday, 19th)

To Maria, for the parish:

Dear children! Today I am calling you to live in humility all the messages I give you. Dear children, when you live the messages do not glorify yourselves by saying: I live the messages. If you carry the messages in your heart and live them everyone will notice it. So, there is no need for words which serve only those who do not wish to hear. For you it is not necessary to speak. For you, my dear children, it is necessary to live and witness by your lives. (DN 4 bis, 67).

THURSDAY, SEPTEMBER 26TH

To Maria, for the parish:

Dear children! Thank you for all your prayers. Thank you for all your sacrifices. I want you to renew the messages that I am giving you. Heed the call to fasting because by fasting you will ensure that the total plan of God here in Medjugorje will be fulfilled. That will give me great joy. Thank you for having responded to my call.

SEPTEMBER

To Maria:

I have given you my love, so that you may give it to others.

THURSDAY, OCTOBER 3RD

To Maria, for the parish:

Dear children! I want to say to you, be thankful to God

*for every grace that God gave you. For all the fruits of grace,
be thankful to the Lord and praise Him. Dear children, learn
to be thankful for little things, and then you will be able to
be thankful for great things.*

THURSDAY, OCTOBER 10TH

To Maria, for the parish:
*I invite you one more time to live the messages in the parish. I invite the young people of this parish particularly, to
do it. Dear children, if you live the messages you will develop
the seeds of holiness. As Mother, I invite all of you to holiness, so that you will be able to transmit it to others. You
are a mirror for others.*

THURSDAY, OCTOBER 17TH

To Maria, for the parish:
*There is a time for each thing. Today, I invite you to begin
to work on your hearts. At present, all the work in the fields
has ended. You find the time to clean the most neglected places,
but you set your hearts aside. Work more now, with love, to
clean each of the recesses of your heart.*

THURSDAY, OCTOBER 24TH

To Maria, for the parish:
*I wish from day to day, to clothe you with sanctity, goodness, obedience and love of God, so that you may be from
day to day, more beautiful and better prepared for your God.
Dear children, listen to my messages and live them. I want
to guide you.*

FRIDAY, OCTOBER 25TH

Mirjana: "When she appeared, the Blessed Virgin greeted
me, 'Praised be Jesus.' Then she spoke of unbelievers;"
*They are my children. I suffer because of them. They do
not know what awaits them. You must pray more for them.*
"We prayed with her for the weak, the unfortunate, the foresaken. After the prayer, she blessed us. Then she showed me,
as in a film, the realization of the first secret. The earth was
desolate.

It is the upheavel of a region of the world. "She was precise. I cried."

"Why so soon," I asked?

In the world, there are so many sins. What can I do, if you do not help me. Remember, that I love you.
"How can God have such a hard heart?"

God does not have a hard heart. Look around you and see what men do, then you will no longer say that God has a hard heart.

How many people come to church, to the house of God, with respect, a strong faith, and love of God? Very few! Here you have a time of grace and conversion. It is necessary to use it well. (DN 5, 39).

To Mirjana:

Pray very much for Father Pero, to whom I send a special blessing. I am a mother, that is why I come. You must not fear for I am there.

Father Pero Ljubicic had been chosen by Mirjana, to unveil to the world, the first three warnings, three days before the event. (DN 5, 40).

THURSDAY, OCTOBER 31ST

To Maria, for the parish:

Dear children, today I love all of you with the same love, and I wish that each one would do all that is possible, according to his own capacity. Dear children, you can do it, I know. But you do not want it, because you feel small and weak. Take courage, and offer little flowers to the Church and to Jesus, so that all of us may be happy.

Message to the prayer group:

God loves you very much. He loves you a hundred-fold more than your parents love you. (and she invited to offer her heart to this love. T. Vlasic, 2 Nov. 1985, VB 3, 179).

THURSDAY, NOVEMBER 7TH

To Maria, for the parish:

I invite you to love your neighbor, especially those who do you harm. In this way, you will be able to discern the intentions of the heart with love. Pray and love, dear children.

It is with the strength of love, that you will be able to accomplish what seems impossible to you.

THURSDAY, NOVEMBER 14TH

To Maria, for the parish:

I, your Mother, love you. I encourage you to pray. I never get tired. I call you even when you are far from my heart. I feel badly for each person who is lost. But I am your Mother; I forgive easily, and I experience joy for each child who returns to me.

THURSDAY, NOVEMBER 21ST

To Maria, for the parish:

I am anxious to tell you that it is a special time for you and for the parish. During the summer, you say that you have to work very much. At this time, there is no work in the fields. Thus, I invite you to work on yourselves. Come to mass; the time is being provided for you.

Dear children, there are many who come, in spite of the bad weather, because they love me, and want to prove their love to me. I ask all of you to prove your love to me by coming to mass. The Lord will reward you generously for it.

THURSDAY, NOVEMBER 28TH

To Maria, for the parish:

I wish to thank all of you for everything you have done for me, especially the young people. I ask you dear children, enter conscientiously into prayer, because it is in prayer, that you will know God's designs.

WEDNESDAY, DECEMBER 4TH

Gianni Sgreva, an Italian Passionist, was inspired to found a "Community of Consecrated" on the message of Medjugorje, and seeking discernment, submitted his case of conscience to Maria, who questioned the Gospa.

I prefer to answer him personally.

It seems that the message was positive, because the community opened May, 18th, 1987, at Priabona in Italy. (There follows another message, which one will find later: June 7, 1986, Archives Sgreval.)

THURSDAY, DECEMBER 5TH

To Maria, for the parish:

I wish to invite you to prepare yourselves for the feast of Christmas, through prayer, penance, and acts of love. Do not worry so much, dear children, about material things, because in this manner, you will not be able to live the feast of Christmas.

SATURDAY, DECEMBER 7TH

To Jelena

I have only one wish for tomorrow's feast. I ask of you to find at least a quarter of an hour, for you to come before me and entrust your problems to me. No one will understand you, as I do. (J).

THURSDAY, DECEMBER 12TH

To Maria, for the parish:

I invite you to praise Jesus, with me, at this time of Christmas. On that day, I give Him to you in a special way, and invite you to celebrate Jesus' birth with me.

Dear children, on that day, pray more, and think more of Jesus.

THURSDAY, DECEMBER 19TH

To Maria, for the parish:

I invite you to love your neighbor. If you love your neighbor, you will feel more the presence of Jesus, especially on Christmas day. God will fill you with great gifts, if you abandon yourselves to Him. On Christmas Day, I will give a special blessing to all the mothers, my maternal blessing. And Jesus will grant His blessing to everyone.

THURSDAY, DECEMBER 26TH

To Maria, for the parish:

I thank all of you who have listened to my messages, and who have lived, on Christmas Day, what I had told you previously. Beginning now, you are purified of your sins, and I would like to continue to guide you in the love of your heart.

TUESDAY, DECEMBER 31ST

To Jelena, during the eve of December 31st:

Next year is the year of peace; not because men have named it so, but because God has programmed it. You will not have peace through the presidents, but through prayer.

Through one of the little seers of the group, during this same vigil, Jesus said:

When you hear the clocks at midnight, you will fall on your knees, bow your head to the ground, so that the King of Peace will come. This year, I will offer my peace to the world. But afterwards, I will ask you where you were when I offered you my peace.

(These two messages were reported by T. Vlasic, February, 6th, 1986. VB 4, 34).

1986

THURSDAY, JANUARY 2ND

Message to the parish:

I invite you to decide totally for God. I beg of you dear children, give yourselves completely, and you will be able to live everything that I have told you. It will not be difficult for you to give yourselves completely to God.

MONDAY, JANUARY 6TH

To Vicka:

If you agree to it, I will not appear to you anymore for 50 days.

Vicka accepts this sacrifice. (DN 5, 107).

THURSDAY, JANUARY 9TH

Message to the parish:

I invite you to help Jesus through your prayer, for the realization of all His plans, which He has already begun here. Offer your sacrifices to Jesus, so that He will realize everything that He has planned, and that Satan will not be able to do anything.

THURSDAY, JANUARY 16TH

Message to the parish:
Today, I still invite you to prayer. I need your prayers so that God may be glorified through all of you. Dear children, I beg of you: Listen to my maternal call, and live it. If I invite you to it, it is only out of love, and in order to be able to help you.

TUESDAY, JANUARY 21ST

It was the second day of retreat for a prayer group, probably that of Jelena, (January 21-24, 1986).
This evening, rest. (T. Vlasic, 23 Jan. 86, VB 4, 24).

WEDNESDAY, JANUARY 22ND

To the same group:
I know that you are tired, but I cannot tell you, rest. Today, I tell you, pray, and do not go to bed before having prayed at least a quarter of a hour, for the group. Tomorrow will be a better day. (T. Vlasic, 23 Jan. 86, VB 4, 24).

THURSDAY, JANUARY 23RD

Message to the parish:
I invite you, again, to prayer of the heart. If you pray with the heart, dear children, the eyes of your brothers will melt, and every barrier will disappear. Conversion will be easy for all those who want to receive it. It is a gift which you must implore for your neighbor.

THURSDAY, JANUARY 30TH

To Maria, for the parish:
I invite all of you to pray, so that all of God's designs on you, may be realized, and all that God pursues through you. Help all the others to be converted, especially all those who come to Medjugorje. Dear children, do not permit Satan to become the master of your heart, because in that case, you will become the image of Satan, and not mine.
I invite you to pray, in order to become witnesses of my presence. Without you, the Lord cannot realize what He wishes.

The Lord has given each one a free will, and you can dispose of it.

THURSDAY, FEBRUARY 6TH

To Maria, for the parish:

This parish, which I have chosen, is a special parish which distinguishes itself from others. I offer some special graces to all those who pray with the heart. Dear children, I give these messages first to the parishioners, and then to all the others. You will be responsible for these messages before my Son, Jesus, and me.

THURSDAY, FEBRUARY 13TH

To Maria, for the parish:

This Lent is for you, a special stimulant to change your life. Begin from this moment. Unplug the television and put aside so many other useless things. Dear children, I invite you to individual conversion. This time belongs to you.

THURSDAY, FEBRUARY 20TH

To Maria, for the parish:

Here is my second message for Lent. Renew your prayer before the cross. Dear children, I offer you special graces and Jesus, the extraordinary merits of the cross. Accept them, and live them. Meditate on the passion of Jesus. Unite your life to Jesus.

SATURDAY, FEBRUARY 22ND

At the end of the meeting of the prayer group, before the blessing:

Dear children, you will be able to receive Divine love, only in proportion to when you understand that, on the cross, God offers you His immense love.

(God's punishment is a sign of love, observes T. Vlasic, March 31, 86. VB 45, 59).

THURSDAY, FEBRUARY 27TH

To Maria, for the parish:

Dear children, live in humility, the messages which I give you.

THURSDAY, MARCH 6TH

To Maria, for the parish:

Even today, I invite you to open up more to God, so that He can work through you. It is in proportion to how you open yourselves, that you will harvest the fruits. I invite you again to prayer.

THURSDAY, MARCH 13TH

To Maria, for the parish:

Today I invite you to live Lent with your small sacrifices. Thank you for each sacrifice which you have brought me. Dear children, continue to live in this way. With love, help me to present your offerings. God will reward you.

THURSDAY, MARCH 20TH

To Maria, for the parish:

Today, I invite you to actively enter into prayer. You wish to live all that I tell you, but, you are not successful in it because you do not pray enough. Dear children, I beseech you, open yourselves and begin to pray. Prayer will be a joy for you. If you begin, you will not be uncomfortable, because you will pray in joy.

MONDAY, MARCH 24TH

To the prayer group:

Dear children, receive all that the Lord offers you. Do not have your hands paralzyed and do not repeat: 'Jesus, give me.' But open your hands, and take everything that the Lord offers you. (T. Vlasic, April 27, 86, VB 4, 64).

THURSDAY, MARCH 27TH

To Maria, for the parish:

Thank you for all the sacrifices, but I invite you to a greater sacrifice: the sacrifice of love. Without love, you cannot receive neither my Son, nor me. Without love, you are not able to convey to others, your experience. For that, I invite you dear children, to begin to live love in your hearts.

THURSDAY, APRIL 3RD

To Maria, for the parish:
Dear children, I am calling you to live the holy Mass. There are many of you who have experienced the beauty of the Mass, but there are others who go unwillingly. I have chosen you, dear children, and Jesus is giving you His graces in the holy Mass. Let everyone who comes to Mass be joyful. Come with love and rejoice in the holy Mass.

THURSDAY, APRIL 10TH

To Maria, for the parish:
Dear children, I invite you to grow in love. A flower cannot grow without water. Neither can you grow without God's blessing. Everyday, you should ask for God's blessing so that you can grow normally, and carry out your works.

THURSDAY, APRIL 17TH

To Maria, for the parish:
Dear children, you are preoccupied with material things, and you lose, thus, everything that God wants to give you. Pray then, dear children, for the gifts of the Holy Spirit. They are necessary for you, in order that you may give witness to my presence here, and to everything that I give you.
Dear children, abandon yourselves to me so that I can guide you fully. Do not worry so much about material things.

THURSDAY, APRIL 24TH

To Maria, for the parish:
Dear children, today I invite you to prayer. You have forgotten that you are all important, especially the elderly in the families. Invite them to pray. Let all the young people, by their lives, be an example for others. Let them be witnesses for Jesus.
Dear children, I beseech you to begin to convert yourselves through prayer, then you will know what you must do.

THURSDAY, MAY 1ST

To Maria, for the parish:

Begin to change your lives in your families. Let your family be a harmonious flower, which I can offer to Jesus. Dear children, let each family be active in prayer. It is my wish that one day, one will be aware of the fruits of prayer in the family. It is only thus, that I will offer you all, as petals to Jesus in fulfillment of God's plan.

THURSDAY, MAY 8TH

To Maria, for the parish:

Dear children, you are responsible for the messages that I give here. Here one finds the fountain of grace, and you are the vessels which convey these gifts. That is why I invite you, dear children, to carry out this work, which is yours, with responsibility. Each one in the measure of his ability. Dear children, I invite you to carry these gifts to others with love. Do not keep them for yourselves.

THURSDAY, MAY 15TH

To Maria, for the pàrish:

Dear children, today I invite you to offer to me your hearts so that I can convert them, and make them similiar to mine. You ask yourselves why you are not able to satisfy my requests? You are not able to because you have not entrusted your hearts to me, so that I can change them. You say, but you do not do it. Do then, everything that I tell you. Only in that way, can I be with you.

THURSDAY, MAY 22ND

To Maria, for the parish:

Today I wish to give you my love. You do not realize, dear children, how great my love is, and you do not know how to receive it. I wish to manifest it to you in many ways dear children, but you do not recognize it. You do not understand my words with your hearts, and because of that you do not understand my love.

Dear children, accept me in your life. Thus, you will be

able to accept everything that I tell you, and everything to which I invite you.

THURSDAY, MAY 29TH

To Maria, for the parish:

Dear children, live the love of God, and toward your neighbor. I invite you to it. Without love, dear children, you are not able to do anything. That is why I invite you to live a mutual love. Only in that way will you be able to love, and to receive me, and all those who are around you and come to your parish. Everyone will feel my love through you. Thus, I beg you to start, as of today, to love with a burning love, the love with which I love you.

THURSDAY, JUNE 6TH

To Maria, for the parish:

Dear children! I invite you to decide whether or not you want to live the messages which I give you. I wish that you live and actively convey my messages to others.

In a very particular way, dear children, I wish that all of you become a reflection of Jesus, and bear witness to this unfaithful world. I desire that you become a light to all, that all of you will testify to the light.

Dear children, you are not called to darkness, but to light. So be a light, by the way you live your life.

JUNE 7TH (First Friday of the month)

Fr. Pere Gianni Sgreva, who wanted to found a new community on the messages of Medjugorje, had questioned Maria on June 6th. On the 7th of June she tells him:

"This is what the Gospa answered."

Yes, one must pray. What you are doing pleases me. For the time being, keep a very active prayer life, and God will then light up the other plans.

"Since the Gospa said that, we are sure that the road is a good one. She was happy when I asked her about it."

The community which opened in 1987, in Italy, is prospering so well, that before the end of the year, it had to move, since the large house at Priabona had become too small.

THURSDAY, JUNE 12TH

To Maria, for the parish:
Dear children! Today I invite you to begin to pray the rosary with a living faith. Only in that way will I be able to help you. You wish to receive graces, but you do not pray. I am not able to help you if you do not decide to begin.

I invite you, dear children, to pray the rosary in such a way that it will be a commitment for you, achieved in joy. In this way, you will understand the reason for which I have been with you, for such a long time. I want to teach you to pray.

THURSDAY, JUNE 19TH

Message for the parish:
These days, Our Lord has permitted me to intercede more for you. I invite you then, to again, pray. Pray without ceasing. In this way, I can give you the joy which Our Lord gives me. Through His graces, dear children, let your sufferings be transformed into joy. I am your Mother, and want to help you.

TUESDAY, JUNE 24TH

Maria and Ivan met with the prayer group on Mt. Krizevac:
You are on a Thabor. You receive blessings, strength and love. Carry them into your families, and into your homes. To each one of you, I grant a special blessing. Continue in joy, prayer, and reconciliation. (DN 5, 14-15).

To the prayer group:
I beseech you, withdraw in silence. Your obligation is not so much to do, but to adore God, to stay with Him. (T. Vlasic, 26 June 86. VB 4, 115).

THURSDAY, JUNE 26TH

To Maria, for the parish:
Dear children, God has given me permission to realize with Him, this oasis of peace. I invite you to keep it intact. Through their indifference, some people destroy prayer and peace. I beseech you, testify and help by your lives to preserve it.

THURSDAY, JULY 3RD

To Maria, for the parish:

Dear children! Today I invite all of you to prayer. Without prayer, dear children, you are not able to perceive neither God, nor me, nor the graces which I give you. Therefore, I ask you to always begin and end each day with prayer.

Dear children, I desire to lead you day after day, as much as possible toward prayer, but you cannot grow, if you do not wish to. I exhort you, dear children, let prayer have the first place.

THURSDAY, JULY 10TH

To Maria, for the parish:

Today I invite you to holiness. You cannot live without holiness. That is why you must, with love, be victorious over every sin. Overcome all difficulty with love. I beseech you, dear children, live love within yourselves.

THURSDAY, JULY 17TH

To Maria, for the parish:

Dear children! Today I invite you to ask yourselves why I have been with you such a long time. I am the intercessor between you and God. For that reason, dear children, I invite you to always live with love, everything that God asks of you. Live all the messages that I give you in complete humility.

THURSDAY, JULY 24TH

To Maria, for the parish:

What joy you give me; you are on the road to holiness. I beg you, help by your witness, all those who do not know how to live in holiness. That is why your family must be the place where holiness is born. Help everyone to live in holiness, especially the members of your own family.

THURSDAY, JULY 31ST

To Maria, for the parish:

Hatred gives rise to division and blinds one to everything and everybody. I invite you to spread harmony and peace, more specially, there where you live.

Dear children, act with love. May love be your only tool. With love, convert into good, all that Satan is trying to destroy and take to himself. It is only thus, that you will be completely mine, and that I will be able to help you.

THURSDAY, AUGUST 7TH

To Maria, for the parish:

You know that I promised you an oasis of peace, but you do not know that around this oasis is a desert, where Satan watches and tries to tempt each one of you.

Dear children, it is only through prayer, that you will be able to overcome every influence of Satan, wherever you may be. I am with you, but I cannot deprive you of your free will.

THURSDAY, AUGUST 14TH

To Maria, for the parish:

May your prayer be the joy of a meeting with the Lord. I cannot guide you there, if you yourselves do not feel the joy of prayer. I wish to guide you every day, more deeply into prayer, but I cannot force you.

THURSDAY, AUGUST 21ST

To Maria, for the parish:

I am grateful for the love that you show me. You know, dear children, I love you immensely, and each day I pray to the Lord to help you to understand the love which I bear for you. That is why, dear children, pray, pray, pray.

THURSDAY, AUGUST 28TH

To Maria, for the parish:

I invite you to be, in everything, an example for others, especially in prayer and bearing witness. Without you, dear children, I cannot help the world. I want your cooperation with me in everything, even the smallest things. Therefore, dear children, help me.

May your prayer be a prayer of the heart, and abandon yourselves completely to me. In this way, I will be able to teach you and to guide you on the path, upon which I have set you.

THURSDAY, SEPTEMBER 4TH

To Maria, for the parish:

Again today, I invite you to prayer and fasting. Be assured, dear children, that with your help, I can do everything and prevent Satan from leading you into sin, and to force him to leave this place.

Dear children, Satan lies in wait for each of you. He tries, each day, to plant doubts in each of you. Therefore, dear children, make each day a prayer and total abandonment to God.

THURSDAY, SEPTEMBER 11TH

To Maria, for the parish:

During these days, when you joyfully celebrate the Feast of the Cross, I wish that your own cross become a source of joy.

Especially, dear children, pray in order to be able to accept sickness and suffering with love, as Jesus did. It is only in this way, that I can experience the joy of giving you the graces and the cures, which Jesus permits me to grant you.

THURSDAY, SEPTEMBER 18TH

To Maria, for the parish:

Again today, I thank you for everything you have done for me in recent days. I thank you more particularly, dear children, in the name of Jesus, for the sacrifices you have offered this last week.

Dear children, you forget that I rely on your sacrifices to help you, and to keep Satan away from you. It is for that reason, that I again invite you to offer your sacrifices to God with a deep reverence.

THURSDAY, SEPTEMBER 25TH

To Maria, for the parish:

I invite you to help others through your peace, so that they see it, and begin to look for peace within themselves. Because you are in peace, dear children, you cannot understand the absence of it. That is why I invite you to help through your prayers and your life, to destroy every evil among men, and to unmask Satan's deceptions. Pray, so that truth may prevail in your hearts.

THURSDAY, OCTOBER 2ND

To Maria, for the parish:
Even today, I invite you to pray. You do not realize, dear children, the value of prayer, so you do not tell yourselves: 'Now is the time for prayer; nothing is more important to me. No one is more important for me than God.'

Dear children, dedicate yourselves to prayer with a special love. In this way, God will be able to give you His graces. Thank you for your response to my call.

THURSDAY, OCTOBER 9TH

To Maria, for the parish:
You know that I wish to lead you on the road to holiness. But I cannot compel you by force to become saints. I wish that everyone of you helps me, and himself, by your small sacrifices. In this way I will be able to guide you, and make you more holy, day by day.

Dear children, I do not want to force you to live my messages, but this long time I have spent with you is the sign of the immense love I bear for you. I wish that each one of you become holy.

THURSDAY, OCTOBER 16TH

To Maria, for the parish:
Today, I wish to show you again, how much I love you. I am sad that I am unable to help each of you to understand my love. That is why, dear children, I invite you to pray and to consecrate yourselves completely to God, because Satan wants to conquer you in daily affairs, and to take first place in your lives. For that, dear children, you must pray without ceasing.

THURSDAY, OCTOBER 23RD

To Maria, for the parish:
Again today, I call you to prayer. More particularly, dear children, I invite you to pray for peace. Without your prayer,

I cannot help you to understand the messages that my Lord has permitted me to give you. That is why, dear children, you must pray, in order to know through prayer, the peace that God gives you.

THURSDAY, OCTOBER 30TH

To Maria, for the parish:
Today, again, I invite you accept and live seriously the messages which I give you. It is for you, dear children, that I have stayed here for such a long time. It is so that I might be able to help you to realize these messages which I give you.

THURSDAY, NOVEMBER 6TH

To Maria, for the parish:
Dear children, today I invite you to pray everyday for the souls in Purgatory. Every soul needs prayer and grace in order to reach God and His love. By this way, dear children, you will gain new intercessors, who will help you during your life to discern that nothing on earth is more important for you, than longing for Heaven.

For that dear children, pray without respite, so that you may be able to help yourselves and others, to whom your prayers will bring joy.

THURSDAY, NOVEMBER 13TH

To Maria, for the parish:
Even today, I invite all of you to pray with all your heart, as well as to reform your life from day to day. I am especially calling you, dear children, to live rightiously through prayer and sacrifice. I wish that each one of you, near this source of grace, (Medjugorje), come to paradise with this special gift which He will give—holiness. Pray and reform your life, dear children, so as to become saintly. I will always be near you.

THURSDAY, NOVEMBER 20TH

To Maria, for the parish:
Today I invite you to live, and to follow all the messages which I give you with my special love. Dear children, God

*does not want you to be restless and indecisive, but totally
abandoned to Him. You know that I love you, and that I burn
with love for you.*

*For that reason, dear children, decide also in favor of love.
May love prevail in all of you so that daily, you may burn
with the love of God and experience it for yourselves. Not
human love, but God's love.*

THURSDAY, NOVEMBER 27TH

To Maria, for the parish:

*Dear children, today I invite you again, to dedicate your
life to me with love, so that I may be able to guide it lovingly.
It is a very special love that I bear for you, dear children,
and it is my desire to lead all of you to Heaven and near
to God. Understand that this life lasts a short time, in comparison with that of Heaven.*

*That is why, dear children, again today, decide in favor
of God. In this way only, can I show you, how dear you are
to me, and how much I desire that all of you be saved, and
be with me in Heaven.*

THURSDAY, DECEMBER 4TH

To Maria, for the parish:

*I invite you still today, to prepare your hearts for these days
when the Lord wants above all, to purify you from all the
sins of your past. You cannot do it alone, dear children, and
for that reason, I am here to help you. Pray, dear children,
because it is only in this way that you will be able to know
all the evil that dwells in you, and abandon it to the Lord,
so that He may purify your hearts completely. So, dear children, pray constantly and prepare your hearts through penance and fasting.*

THURSDAY, DECEMBER 11TH

To Maria, for the parish:

*Dear children, I invite you to pray during this special time,
so that you may taste the joy of meeting with the newborn Jesus.*

*Dear children, I wish that you live these days as I lived
them. I want to guide you and show you this joy, to which*

I want to bring all of you. That is why, dear children, pray and abandon yourselves totally to me.

THURSDAY, DECEMBER 18TH

To Maria, for the parish:

Today I call you again, to prayer. When you pray, you are so much more beautiful. You are like flowers, which after the snows, are bursting with beauty in their indescribable colors. In the same way, dear children, after prayer, display more before God, all that is beautiful, in order to please Him. That is why dear children, pray and open your life to the Lord, so that He may make of you a beautiful and harmonious flower for paradise.

THURSDAY, DECEMBER 25TH

To Maria, for the parish:

I thank the Lord today for all that He does, and especially for the gift of permitting me to remain with you. Dear children, these are the days when the Lord grants special graces to all those who open their hearts to Him. I bless you and I wish that you also know these graces. Place yourselves at the disposition of the Lord, so that He may be glorified through you. My heart follows attentively, your progress.

1987

THURSDAY, JANUARY 1ST

To Maria, for the parish:

Dear Children! Today, the day of the new year, I invite all of you to live the messages which I give you. You know, dear children, that because of you, I have stayed here this long, in order to teach you to walk on the road to holiness. Therefore, dear children, pray constantly, and live all the messages which I give you. I do it with a great love for God, and for you.

THURSDAY, JANUARY 8TH

To Maria, for the parish:

I would like to thank you for your response to my messages; especially, dear children, thank you for all the sacrifices and all the prayers you have presented to me. I wish to continue to give you messages, no longer each Thursday, but on the 25th of each month. The time has come when, what my Lord wanted, has been accomplished. From now on, I will give you fewer messages, but I will remain with you.

Also, I ask you dear children, to listen to my messages and to live them so that I can guide you.

SUNDAY, JANUARY 25TH

The first apparition of the 25th of the month, (the anniversary day of the month of the first apparition on the hill), given to Maria, for the parish:

Today I want to appeal to all of you to start living a new life from this day on. Dear Children, I wish that you would understand that God has chosen each one of you to have a part in the great plan for the salvation of mankind. You cannot fully understand how great your role is in God's design. For that reason, pray, dear children, so that through prayer, you may be able to know your role in God's plan. I am with you, so that you may be able to realize it fully

Beginning January 25th, the messages are now monthly, each 25th of the month, monthly anniversary date of the first apparition. As in the case of the Thursday messages, we do not give any reference. These messages have been transmitted by benevolent organizations to the whole world.

WEDNESDAY, JANUARY 28TH

To Mirjana, at Sarajevo:

My dear children! I came to you in order to lead you to purity of soul, and then to God. How did you receive me? At the beginning you were fearful, suspicious of the children I had chosen. Later on, the majority received me in their heart. They began to put into practice, my maternal recommendation. Unfortunately, that did not last a long time. Whatever be the place where I appear, and with me also my Son, Satan also comes. You permitted him to subdue you without realizing that you were being led by him.

It is up to you to realize that your behavior is not permitted by God, but you immediately stifle the thought.

Do not give in dear children. Wipe away from my face, the tears which I shed on seeing you act in this manner. Look around you. Take the time to come to God in the Church. Come into your Father's house. Take the time to meet for family prayer, in order to obtain the grace from God. Remember your deceased; make them happy by offering the Mass. Do not look with scorn on the poor man who is begging a morsel of bread. Do not send him away from your abundant table. Help him and God will help you. It could very well happen that the blessing he leaves you as a sign of gratitude, will be fulfilled for you. God may listen to him.

You have forgotten all that my children. Satan has influenced you in that. Do not give in. Pray with me! Do not deceive yourselves in thinking, I am good, but my brother, who lives next to me is not good. You will be mistaken. I love you because I am your mother, and I warn you. There are the secrets my children. One does not know what they are; when they learn, it will be too late. Return to prayer! Nothing is more necessary. I would like it if the Lord would have permitted me to show you just a little about the secrets, but, He already gives you enough graces.

Think! What do you offer to Him in return. When was the last time you gave up something for the Lord? I will not blame you further, but once again call you to prayer, fasting, and to penance. If you wish to obtain a grace from the Lord by fasting, then let no one know that you are fasting. If you wish to obtain the grace of God through a gift to the poor, let no one know it, except you and the Lord. Listen to me, my children! Meditate on my message in prayer.

WEDNESDAY, FEBRUARY 25TH

Message to the parish:
Dear children! I wish to cover all of you with my mantle,

and to lead all of you on the road to conversion. I beg you, dear children, entrust all your past to the Lord, with all the evil that has accumulated in your hearts. I wish each one of you to be happy, but with sin, that is never possible.

Pray, dear children, and in prayer you will know the new road of joy. Joy will shine forth in your hearts, and in joy, you will be the witnesses of what my Son and I expect of each one of you. I bless you.

WEDNESDAY, MARCH 25TH (Feast of the Annunciation)

Message to the parish:

Today I thank you for your presence in this place where I give you special graces. I call each of you to begin to live, starting today, the life which God desires of you, and to start doing good deeds of love and mercy. I do not wish, dear children, that you live the message while at the same time displeasing me by committing sins.

Also, dear children, I wish that each of you live a new life, without destroying all that God has done in you, and what He gives to you. I give you my special blessing, and I remain with you on your road to conversion.

SATURDAY, APRIL 25TH

Message for the parish:

Dear children! Today I once again invite all of you to pray. You know that God grants special graces through prayer. Therefore, dear children, try to pray so that you will be able to understand all that I give you here.

I invite you, dear children, to prayer of the heart. You know that without prayer you cannot comprehend all that God has planned through each one of you. So Pray! It is my wish that God's plan be fulfilled in and through each of you, and that all He has placed in your hearts will increase. Pray that God's blessing may protect you from all the evil that threatens you. I give you my blessing.

MONDAY, MAY 25TH

Message to the parish:

I call on each of you to begin to live in God's love. Dear

children, you are ready to commit sin, and to place your-
selves in Satan's hands without reflection. I call you so each
of you will decide knowingly for God, and against Satan.

I am your mother, and I desire to lead all of you to com-
plete holiness. I wish for each of you to be happy on earth
and then to be with me in Heaven. This, dear children, is
my purpose in coming here, and my desire. Thank you for
having responded to my call.

WEDNESDAY, JUNE 24TH

Sixth anniversary of the prelude to the apparitions:

Maria invited the pilgrims to climb Krizevac at 11:30 at
night. A crowd of thousands of people climbed the rocky foot
path, without accident, (One wonders how!). After reciting
the rosary, toward midnight, Maria confided in those who
surrounded her.

"The Blessed Virgin was joyful. First of all, she prayed
over all of us. We asked her to bless us. She did. Then she
gave us, in substance, this message:"

Dear children! I want to lead you on the road to conver-
sion. I desire that you convert the world and that your life
be a conversion for others. Do not fall into infidelity. Let each
one of you be completely submitted to my will and to the will
of God. Beginning this day, I give you special graces, and
in particular the gift of conversion. Let each one of you take
home my blessing, and motivate the others to a real conversion.

"Through her," Maria concluded, "God gives us this gift
this evening. Before leaving us, Our Lady prayed again over
all of us for a moment. We prayed with her for all our needs,
for all your needs, for each of you here present. Finally the
Blessed Virgin said:"

Go in the peace of God! (Transcribed the same day at
Medjugorje.)

THURSDAY, JUNE 25TH

Message to the parish:

Dear children! Today I thank you all, and wish to call all
of you to the peace of God. I wish that each one of you may
know, in his heart, this peace which God gives. Today, I bless

all of you. I bless you with God's blessing, and ask you, dear children, to follow and to live my way.

I love you all, dear children. That is why I have called you so many times. I thank you for all that you have done according to my intentions. Please help me, so that I may be able to present you to God, and guide you on the path to salvation. Thank you for having responded to my call.

SATURDAY, JULY 25TH

Message to the parish:

Dear children! I beseech you from this day on, take up the way of holiness. I love you and therefore, I wish you to be holy. Do not let Satan block you on the way. Dear children, pray and accept all that God is offering you on this way which is bitter, but to whomever is engaged in it, God reveals joy and the sweetness to respond in good heart, to His calls. Do not measure the importance of little things, but long for Heaven and holiness.

TUESDAY, AUGUST 25TH

Message to the parish:

Dear children! Today also I call upon you again to decide to live the messages. God has permitted me, in this year which the Church has dedicated to me, to be able to speak to you and to encourage you on the way to holiness.

Dear children, ask God for the graces which He wants to give you through me. I am ready to intercede with God for all that you ask, so that your holiness may be complete. Therefore, dear children, do not forget to ask, because God has permitted me to obtain graces for you.

CHAPTER 5

The Apparitions, Forbidden in the Rectory In Search of A Discreet Place

A solution: The choir loft in the church, without eyewitnesses, starting the beginning of September, 1987.

FRIDAY, SEPTEMBER 25TH

Message to the parish:
Dear children! Today, I wish to invite all of you to prayer. Let prayer be <u>LIFE</u> for you. Dear children, devote your time to Jesus only, and He will give you everything that you search for. He will reveal Himself to you completely.

Dear children, Satan is strong, and he watches over each of you in order to tempt you. Pray, and this way he will not be able to harm you nor to block your way on the road to holiness. Dear children, make progress as much as possible, toward God and in prayer, from day to day. Thank you for having responded to my call.

SUNDAY, OCTOBER 25TH

Message to the parish:
Today I invite all of you to decide for paradise. The way is difficult for those who have not decided for God. Dear children, decide and believe. God offers Himself to you in His fullness. you are called and you need to respond to the call of the Father, who is calling you, through me. Pray, because in prayer, each one of you will be able to achieve perfect love. I am blessing you and I want to help each one of you, so that you will be under my motherly mantle.

WEDNESDAY, NOVEMBER 25TH

Message to the parish:

Even today again, I invite you. May each of you decide to abandon yourself completely to me. Only thus, can I in turn, present each of you to God. Dear children, you know that I love you immeasurably, and I wish for each one of you to be mine. But God gives everyone freedom, which I lovingly respect, and to which I humbly submit.

Dear children, I wish that God's plan regarding this parish be realized. But, if you do not pray, you will not be able to recognize my love, nor God's plan for this parish, and for each of you. Pray that Satan does not entice you with his pride and deceptive strength. I am with you and want you to believe that I love you.

FRIDAY, DECEMBER 25TH

Message to the parish:

Rejoice with me. My heart is rejoicing because of Jesus, and it is He, whom I want to present to you today. Dear children, I want each one of you to open your heart to Jesus, and I will give Him to you with love. It is He who transforms you, teaches you and protects you.

Today I pray for each one of you in a special way, and I present you to God that He may manifest Himself to you. I invite you to sincere prayer with the heart. Let each one of your prayers be an encounter with God. In your work, and in your everyday life, put God in the first place. I ask you with great seriousness to obey me, I beseech you.

1988

JANUARY, 25TH

Message to the parish:

Dear children, today I again am calling you to complete conversion, which is difficult for those who have not chosen God. I am inviting you, dear children, to convert fully to God. God can give you everything that you seek from Him. But you seek God only when sicknesses, problems and difficulties come to you, and you think that God is far from you and is not listening and does not hear your prayers.

No, dear children, that is not the truth. When you are far from God, you cannot receive graces, because you do not seek them with a firm faith. Day by day, I am praying for you, and I want to draw you evermore near to God. I cannot, if you do not desire it. Therefore, dear children, put your life in God's hands. I bless you all. Thank you for responding to my call.

FEBRUARY 25TH,

Message to the parish:

Dear children, I am calling you to prayer and complete surrender to God. You know that I love you and am coming here out of love, so I could show you the path of peace and salvation for your souls. I want you to obey me and not permit Satan to seduce you. Satan is very strong and therefore I wish you to dedicate your prayers to me, so that those who are under his influence may be saved. Give witness by your life; sacrifice your life for the salvation of the world. I am with you and am grateful to you, but in Heaven you shall receive the Father's reward, which He has promised to you.

Therefore, dear children, do not be afraid. If you pray, Satan cannot injure you even a little, because you are God's children and He is watching over you. Pray and let the rosary always be in your hands as a sign to Satan that you belong to me.

MARCH 25TH,

Message to the parish:

Today, I invite you dear children, to complete surrender to God. You are not conscious of how God loves you with such a great love. He permits me to be with you so I can instruct you and help you to find the way of Peace. This way, however, you cannot discover if you do not pray. Dear children, forsake everything to consecrate your time to God; and then God will bestow gifts upon you and bless you.

Little children, do not forget that your life is fleeting like a spring flower, which today is wondrously beautiful but tomorrow has vanished. Therefore, pray in such a way that your prayer, your surrender to God, may become like a road sign. That way, your witness will not only have value for yourself, but for others, and for all eternity.

APRIL 25TH

Message for the parish:

Dear children, God wants to make you holy. Through me, He is inviting you to complete surrender. Let Holy Mass be your life. Understand that the Church is God's palace, the place in which I gather you and want to show you the way to God. Come and pray! Neither look at others, nor slander them. Rather let your life be a testimony on the way of holiness. Churches deserve respect and are set apart as holy because God, who became man, dwells in them day and night.

Little children, believe and pray that the Father will increase your faith; then you can ask for whatever you need. I am with you and I am rejoicing because of your conversion; and I am protecting you with my motherly mantle. Thank you for your response to my call.

CHAPTER 6

Messages Undated or Approximated

Gathered by different authors

We give in an appendix, the messages which have been gathered by authors, who had made inquiry into the messages of Medjugorje. These messages, which they generally did not date, (nor give the means for dating) are presented in a chronological order, per each book. This provides a "date limit." As an exception, we group at the end, the four volumes of homilies of Father T. Vlasic and Father Slavko Barbaric, which are remarkable for the quality of their information.

APOCALYPTIC MESSAGES

Received by Mirjana before December 26, 1982, confided on November 5, 1983 to Tomislav Vlasic, who conveyed them to the Pope on December 16, 1983.

In his letter of December 16, 1983, to the Pope, and published in "Is The Virgin Mary Appearing at Medjugorje?" (Paris, 1984), Tomislav Vlasic reports some revelations received by Mirjana in 1982, and confided to him November 5, 1983, with this significant introduction:

"During the apparition of December 25, 1982, according to Mirjana, the Madonna confided to her the tenth and last secret, and revealed to her, the dates in which the different secrets will be realized. The Blessed Virgin revealed to Mirjana some aspects of the future, up to this point, in greater detail than to the other seers. For this reason, I am reporting here what Mirjana told me in a conversation of November

5, 1983. I summarized the essentials of her account, without literal quotation. Mirjana told me:"

> Before the visible sign is given to humanity, there will be three warnings to the world. The warnings will be in the form of events on earth. Mirjana will be a witness to them. Ten days before one of the admonitions, Mirjana will notify a priest of her choice. The witness of Mirjana will be a confirmation of the apparitions and a stimulus for the conversion of the world.
>
> After the admonitions, the visible sign will appear on the site of the apparitions in Medjugorje for all the world to see. The sign will be given as a testimony to the apparitions and in order to call people back to faith.
>
> The ninth and tenth secrets are serious. They concern chastisement for the sins of the world. Punishment is inevitable, for we cannot expect the whole world to be converted. The punishment can be diminished by prayer and penance, but it cannot be eliminated. Mirjana says that one of the evils that threatened the world, the one contained in the seventh secret, has been averted thanks to prayer and fasting. That is why the Blessed Virgin continues to encourage prayer and fasting: *You have forgotten that through prayer and fasting you can avert wars and suspend the laws of nature.*
>
> After the first admonition, the others will follow in a rather short time. Thus, people will have some time for conversion.
>
> That interval will be a period of grace and conversion. After the visible sign appears, those who are still alive will have little time for conversion. For that reason, the Blessed Virgin invites us to urgent conversion and reconciliation.
>
> The invitation to prayer and penance is meant to avert evil and war, but most of all to save souls.
>
> According to Mirjana, the events predicted by the

Blessed Virgin are near. By virtue of this experience, Mirjana proclaims to the world: "Convert as quickly as possible. Open your hearts to God."

"In addition to this basic message, Mirjana related an apparition she had in 1982 which we believe sheds some light on some aspects of Church history. She spoke of an apparition in which Satan appeared to her. Satan asked Mirjana to renounce the Madonna and follow him. That way she could be happy in love and in life. He said that following the Virgin, on the contrary, would only lead to suffering. Mirjana rejected him, and immediately the Virgin arrived and Satan disappeared. Then the Blessed Virgin gave her the following message, in substance:"

Excuse me for this, but you must realize that Satan exists. One day he appeared before the throne of God and asked permission to submit the Church to a period of trial. God gave him permission to try the Church for one century. This century is under the power of the Devil, but when the secrets confided to you come to pass, his power will be destroyed. Even now he is beginning to lose his power and has become aggressive. He is destroying marriages, creating division among priests and is responsible for obsessions and murder. You must protect yourselves against these things through fasting and prayer, especially community prayer. Carry blessed objects with you. Put them in your house, and restore the use of holy water.

KRALJEVIC (1983)

The Virgin tells the children:
I know that many will not believe you, and that many who have an impassioned faith will cool off. You remain firm, and motivate people to instant prayer, penance and conversion. At the end, you will be happier. (K.56).

Messages approximately grouped on Ecumenism (see annex #2):
In God differences do not exist among his people; religion

need not separate people. *Every person must be respected,
despite his or her particular profession of faith.*

*God presides over all religions, as a king controls his sub-
jects, through his priests and ministers. The sole mediator
of salvation is Jesus Christ.*

Do differences exist among the believers of different
churches? (A question asked in reference to a certain Protestant community.)

*It is not equally efficacious to belong to or pray in any
church or community, because the Holy Spirit grants his power
differently among the churches and ministers. All believers
do not pray the same way. It is intentional that all apparitions
are under the auspices of the Catholic Church.* (K.59).

To the seers:
*When you will suffer difficulties, and need something, come
to me.* (K.72).

*I cannot cure. God alone cures. Pray! I will pray with you.
Believe firmly. Fast, do penance. I will help you as long as
it is in my power to do it. God comes to help everyone. I
am not God. I need your sacrifices and your prayers to help
me.* (K.86, and F.1,45).

Faith cannot be alive without prayer. (K.86).

*The Mass is the greatest prayer of God. You will never be
able to understand its greatness. That is why you must be
perfect and humble at Mass, and you should prepare yourselves there.* (K.86).

For a Priest who questions:
"Is it preferable to pray to you or to pray to Jesus?"

*I beseech you, pray to Jesus! I am His Mother, and I inter-
cede for you with Him. But all prayers go to Jesus. I will
help, I will pray, but everything does not depend solely on
me, but also on your strength, and the strength of those who
pray.* (K.87).

With respect to the souls in Purgatory:
These persons wait for your prayers and your sacrifices.
(K.87).

The most beautiful prayer is the "Creed." (K.94).
The most important thing, is to believe. (K.94).
All prayers are good, if they are said with faith. (K.95).
My Son wants to win all souls to Him, but the Devil strives to obtain something. The Devil makes a great effort to infiltrate among you, at all costs. (K.116).

JOURNAL OF JELENA

Questioned on the similarity between the signs announced at Medjugorje, and the third secret of Fatima, Jelena responds, "Toward these things the Gospa told us:"
Do not fear anything. You must forget what is behind you in your life. I only want that from now on, you be new people. Do not fear anything when I am near you. I love you.

Conversation with Fr. Bonifacio and Fr. Petar Ljubicic:
It does not suffice to pray. You must change your life, your heart. Love the others, have love for others. Love what you do and always think about Jesus and you will understand what is good, and what is bad. (ibid).

FATHER BUBALO (1981)

Vicka: "At the very beginning, the Gospa tells us:"
You may leave, but let little Jakov stay with me.
And **Vicka** adds: "Jakov is an extraordinary boy; the Gospa knew it." (Bu.52).

During the times of the first apparitions:
To Mirjana:
My Son struggles for each of you, but Satan fights Him also. He prowls around you, sets traps for you. He tries to divide you, you the seers, to plant discord among you; to confuse you so you will detest yourselves, and will abandon yourselves to him.

Vicka adds: "Our Lady has said it to us on several occasions." (Bu.71).

BOTTA-FRIGERIO (1984)

The world can only be saved through peace. But it will only have peace in its meeting with God. (Bo.75).

The world lives amidst very strong tensions. It is on the edge of catastrophe. (Bo.75).

I have come here because there are many believers. I want to remain with you in order to convert many and to bring peace to everyone. Begin by loving your enemies. Do not judge, do not slander, and do not despise, but give only love. Bless your adversaries and pray for them.

I know well that you are not capable of doing it; I advise you to pray each day at least five minutes to the Sacred Heart, so that you can receive the gift of Divine Love, with which you will be able to love your enemies. (Bo.75).

It is necessary to convert oneself to God, in order to obtain peace. Tell the whole world; tell it without delay, that I ardently wish conversion. Be converted, do not wait. I will ask my Son that He not chastise the world. Convert yourselves, renounce everything, and be ready for everything.

Do not go in search of extraordinary ways, take rather, the Gospel and read it. There, everything will be clear. (Bo.76).

You only learn to pray, through praying. (Bo.76).

Offer your time to God and let yourself be guided by the Holy Spirit. Then, your work will go well and you will have free time. Those who abandon themselves to God, do not have place in their hearts for fear. The difficulties which you will face, will contribute to your growth and to the glory of the Lord. For that, reject fear. (Bo.77).

Prayer always leads to peace and serenity. (Bo.78, cfBl 298).

No one is dispensed from fasting, except those who are gravely ill. Prayer and works of charity cannot replace fasting. I recommend to you in a special way, to attend Holy Mass every day. (Bo.79).

Mass represents the highest form of prayer. You must be humble and respectful during Holy Mass, and prepare yourself for it with care. (Bo.79, cf Bl 238).

May the Holy Father announce with courage, peace and

love to the world. May He not consider Himself the Father of Catholics, but of all mankind. (Bo.80).

CASTELLA–LJUBIC (1984-85)

Reported by *Mirjana:*
Tell the faithful that I need their prayers, and prayers from all the people. It is necessary to pray as much as possible and do penance because very few people have been converted up until now. There are many Christians who live like pagans. There are always so few, true believers. (C.49, cf. Bl 213).

To the priest who asked what they should do:
Carry out well your responsibility, and do what the Church asks you to do. (C52).

One day the Gospa reproached Jakov for his behavior at school towards his friends:
You must love them all.
"I love them all. But they are so annoying to me."
Then accept it as a sacrifice, and offer it. (C.64).

A group of seminarians from Zagreb and Djakovo, attended an apparition.
Maria: "The Gospa looked at each one of us, and told us with a smile:"
Tell them, that with prayer, one obtains everything. (C.68).

The Blessed Virgin received a young nun with open arms, while she kept her hands joined before the others. Questioned by *Mirjana,* she said:
I will take with me very soon, all those to whom I extended my arms. (C.69).

To a nun who asked about her brother, who had died in an accident:
I understand the question, answered the Blessed Virgin. *He died in the state of grace. He needs Masses and prayers.* (C.70).

Asked by *the seers* why her choice had fallen upon them,

the Blessed Virgin replied:

I do not choose the best. Are you angry with my choice, my angels? (C.75).

Mirjana reports to a religious, a close friend, this word from the Gospa:

The hour has come when the demon is authorized to act with all his force and power. The present hour, is the hour of Satan. (C.99).

Many pretend to see Jesus and the Mother of God, and to understand their words, but they are, in fact, lying. It is a very grave sin, and it is necessary to pray very much for them. (C.123).

I am anxious for people to know what is happening in Medjugorje. Speak about it, so that all will be converted. (C.134).

To Mirjana, who asks the Gospa on her insistence in saying, "It presses me to. . .:"

When you will be in Heaven, you will understand why I am so pressed. (C.214).

To the seers who ask regarding the apparitions and their purpose:

Is it, after all, that I bore you? Everything passes exactly according to God's plan. Have patience, persevere in prayer and in penance. Everything happens in its own time. (C.215).

On the matter of a Catholic priest, confused because of the cure of an Orthodox child:

Tell this priest, tell everyone, that it is you who is divided on earth. The Muslims and the Orthodox, for the same reason as Catholics, are equal before my Son and me. You are all my children. Certainly, all religions are not equal, but all men are equal before God, as St. Paul says. It does not suffice to belong to the Catholic Church to be saved, but it is necessary to respect the commandments of God in following one's conscience.

Those who are not Catholics, are no less creatures made in the image of God, and destined to rejoin someday, the

House of the Father. Salvation is available to everyone, without exception. Only those who refuse God deliberately, are condemned. To him, who has been given little, little will be asked for. To whomever has been given much (to Catholics), very much will be required. It is God alone, in His infinite justice, Who determines the degree of responsibility and pronounces judgment. (C 128).

FR. ROBERT FARICY (1985)

On the subject of Christ:
I am His Mother, and I intercede for you, near to Him. (F2,134).

TUTTO (1985)

Let the faithful meditate each day on the life of Jesus, while praying the rosary. (T.43).

Every prayer, which comes from the heart, is agreeable to God. (T.58).

You do not celebrate the Eucharist, as you should. If you would know what grace, and what gifts you receive, you would prepare yourselves for it each day, for an hour at least. You should go to confession once a month. You should consecrate three days to reconciliation, each month: the first Friday of the month, followed by Saturday, and Sunday.

The parish at Medjugorje had established an hour of adoration, before the Most Blessed Sacrament, the first Friday of the month. On the Saturday which followed, an hour of devotion before the cross, with prayers for sinners. And on Sunday, the Holy Mass was followed by a meal of reconciliation. (T.58).

BLAIS (1986)

I do not have the right to impose on anyone, what they should do. You have reason, and a will. You should, after having prayed, reflect and decide. (Bl.37).

Receive the peace of my Son. Live it, and spread it. (Bl.90).

Permit Jesus to perform great works in you. The door of your heart, the lock is rusted. Permit Him to open it. May it be open through your prayer, your fasting, your conversion. (Bl.143).

Pray slowly, and meditate while saying the prayers of the

rosary. Take a quarter of an hour to recite: 5 Our Father's, Haiḷ Mary's, and Glory Be's. (Bl.173).

I love you so much. And if you love me, you will be able to feel it. I bless you in the name of the Most Holy Trinity, and in my name. Remain in peace. (Bl.183).

You will find everything in the Gospels. (Bl.244).

Let the word of God begin to speak in your heart. (Bl.245).

Begin to love your enemies. Do not judge or slander. Do not scorn. Do not curse. Only give your adversaries love. Bless them, and pray for them. I know that you are not capable of doing it, but I advise you to pray each day at least five minutes, to the Sacred Heart, so that He can give you Divine love, with which you will be able to love, even your enemies. (Bl.301). (Another version of the message previously shown in Botta.)

You can direct your prayers not only to those who are already in Heaven, but also to those who are in Purgatory, because with their prayer, they can help you to reach eternal happiness. (Bl.326).

One must follow the authority of the Church with certainty. Yet, before she expresses an opinion, it is necessary to advance spiritually, because she will not be able to express a judgment in a vacuum, but in a confirmation which presupposes growth of the child. First comes birth, followed by Baptism, then Confirmation. The Church comes to confirm him, who is born of God. We must walk and advance in the spiritual life, affected by these messages. (Bl.330).

MIRAVALLE (1986)

Before December, 1983:

So many believers never pray. Have the people pray! Faith cannot be alive without prayer. (M 8).

I am not able to cure you. God alone, can cure you. Pray! I will pray with you. Believe firmly, fast, do penance. God comes to help each one. I am not God. I need your prayers and your sacrifices to help me. (M 8).

You do not need a sign; you yourselves must be a sign. (M 9).

Peace is necessary for prayer. Peace should be present before prayer, and while one is praying. Prayer should, of course, lead to peace and reflection. (M 30).

Why ask so many questions? The answer is found in the Gospels. (M 31).

To Jelena:
The subject on the certainties of catastrophies comes from false prophets. They say, on such a day, at such an hour, there will be a catastrophe. I have always said: Punishment will come about, if the world is not converted. Call all mankind to conversion. Everything depends on your conversion. (M 31).

To Jelena:
When others cause you some difficulty, do not defend it, rather, pray. (M 31).

To Jelena:
I desire that you be a flower, which blossoms for Jesus at Christmas. A flower which does not cease to bloom when Christmas has passed. I wish that you have a shepherd's, heart for Jesus. (M 31).

Dear children, when someone comes to you and asks you a favor, answer by giving. I find myself before so many hearts which do not open themselves to me. Pray, so that the world willingly wants to accept my love. (M 39).

Between June and December, 1984:
Dear children, the love of God has not spread over all the earth. That is why, pray! (M 40).

Dear children, I wish that the whole world become my children, but they do not want to. I want to give them all things. That is why, pray! (M 40).

Dear children, I love you so much. When you love me, you will be able to feel it. I bless you in the name of the Most Holy Trinity, and in my name. Go in peace. (M 40).

BOA NOVA

These are my last apparitions to mankind. With the events which are preparing themselves, and which are near, the power which Satan still holds, will be withdrawn from him. The present century has been under his power. Now that he is conscious of losing the battle, he is becoming more aggressive. He attacks the family, separates husband and wife. He creates divisions among the priests, and even gives himself to physical attacks. Protect yourselves, above all through prayer, through blessed sacred objects, through community prayer. (BN 20, 10).

LATEST NEWS (1987)

Love your Serbian, Orthodox and Muslim brothers, and the atheists who persecute you. (DN 2, 73). (Concerning information from Bishop Franic.

All your prayers touch me very much, especially your daily rosary. (DN 6, 15).

FR'S. TOMISLAV VLASIC AND SLAVKO BARBARIC (VB)

The weekly information given by Fr. Tomislav Vlasic and Fr. Slavko Barbaric, to Italian pilgrims, have been edited, in four volumes which we have designated through the abbreviations: VB 1, VB 2, VB 3, VB 4.

Here, we re-group the messages, which are not dated, in these four volumes. Each volume gives way to a "limit date" as follows. The first gives some communication from May 24 to December 29, 1984. The second, January 4 to June 25, 1985; the third from July to December, 1985; and the fourth, from January 4, 1986, to January 8, 1987.

VB 1 (1984)

I've already said many times, that peace in the world is in a state of crisis. Become again, brothers to one another. Pray and fast more, in order to be saved. (Sept. 1983, VB 1, 15).

Pray, fast, and let God act.

If you want to be very happy, lead a simple, humble life, pray very much, and do not sink into problems. Let God resolve them. (message also in M 30).

Peace should follow your prayer.

Often, prayer said in a loud voice keeps Jesus at a distance, because men want to conquer with their own strength. Then there is no more place for God. Prayers said in a loud voice are good, but they must come from peace in the heart.

Even joy and songs can hinder the rise of the groups, if

the people deliver themselves only to emotion. (T. Vlasic, May 24, 1984; collects these teachings as a rule of life, given by Our Lady, VB 133).

When I tell you, pray, pray, do not understand it only as an increase in quantity. What I want is to carry you to a profound continuous desire of God. (T. Vlasic, VB 1, 39).

The most important thing is to believe. That is, to open one's self to God; pray and fast. (T. Vlasic, June 1, 1984, VB 1, 41).

Response from Our Lady to two questions from Tomislav Vlasic:
"Have you come to purify the new renewal movements, which are multiplying?"
It is exactly so.

"How could Jesus pray all night, without getting tired. What was His method?"
He had a great desire for God, and for the salvation of souls. Prayer is a dialogue with God, a meeting with the Gospel.

"What do you say about Oriental meditations?" (Zen, Transcendental meditation):
Why do you call them 'meditations,' when it deals with human works? The true meditation is a meeting with Jesus. When you discover joy, interior peace, you must know there is only one God, and only one Mediator, Jesus Christ. (VB 1, 45).
Your days will not be the same according to whether you pray, or you do not pray. (VB 1 51).

Responses to questions asked by the seers at the request of Tomislav Vlasic:
What do you tell the priests and religious?
Be strong in faith and protect the faith of your people.
What do you advise us for advent?
Do what the Church tells you.
Do you want to give a sign for priests?
Have them take the Gospel and they will understand everything. (T. Vlasic, June 20, 1984. VB 1, 51).
Go to the heart. Words are not sufficient. Go to the heart. (VB 1, 52).

In the past autumn (1983), Our Lady said:

I would be happy for people, families, to pray a minimum of half-an-hour, in the morning and in the evening.

The people shook their heads at this, stated Fr. Vlasic.

But in the spring of 1984, Our Lady said:

I know that in the parish and in all the parishes, you can pray four hours a day, but you do not understand it yet because you live only for your work. One does not live from work alone, but also from prayer.

As I objected to her: "If one asks so much, people will go away." She replied:

Not even you understand. That makes hardly a sixth of your day. (T. Vlasic, July 31, 1984. VB 1, 55).

You, do not think of wars, of evil, of chastisements. If you think about evil, you are on the road where one meets it. Your role is to accept Divine peace, to live it and spread it. (VB 1, 61).

To Jelena:

Christians make a mistake in considering the future because they think of wars and of evil. For a Christian, there is only one attitude toward the future. It is hope of salvation. (ibid).

Your responsibility is to accept Divine peace, to live, and to spread it not through words, but through your life. (Same communication of T. Vlasic Aug. 2, 1984. VB 1, 63).

To Jelena:

The only attitude of the Christian toward the future is hope of salvation. Those who think only of wars, evils, punishment, do not do well.

If you think of evil, punishment, wars, you are on the road to meeting them. Your responsibility is to accept Divine peace, live it and spread it. (A more ample transmission of the word already cited in VB 1, 61. T. Vlasic, Aug. 12, 1984. VB 1, 81).

If you have not listened to my messages, the day of joy will become for me, a day of sadness. (S. Barbaric, Dec. 8, 1985. VB 1, 135).

VB 2 (1985)

To Ivan's prayer group:
Even the little things, entrust them to me. Consecrate them to my mission. (S. Barbaric, Mar. 2, 1985. VB 2, p.40).

To the question:
How does one behave before Satan?
Fervent prayer, humility, reciprocal love will prevent Satan from approaching you.

To a question conveyed through Tomislav Vlasic at the beginning of Lent, 1985:
What do you most wish for the fast?
The Gospa responds insisting on something else:
Honesty, love, humility and sincerity will lead you to me.
(T. Vlasic, Mar. 9, 1985. VB 2, 45).

What should one do in the midst of so many discussions and publications on Medjugorje?
See! Now I am there, in each family, in each home. I am everywhere because I love. Do the same. The world lives from love.
After having repeated a song three times:
Excuse me for making you repeat, but I wish you to sing with the heart. You must really do everything with the heart.
And afterwards, (the seers continue, quoted by T. Vlasic), she made us know this at the beginning of prayer:
One has to be already prepared. If there are some sins, one must pull them out, otherwise, one will not be able to enter into prayer. If one has concerns, he should submit them to God.
That same evening she said:
Take off your jackets. Here it is warm. Remember what Jesus said: Have faith. You must abandon yourselves to God. (All that in preparation for prayer.).
You must not preoccupy yourselves during prayer. During prayer, you must not be preoccupied with your sins. Sins must remain behind. (Words at the beginning of Lent, at the end of Feb. or the beginning of Mar. 1985, reported by T. Vlasic, VB 2, 66).

Many come to pray, but do not enter into prayer. (T. Vlasic, Apr. 5, 1985. VB 2, 74).

When you have entered into prayer, then you are able to pray for God's plans, because when God is there, he inspires your plans.

Do not ask for the blessing, just as you have done the last time. You asked for it and you did not obtain it. (Because it is not a magic thing, she crowns what God has inspired in you in prayer, observes T. Vlasic, Apr. 5, 1985. VB 2, 75).

Prayer must be enjoyment in God, blossoming in God, be full of peace, be full of joy. (T. Vlasic, Apr. 10, 1985. VB 2, 107).

Many Christians do not ever enter into prayer. They arrive at the beginning, but they remain there. (ibid).

(If you enter into prayer after you have been relieved of all your concerns, remorse, analysis), *then you will be able to ask God to inspire your plans from within. You will feel what God wants,* (inside of you, yourself and your group), *and then ask for the blessing.* (T. Vlasic, Apr. 10, 1985. VB 2, 112).

Your work will not go well without prayer in the morning. Pray then in the morning, and pray in the evening. Understand that your work cannot be done well without prayer. (Message of autumn 1983, T. Vlasic, Apr. 29, 1985. VB 2, 137).

Come early to church.

Sometimes it is better not to come to Mass than to come in a hurry and to return home in a hurry, (S. Barbaric, May 18, 1985, VB 2, 147).

These apparitions are the last for humanity. (T. Vlasic, May 31, 1985, VB 2, 165).

To Jelena, message of 1983:

Take me seriously. When God comes among men, he does not come to joke, but to say serious things.

It is better to stay in church and pray with faith than to gather together with onlookers near the seers during an apparition. (Which had then taken place in the presbytery).

Message to the prayer group which had received many messages during Lent and was surprised not to receive any more after Easter:

Thank you to all those who pray and feel my presence. I regret that some individuals say the Gospa is no longer among us. Pray, and you will feel that I am present.

In a meeting of her prayer group, Jelena saw the desert, and in the desert, a tree, and under the tree, where the sun was shining. In this sun, she recognized Jesus Christ.

The Gospa told her, among other things:

To this group, many graces have been given, but you must not reject them. (T. Vlasic, June 15, 1985, VB 2, 18).

VB 3 (1986)

To Jelena's group, toward the beginning of July 1985:

I cannot speak to you. Your hearts are closed.

You have not done what I told you, I cannot speak to you. I cannot give you graces as long as you remain closed. (T. Vlasic, July 13, 1985, VB 3, 15).

To Jelena for her group:

Each of you has a special gift which is your own, and can alone understand it interiorly.

To Jelena's prayer group:

It seems when you carry my messages, be on your guard that they are not lost. Carry my messages with humility, in such a way that on seeing happiness in you, persons will desire to be like you. Do not carry my messages to simply throw them to others.

T. Vlasic, July 15, 1985 comments: "Don't go to the cities: Milan, Rome or Turin to cry: 'The Madonna has appeared.' Have them understand it through what you are."

In the middle of June, 1985, Jelena saw a splendid pearl which divided itself, and each part glittered, then it faded. And she heard this explanation:

Jelena, man's heart is like this splendid pearl. When he belongs completely to the Lord, he shines even in the darkness. But when he is divided, a little to Satan, a little to sin, a little to everything, he fades and is no longer worth anything. (S. Barbaric, Aug. 4, 1985, VB 3, 37).

To Jelena, during the week of July 28th to August the 4th:

During these days, I wish that you consider this idea: After so long and so much time, I have not met Jesus, my friend. After so long and so much time, I have not encountered my Mother, Mary. In these days, I want to encounter them. (T. Vlasic, Aug. 5, 1985, VB 3, 39).

Do not be afraid of Satan. That isn't worth the trouble, because with a humble prayer, and an ardent love, one can disarm him. (S. Barbaric, Aug. 8, 1985, VB 3, 57).

Prayer given to Jelena for her group:
My soul is full of love like the sea. My heart is full of peace like the river. I am not a saint, but I am invited to be one. (T. Vlasic, Sept. 10, 1985, VB 3, 97).

Against temptations of analysis, which are temptations from the devil:
With respect to sin, it suffices to give it serious considera-tion, and soon, move ahead and correct the sin.

Your humility must be proud (high minded). *Your pride should be humble.*

If you have received a gift from God, you must be proud but do not say that it is yours. Say, rather, that it is God's. (T. Vlasic, Sept. 10, 1985, VB 3, 98).

To Mirjana, in 1984 (Probably Aug. - Sept.):
Every adult is capable of knowing God. The sin of the world lies in this: It does not look for God. (T. Vlasic, Sept. 10, 1985, VB 3, 98).

To Maria, during her retreat of one week, beginning of Sep-tember, in response to her question:
Have you anything concrete for me?
Yes. I give you my love so that you can give it to others. (S. Barbaric, Oct. 7, 1985, VB 3, 121).

The Gospa said with sadness:
Those who say, 'I do not believe in God,' how difficult it will be for them when they will approach the Throne of God and hear the voice: Enter into Hell. (T. Vlasic, Oct. 8, 1985, VB 3, 127).

To Jelena, three evenings in succession, toward October 10th
to 15th:
If you wanted to accept my love, you would never sin.

On the following evening (the fourth day), **Jelena** asks:
Why do you always repeat the same message?
But I don't have anything else to say to you.
And she cries. (T. Vlasic, Oct. 19, 1985, VB 3, 151).
*There are many who finish their prayers, even without en-
tering into them.* (ibid 3, 158).

A question from the pilgrims of Milan to Jelena:
We have come to you, Dear Mother. When will you come
to Milan?

The Gospa's answer through Jelena:
When you open your hearts to me. (T. Vlasic, Oct. 25, 1985,
3, 167).

Tomislav Vlasic, whom the Blessed Virgin had entrusted
with a responsibility through Jelena, asks through the seer,
Maria:
How should I do it?
Do not worry, I will help you.
*If you want to be stronger than evil, and grow in goodness,
then develop an active conscience.* (T. Vlasic, Nov. 2, 1985, VB
3, 179).

To a prayer group, after an hour in which prayer of petition
had prevailed:
Have you forgotten that you are in my hands? (T. Vlasic, Nov.
16, 1985, VB 3, 201).

VB 4 (1987)

To Jelena and Marijana, a little before February 25th:
*Understand that you are nothing, incapable, really nothing.
It is the Father who will do everything.* (T. Vlasic, Feb. 25, 1986,
VB 4, 39).

To Jelena, for her prayer group, after prayer and fasting:
I have listened to your prayer and yet you will not receive what you have wished. You will receive other things because it is not up to you to glorify yourself, but to me to glorify myself in you. (ibid VB 4, 39).

Do not be afraid. Confide yourself to the Father. Pray, until you are sure that He guides everything.

In difficulties, when you carry the cross, sing, be full of joy.

To a group who was praying for a person in crisis:
You cannot do anything. I can change her. You must only love her. Do not create any barriers in her life, because as long as there are barriers, the river foams and rises. Leave her free, like the river. Do not build any more bridges because as long as one builds bridges, the river is restricted and does not flow freely. Leave her free to flow like the river flows.

A month later the group, frustrated in its prayer, asks: "But how is it that this girl (in crisis) does not change?" Answer, after a long moment of prayer:
Let her run like the river. Do not create any barriers. Do not build any bridges. Consider well and see how many barriers you have already created, how many bridges you have built. Be attentive not to close her. This young girl is at the point of opening up. She has confidence in you. Be patient still. Understand that you can do nothing. You must only love and leave everything to me.

To Jelena:
When people ask you to speak about the apparition, say: 'Let us pray together to understand the apparitions of the Gospa.'

In the prayer group which found the advice from the Gospa too rigid:
Why shut down the television? Why not even read the newspaper?
If you look at the programs, if you look at the newspapers,

your heads are filled with news, then there is no longer any place for me in your hearts.

Pray. Fast. Let God act!

Pray for the gift of love, for the gift of faith, for the gift of prayer, for the gift of fasting. (T. Vlasic, Apr. 17, 1986, VB 4, 63).

To Jelena, for her group:

I beg you, destroy your house made of cardboard which you have built on desires. Thus I will be able to act for you. (T. Vlasic, Apr. 17, 1986, VB 4, 63).

To Maria, for her prayer group:

Dear Children, seek to make your hearts happy through the means of prayer. Dear Children, be the joy for all mankind, be the hope of mankind. You will only be able to obtain it through the means of prayer. Pray, pray! (T. Vlasic, May 3, 1986, VB 4, 82).

To the prayer group during the week preceding May 3rd:

I give you the best that I can give anyone. I give myself and my Son.

To the group on March 25th, on the Feast of the Annunciation:

Today, before God, I say my 'Fiat' for all of you. I repeat it: I say my 'Fiat' for all of you.

Dear Children, pray, so that in the whole world may come the Kingdom of Love. How mankind would be happy if love reigned!

To Jelena, during the autumn of 1983:

Dear Children, one lives not only from work, one lives also from prayer.

Toward May 12th (at the beginning of the Novena of Pentecost) to the prayer group:

You will be happy if you do not judge yourselves according to your faults, but if you understand that in your faults even graces are offered to you. (T. Vlasic, May 18, 1986, VB 4, 93).

Love. If you do not love, you are not able to transmit the testimony. You are not able to witness, neither for me, nor for Jesus. (S. Barbaric, June 6, 1986, VB 4, 105).

I wish for all of you to be the reflection of Jesus. He will thus illuminate this unfaithful world which moves in darkness. (ibid VB 4, 105).

Pray before the Cross. Special graces come from the Cross. Consecrate yourselves to the Cross. Do not blaspheme neither Jesus nor the Cross. (S. Barbaric, June 20, 1986, VB 4, 109).

You will have as many graces as you want. That depends on you. You will have love when you want it, as long as you want it. That depends on you. (T. Vlasic, June 26, 1986, VB 4, 110).

To the prayer group (July 10, 1986), before giving her blessing, at the end of an evaluation of the group:

I thank you for that. You have done well, but do not forget (. . .); basically, God's will is decisive. (T. Vlasic, July 20, 1986, VB 4, 121).

I wish only that for you the Rosary become your life. (T. Vlasic, Aug. 4, 1986, VB 4, 134).

Read each Thursday the Gospel of Matthew, where it is said: No one can serve two masters (. . .). You cannot serve God and money. (Mt. 6, 24-34.—T. Vlasic, Aug. 5, 1986, VB 4, 14).

To Jelena, for her group:

I wish only that you would be happy, that you would be filled with joy, that you be filled with peace and announce this joy. (ibid).

To the prayer group:

If you would abandon yourselves to me, you will not even feel the passage from this life to the next life. You will begin to live the life of Heaven from this earth. (T. Vlasic, Aug, 7, 1986, VB 4, 142).

To Jelena, the beginning of September 1986:

Today it is not words nor deeds which are important. The important thing is only to pray, to remain in God. (T. Vlasic, Sept. 9, 1986, VB 4, 156).

Many have begun to pray for healing here at Medjugorje, but, when they have returned to their homes, they abandon prayer, forget, and also lose many graces. (S. Barbaric, Sept. 12, 1986 VB 4, 158).

Message of Jesus through Jelena:
I am joyful, but my joy is not complete until you are filled with joy. You are not yet filled with joy because you are not yet at the stage of understanding my immense love. (T. Vlasic, Oct. 8, 1986, VB 4, 167).

Answer from the Gospa through a seer, to Tomislav Vlasic, who was confronted with problems dealing with truth:
"Should I write, answer these injustices, these lies?"
Do not waste your time. Pray and love. You cannot even imagine how powerful God is. (T. Vlasic, Dec. 29, 1986, VB 4, 213).

To Vicka:
Do you want to offer yourself, also, for the salvation of the world? I need your sacrifices.

To a group from the parish of Medjugorje:
Come at 11 o'clock at night to the place of the apparitions (...). Come at three o'clock in the morning to pray at the place of the Apparition.
Come at one o'clock in the morning to Krizevac.
Come and pray all night.
It is to Ivan's group that these messages of nocturnal prayer were addressed on the hill of the first apparitions, or at Krizevac. (T. Vlasic, Dec. 31, 1986, VB 4, 220).

PART IV
Appendices

APPENDIX 1

An Unfortunate Interference

WHICH OBSCURES THE MESSAGE OF MEDJUGORJE

It is deliberately that we present in an appendix, outside of the corpus, a very special series of texts which do not belong to the message, but at the same time, constitute an unfortunate interference and a cause of confusion.

It deals with the words attributed to the Blessed Virgin on the famous "Hercegovina Question:" a painful and inextricable question which is centered in the diocese of Mostar. It is the difficult redistribution of parishes between:

The Franciscans, the only priests of this country for centuries, and the secular clergy established after the end of the Turkish occupation in 1881.

There has been a prolonged disagreement over this redistribution. This matter has nothing to do with the apparitions themselves, though some forces have worked desperately hard to imply it does. It does not involve the issue of whether the Virgin appears here, or whether she doesn't.

Some newspapers, usually better informed, said that the priests at Medjugorje were "suspended, and in conflict with the bishop." ("Derneieres Nouvelles" #2, Pg. 19). That is false. The parish of Medjugorje is a normal, fervent, exemplary parish. The bishop himself recognizes the marvelous fruits which the Lord accomplishes there. He successively transferred several priests from this parish, whose influence served the apparitions which he fought, (including Tomislav Vlasic). They obeyed, and he replaced them regularly with the agreement of the Franciscan Provincial, named by Rome, to be its right arm in this matter.

Two Friars, who were suspended and the object of so many questions to the Gospa, do not belong to the parish of Medjugorje. They live in the episcopal city, in the provincial house of the Franciscans. And the provincial, a declared ally of the Bishop, did not expell them according to directives from Rome.

The words attributed to the Blessed Virgin with respect to the conflict of Hercegovina must be situated within this context.

1. It is an inveterate and passionate conflict in spite of virtuous efforts to peacefully defuse this tension. Anyone who speaks about it successively, to the bishop, then to the Franciscans, as I have done several times, has the feeling of attending Pirandello's drama, "Each In His Own Way." The two points of view hardly tally in their respective coherence:

The Franciscans see and live their secular ties with a people. They continue the heroic and fervent tradition of the faith spread, then maintained by them, during the four centuries of Muslim persecution not without apostacies. There were some religious and laity martyrs. From that, there results a filial attachment of the people to the Franciscans. Even when the latter accepted to yield parishes to the secular clergy, their parishoners often did not follow. They are like children to whom one would say: "Change parents." And, according to the radical and impetuous temperament of this country, they are ready to abandon the Church if it cuts this umbilical cord so vital for them.

At Grude, the parishoners blocked the doors of the church when the bishop named a secular priest to it. The problem then is inextricable, agonizing, insurmountable on the surface.

The bishop himself, sees the importance of regulating boldly and quickly, the matter of distribution of the contested parishes, according to plans from Rome, in spite of the irresistable obstacles and dialogues which have been without solution for 40 years. To wit: He has engaged all his power intrepidly, and has acquired very high support to force those who resist him; and through his means of authority, and procedures of urgency, he sometimes short-circuited canonical rules and good uses of the Church. He can do it much better through local awareness, as if the measures of authority were taken in Rome itself, and not by virtue of his diocesan powers.

2. At the time when the apparitions began, two young Franciscan Friars, Ivan Prusina and Ivica Vego, were excluded from the Franciscan Order, and suspended—(they were forbidden from administering the sacraments). They were accused of having administered them in the Franciscan chapels in Mostar, to people who did not want to attend the new parish under the secular clergy at the Cathedral.

This new parish was created by Bishop Zanic, September 14, 1980, the same day he became Bishop of Mostar, after having been coadjutor. Through this ligitimate act of authority, he took away from the Franciscans, 80 percent of their principal parish.

Many other Franciscans also administered the sacraments to other recalcitrant parishioners in the same Franciscan chapels, but without being punished. Ivan and Ivica served as scapegoats to set an example. They received orders to leave Mostar, with threats of sanctions, in April of 1981, two months before the apparitions began.

After the apparitions began, some of their parishioners, who had supported the two, spoke about it to the seers and asked them to consult the Blessed Virgin with regard to this matter. It seemed to them that the Friars were suffering an injustice. The two Friars themselves, had visited the place of the apparitions since the end of June, 1981. They also questioned the seers when the canonical sanctions fell on them, progressively from December 29th, 1981, to April 29th, 1982.

First of all, from July 22, 1981, a decree from the vicar and procurator general of the Franciscans, Father Honorious Pontoglio, special delegate from the Holy See, threatened them with suspension and exclusion from the Franciscan order if they did not cease their ministry, and if they refused to leave Mostar.

They ceased to administer the sacraments, but stayed in Mostar. Other Franciscans continued to administer the sacraments in the same chapels, something that they do even to this day, without having any worries with the tacit agreement of the provincial and the bishop.

On December 29, 1981, a "final admonition" was communicated to the two Friars by the provincial delegate, Nikola Radic.

On February 18, and April 22, the Friars submitted their protests and justifications, which were not taken into consideration. The decree of July 22, 1981, excluded all possibility of recourse.

Considering that their vows, which had been made before God and duly recorded in the Church, could not be annulled in such a summary fashion, the two Friars appealed this decision as invalid, with respect to "fundamental rights," and under canon law of the Church. They remained in Mostar, ready to leave, they said, should a normal, canonical judgment be pronouced. Thus, the vicar general of the Franciscan Order (H. Pontaglio) informed them on April 29, 1982, of their suspension from the Order, of which they had been previously threatened.

It is in these complex conditions, and in this conflicting, painful and passionate climate, that the Gospa was consulted by the seers after successive requests of the parishoners regarding the two Friars; then by the two Friars themselves, and finally, by Father Tomislav Vlasic, spiritual director of Medjugorje, concerned with clarifying these inextricable "oracles."

What is the value or purpose of it?:

"It is the Virgin! It is then absolutely true," said some.

"This support given against the authority of the Church, proves that it is not the Virgin," said the bishop.

These two radical conclusions had the error of simplifying a very complex problem. In order to judge it beyond the slogans, producing the file is necessary, though it be painful. It shows the complexity of the problem, and the marginal character and limits of this file, and which the Bishop of Mostar has used well to prepare for a negative judgment, which he thought he had to rapidly disseminate.

The file should not have to be included in this text as it is certainly not part of the messages of Medjugorje. However, in attempting to list the dialogue of Our Lady during these last seven years, it becomes necessary to offer a full explanation regarding those passages which we list in the messages, that pertain to the Hercegovina question. Here we present the documents of the file, which will permit one to judge this matter in a less summary and less passionate manner.

Chronological Series of the Texts

Relative to the *"Conflict of Hercegovina"*

1. SATURDAY, DECEMBER 19, 1981:

A. *(A narrative from Fr. Tomislav Vlasic)*

"It is only this December 19th, 1981, that Vicka has talked to me on the matter of the Friars. And that, entirely by accident, because someone had asked me a question in relation to this matter.

I verified what the Blessed Virgin allegedly said. Did she say that the bishop was guilty of a disturbance, or of false conclusions?

On that which concerns Ivica and Ivan (the two Franciscans who were punished), the Blessed Virgin told Vicka, she said to me, that the bishop had made false conclusions, but she could not repeat that literally.

It then became evident to me that the young seers do not convey the responses literally, but say them with their vocabulary, (sometimes their words, a little archaic, give the answer an entirely different tone.) Because of that, in this case, it is necessary to remember that one is dealing with children, with all the imperfections which they can have as children in memorization, transmission, and behavior." (Parish Chronicle p.40).

B. *(Account of Friar Ivica Vego)*

The diary of Friar Ivica Vego (probably from December 20, in any case before the 23rd), noted in an analogous manner, the statement of Vicka:

"I was at Vicka's home, obligatory coffee, and maybe embarrassed hosts. Later, I spoke with her privately in her room. She told me:

'I asked the Gospa.' She was answered:

'The bishop is responsible.'

'She repeated that several times,' Vicka added.

Several times I asked Vicka whether she answered me that way because of her love for the priests. With the vividness which is her character, she denied it.

She promised me to go to the bishop and tell him everything. She spoke to me about her last meeting with him (the bishop). She had to leave when Tomislav Vlasic had asked for jurisdiction for me. He would have wanted for me to go to Medjugorje, where it would be too much for both of us."

2. DECEMBER 23, 1981

(Ivica Vego's Account)

"I was again in Medjugorje. They told me we are not guilty of anything. We can stay."

3. SUNDAY, JANUARY 3, 1982

A. *Vicka's Account (as recorded by the two Friars, Ivan and Ivica):*

Vicka: "We (the seers) have interrogated the Gospa with respect to Father Ivica Vego. The Gospa answered:

Ivica is not guilty. Have him keep the faith even if the Franciscans expel him. I do not cease to repeat: Peace, Peace, and in the meantime, agitation increases. He is not guilty. (She repeated this three times. We all heard her.) The bishop does not see to it enough that there is order. It is his fault. But he will not always be bishop. I will show justice in the Kingdom.

That lasted 10 minutes, everything concerning Ivica."

B. *Monsignor Zanic's Version:*

(In the official statement, where he publically disseminated the subversive messages of Medjugorje, Monsignor Zanic gives here a very faithful version of the last paragraph, the one which Father Grafenauer gathered from the two Franciscans, and which the bishop always attributes to the hidden diary of Vicka.)

"Ivica is not guilty. If one drives him out of the Order may he be courageous. I repeat every day: Peace, peace, peace, but every day, more disorder. Ivica must remain. He is not guilty. (The Lady repeated that three times. All of us heard it, and we told it to Ivica.) The bishop does not keep order. That is why he is responsible. He will not always be bishop. I will show justice in the Kingdom.

That lasted 10 minutes, everything on the problem of Ivica."

C. *Ivica Vego's Diary: (This text details which seers were there):*

January 3, 1982—Vicka, Ivanka, Jakov:

1. "Three times, the Gospa repeated: They are not responsible and he (the bishop) is responsible.

2. Have them stay. May they be courageous and not fear. Question: Will they be expelled from the Order? Answer: If one expels them, let them be proud of it.

3. It is also to the bishop that the call is addressed: MIR (Peace). If he does not want, he will be punished before or afterwards.

4. He does an injustice.

I was thankful, happy and exhausted. I returned to Mostar."

D. *Tomislav Vlasic's Account:*

"I asked the seers to once again ask the Gospa for a confirmation of her intentions of December 19th, on the matter of the Friars. Here is the response from the seers:

Our Mother wants it said to the bishop that he has made a precipitous decision. Let him reflect again, and listen well to both parties. He must be just and patient. She says that both priests are not guilty." (Parish Chronicle, p.43).

(The above text of Bishop Zanic, as well as those of (January 11th and 20th, April 16th and 26th, September 29th, and the end of August) are reproduced by Bishop Zanic with the reference: "Vicka's Diary." But Vicka's diary had not been available for this period. Bishop Zanic only received from his investigator, Father Grafenauer, (who confirms it), answers which Friars Ivan and Ivica obtained from Vicka. Bishop Zanic supposed that they were extracted from some mysterious diary which Vicka hid, and of which Father Grafenauer would be an eyewitness. But Father Grafenauer had lied on several occasions regarding seeing the supposed diary. The above text of the bishop was disseminated by him as testimony to the charge against the Friars.)

4. MONDAY, JANUARY 11, 1982

Vicka's account as transmitted by Fathers Ivan and Ivica:

"We (the seers) again asked questions concerning the two Franciscan Friars from Mostar, and our Lady repeated twice what she had already said."

JANUARY 14, 1982

Monsignor Zanic's narrative on his meeting with Vicka:

"My doubts increased when I met Vicka, and everything was recorded on this tape recorder, January 14, 1982. Vicka told me:
'The Gospa sent me to tell you that you have acted precipitously against the Franciscans.'
What did she tell you?
'I do not know. She said that only.'
I knew, through the government of the province, that the two Friars had been expelled (from the Franciscan Order) through a decision of their general, and it persisted in spite of the will of their superiors that they stay in Mostar, because the Gospa had allegedly said: They are innocent and they must stay.
I heard say that the Gospa had given a message for the two chaplains, I remarked.
'Which chaplains,' responded Vicka?
Then we spoke at some length during a half-hour."

5. WEDNESDAY, JANUARY 20, 1982

Texts transmitted by Monsignor Zanic:

(It always deals with reports which Father Grafenauer had gathered from the two Franciscans or the seers, and which the bishop considered as copies of a self-styled hidden diary of Vicka.)

"We asked what Father Ivica Vego and Father Ivan Prusina would do after they were expelled. Our Lady answered:
They are not guilty. The bishop has made a decision in a precipitous fashion. Let them stay. Let them pray very much, and have the others pray for them."

6. APRIL 4, 1982

A new meeting of Monsignor Zanic with Vicka:

"On April 4, Vicka came and told me:

'The last time that we were here, the Gospa reproached us for not having spoken about the two chaplains from Mostar.'

What then?

'She said that they were also priests, and that they should celebrate Mass and hear confessions.'

But had not the Gospa said that when you were here on January 14th, I asked her?

'She invited us to speak about the two chaplains.'

I saw that was a lie, because she said:

'We spoke so much that we forgot the message of the Gospa which related to the two chaplains.'

Vicka could not have forgotten, since I had asked her specifically if they had messages concerning them.

The young girl talked, talked, talked, and I asked her again.

This message for the chaplains, when was it given to you? Before you came?

'Yes, before.'

That fact convinced me that it did not deal with the Madonna, and that she could not defend the two priests expelled by the Order (Franciscan) and released from their vows. That would be to destroy the hierarchy and the Church, and I knew that Vicka spoke evil of her bishop."

7. THURSDAY, APRIL 15, 1982

Vicka's statement as recorded by the two Priests, Ivan and Ivica:

(It is very difficult to unravel in it, the intentions attributed to the Gospa, and the explanations and commentaries of Vicka herself).

"Thus I asked the questions of the Gospa; that she tell me everything about both of you. First of all she smiled, then she began to speak...

1. They are not guilty of anything (that she repeated twice). For that, let them not worry.

2. Many are against the two of you, and are waiting only for your expulsion and your departure from Mostar.

3. The bishop holds responsibility. Many support him and speak to him each day about expelling you so as not to see you any more.

4. Do not listen to anyone. Do not blame anything. It is important, in any case, that you not leave Mostar.

5. They are doing a grave injustice against you. They are not acting according to God's law, but against it, which gives tremendous blows to the faith of the Church, and introduces even more confusion.

I asked: Dear Gospa, you have told the bishop in some way to permit them to stay. I beg you to do it as soon as possible, because we are in a hurry and wish that everything finishes. Everyday, many people pass near Ivica and Ivan, and do not even look at them, as if they did not exist. Dear Gospa, you knew their situation. I will ask you to help them and to free them from their problems so that they be like other priests.

The Gospa smiles and slowly says:

I will calm it down and there will be no problem. The Masses, they can celebrate them provided they remain inconspicuous until everything returns to normal. They are not to blame. If they were guilty, I would tell them. They are not to be disturbed.

Then I said:

No one can calm things except you. If you do not do anything, nothing will change.

Then she answered me:

Everything will be done, but slowly."

8. FRIDAY, APRIL 16, 1982

A. *Vicka's statement reported by Fathers Ivan and Ivica.*

(The date of April 16, 1982, seems only probable.)

"Another evening, I asked the Gospa about Ivica Vego and Ivan Prusina, and she answered some of my questions:

Dear Gospa, the newspapers write that Ivica and Ivan have been expelled from the Franciscan Order.

She answered me:

They have not been expelled (and she smiled). Tell them to persevere. Let the newspapers write what they want. One does not have to worry. It is not important.

Dear Gospa, make things peaceful so that Ivica and Ivan have no more problems.

She answered: I will calm everything.

She mentioned some priests (Franciscans from Mostar), I will have the opportunity to talk to them. They are three principal ones.

I asked:

Dear Gospa, what is the matter with the bishop? Acquaint him with the facts. In my heart I see that as the only solution.

The Gospa answered:

I am not in a hurry. I am still waiting to know if he is going to yield soon to the message which I gave him through you.

I said:

That means that I still have some business with the bishop. I have had enough of it. I, at least, and more so Ivan and Ivica.

Yesterday, during the apparition, we asked if we could say an Our Father for both of them. She immediately said yes, and she began to pray. When we finished, she smiled and said to me:

You have only those two in your head.

(Vicka adds to the Friars): Many priests are unhappy because of both of you. That will be known; it will be learned. Our Lady stressed that in the meantime, do not pay attention to them. Do what you have to do."

"Is there anything else?" ask the two priests.

"Then she spoke to us of something else, changing the subject or simply praying. She again told us that the most important thing is to be calm, and that everything will work out in good order.

Then I said to her:

Dear Gospa, you always say that everything will be in good order, but it lasts longer. She smiles and says, Slowly, slowly."

The comparison of the two statements, following the two conversations on successive days, shows how these intentions were reported freely and similarly, even coinciding on the essential points without contradicting themselves.

The common denominator is that it shows a fervent, friendly (yet militant) Vicka with regard to the two priests, and her impatience, in which the Gospa catches her with a smile, "You are thinking only of those two," etc.

B. Monsignor Zanic's version of Vicka's statement:

"I, Vicka, asked about Ivica Vego and Ivan Prusina; and Our Lady answered some of my questions.

My Lady, the newspapers write that Ivica and Ivan have been expelled from the Order.

She answered me:

They have not been expelled. And she smiled. Tell them to be persevering. The newspapers can write whatever they want. Do not let that distract them. It is not important.

I said: My Lady, make peace so that Ivica and Ivan may have no problems.

The Lady answered me:

I will calm everything.

She mentioned some priests from Mostar, and said I will have the occasion to tell them. There are three who are important.

I asked her:

My Lady, what is the matter with the bishop? Will he change his behavior?

The Lady answered:

I am not in a hurry. I am waiting for him to obey the order which I have given him through you.

I said: But it is painful for me. It is too much for me, and especially for Ivan and Ivica.

Yesterday (April 15, 1982), at the meeting with Our Lady, we asked her if we could say the Our Father for these two priests. She answered immediately, yes, and she began to pray.

When the prayer was finished, she smiled as she said to me:

You do not have anything else on your mind except the two priests. It is true, I responded."

9. APRIL 16, 1982

A. A New Response from Vicka reported by the two Franciscans.

(Vicka): "On the third evening (April 16, 1982), the Gospa said to me: The bishop is not acting on it with God, neither in charity nor in love of God. Let Ivica and Ivan not polarize themselves with the bishop, who charges them with a heavy burden in order to rid himself of them. He has begun with the youngest one and follows his plan. I know that it is a very hard blow for them. Do not let them be troubled. Have them free that from their minds and know that they are suffering for justice. What the bishop is doing is not according to the will of God; with reference to their innocence, being blamed without any fault. God would not permit that, but the grace of God is not in his actions and he can do what he wants. But one day, one will see the justice which he has not been able to see for a long time. I will begin slowly to calm it, and many priests will radiate with great happiness."

B. Monsignor Zanic's Version: (This version is substantially similar even if the tone appears hardened. But, again, it does not deal with Vicka's diary, but with the oral version reported by the two priests, and transmitted by Father Grafenauer.)

"The bishop does not have any true love at all for the two priests, Ivica and Ivan. He imposes on them a very heavy burden in order to rid himself of them. He began with the youngest and then he is going to continue. I know it is a painful blow for them. Do not let them be troubled. Have them strike that from their minds. Let them know that they are suffering for justice. What the bishop is doing is not the will of God. They are innocent, without guilt, and so punished. God would not do that, but the bishop is not following the grace of God; the bishop is doing what he wants. But one day, the justice which you have not seen in a long time will come forth. I will bring peace little by little, and several priests will feel a great joy."

C. Narrative by Vicka to Ivica (of a response to Father Tomislav Vlasic):

"Ivica, I send you in writing two questions of Tomislav Vlasic and answers of the Gospa:
Tomislav: 'Is it time for priests to reconcile among themselves?'
The Gospa's answer: 'Yes.'
'Is it necessary, among priests, to set up a petition, or would that be harmful?'
The Gospa responds:
'There is no need for any petition. For the time being, let it rest there, then we shall see."

APRIL 29, 1982: Expulsion from the Franciscan Order for the two priests.

This decision was signed by the vicar general, Procurator of the Franciscan Order, Father Honorius Pontoglio.

Here are the factors, which places the elements of the question of Hercegovina, in its proper context:

On September 14, 1980, in the city of Mostar, (Hercegovina, Yugoslavia), the Cathedral parish was founded. This parish was made up through the division of a Franciscan parish already in existence, of which three-fourths was separated in order to form the new parish. A fourth of the Franciscan parish remained.

A great number of the Franciscans of the Province of the Assumption in Hercegovina, did not agree with this division, which had already been established through a contract made between the representatives of the diocesan clergy and the Franciscans. This decree, "Romanis Pontificibus" (June 6, 1975), examined and confirmed everything. But, according to the thinking of the Franciscans, the decree, "Romanis Pontificibus," put into effect only a part of the above mentioned contract, and on the other hand, it eliminated other points of the contract. For these reasons, the above-mentioned contract, according to the arguments of the Franciscans, was made "as a global solution to a problem of the parishes."

In the City of Mostar, it created a great problem: the pastoral of some filial churches. There, after some centuries, some liturgies had to be carried out in the cemeteries. These filial churches had to belong to the new Cathedral parish according to the new decree. The faithful refused to receive the legal diocesan priests, but they received and demanded the Franciscans, (even illegally), as their pastoral ministers.

The bishop ordinary, Monsignor Pavao Zanic, took up this illegal action in words and in his writings. The Franciscan Order, through its superiors, also insisted on turning away the priests from this illegal action through words, persuasion, threats, and decrees. Thus, two Friars in particular (Ivan Prusina and Ivica Vego, parish fellow workers in the Franciscan parish), were in the foreground. At the end, the Sovereign Pontiff, John Paul II, himself, ordered through his authority, that this problem be resolved as soon as possible.

There followed a list of 11 documents issued by the Franciscan Order on this matter, from April 14, 1981 to December 29, finally the decision.

Statement of Expulsion: (April 29, 1982)

"Father Ivan Prusina has been disobedient to all the decrees aforementioned of the Franciscan Order, in part or completely, as well as having been informed in words and in writing of the grave consequences (Document Number 11). Even this 'last warning,' through which 'in the space of three days well utilized,' everything could have been resolved to a good conclusion. He has refused it and has persevered in the state of disobedience. That is why it is declared that Father Ivan Prusina be submitted to all the consequences enumerated in the decree of Reverend Father Honorius Pontoglio, Vicar and the Procurator General, and dated April 29, 1981.

He is thus expelled from the Franciscan Order, freed from the bonds of his religious vows, and suspended 'a divinis' according to the norm of the rescript of the Holy See, dated December 11, 1980."

Father Honorius Pontoglio.

An identical decree was transmitted to Father Ivica Vego.

10. MAY 4, 1982

Response collected by the two priests:

(This text inextricably combines responses of the Gospa with the commentaries by Vicka).

"For Ivan and Ivica, they must always pray more so as to be able to endure all the persecutions. It is a great weariness for them. They will have even more, but let them be proud, smiling, and not to worry about them. I see everything, and I know what they are doing to make you leave. But that cannot be done very easily. Justice must manifest itself.

These priests, if they were sure of them, would act differently. They are not sure at all, and that hurts them. But all this will end well."

Vicka: "But, dear Gospa, show those three [who want to make them leave], in the absence of something better, some warning so that they can permit them to stay [in Mostar]. They have support, and because of that, they try not to see you.

I know that Ivan and Ivica are very worried about it. But it would be easier for them if, very sweetly, they would drive it away as if it did not exist, and they would be priests like the others.

There are many who, because of you, cannot sleep for thinking of it. It is their punishment. But it is nothing in comparison to what could happen to them.

Then she said:

If they are so, that is their fault. It is a great shame that among them [in the community of Friars], they initiate disorder. There is no disorder. There are only blows which some individuals strike against the Church, and even against the faith of the faithful.

Then she added:

For those who are not guilty, there are always reproaches, though they are good priests. I do not see any fault in them.

Vicka: I know all the reproaches which are made behind your back. How they avoid you and try not to see you at all. They can do whatever they want, but how long? No more. That is enough."

11. A LITTLE BEFORE JUNE 24, 1982:

The seers:

"The bishop is protesting because you said that Father Ivica Vego and Father Ivan Prusina are not guilty. He has the feeling that you are not the Blessed Virgin because you do not respect the decision of the leaders. Do you want us to explain your point of view?"

Answer: "It is necessary to respect the leaders and to obey them, but they also make mistakes. They must do penance for their mistakes and rectify their errors. The bishop and those who influence him in this regard, do harm to the faith. I do not find fault with Father Vego and Father Prusina."

12. THE END OF AUGUST 1982

(A Note from Fathers Ivan and Ivica)

"Vicka told us approximately this:

The Gospa has communicated to me the message that Ivan and Ivica not go away from Mostar."

13. WEDNESDAY, SEPTEMBER 29, 1982

(Notation from Father Tomislav Vlasic)

"The answer from the Gospa on the matter of Fathers Ivica Vego and Ivan Prusina is interesting: The bishop has threatened them with secularization. Father Ivica asks:

Must we leave Mostar or stay?

The Gospa answers:

Let them stay." (Parish Chronicle, p. 83).

14. DECEMBER, 1982

(Notation from Fathers Ivan and Ivica)

"After the last pressure on us to leave the province, Father Tomislav had this question asked:
Must Fathers Ivica Vego and Ivan Prussina leave Mostar or must they stay?
Let them stay in Mostar.
She said that and nothing more."

15. SUNDAY, JUNE 19, 1983

A Message Written by Father Ivan for Monsignor Zanic, signed, and transmitted on the 21st:

"On June 19, 1983, the Gospa appeared to the seers Jakov, Marija, Ivica (written meaning "Ivanka.") First of all, she answered some of my questions concerning the sick, then on her own, she began to speak of you, bishop, my Father. Here are the words which she said:
Tell the Father Bishop that I ask him not to delay to acknowledge the events of the Parish of Medjugorje, before it is not too late. Let him consider these events with understanding and love, as well as with a profound sense of his responsibilities. I wish that he will not bring about a conflict among the priests, and that he not stress the negative aspects. The Holy Father has given the bishops directives concerning the problems and the conflicts of their bishoprics. The bishop is a priest for Hercegovina; he is at the head of the churches of Hercegovina. It is because of that that I ask him to concern himself with these events. It is, the time before last, that I address myself to him. If he does not change, if he does not return to the good path, he will be subjected to my judgment and to that of my Son. If he does not listen to me, it will mean that he has not found the way of my Son, Jesus."
Ivan said that the Blessed Virgin asked him to transmit that to the Father Bishop. (Parish Chronicle, p. 149).

16. THE BEGINNING OF JULY 1983

(With Respect to the Tensions Between the Bishopric and the Franciscans)

"Fast twice a week for the intention of the bishop who bears a heavy burden. If there is a need for it, I will ask for a third day. Pray each day for the bishop."

17. TUESDAY, JANUARY 17, 1984

(Inquiry of T. Vlasic, transmitted to Monsignor Zanic on January 22.)

Father Tomislav Vlasic questioned the seers for the last time (except Vicka, who expressed herself on that very much, and whose remarks he wanted to control). He also questioned Jelena, and conveyed all her answers to the bishop in a letter of January 22, 1984 with this explanation:
"Given the fact that you, yourself, have expressed on several occasions that the problem of the 'Friars of Mostar is the essential point for the

understanding and acceptance of the apparitions at Medjugorje,' I asked the seers several questions regarding this problem. I convey to you here, faithfully, the questions and the responses just as they were formulated."

QUESTION 1:

"Dear Gospa, why did you tell Fathers Ivica Vego and Ivan Prusina to stay?"
Response conveyed by Ivan:
"They were not guilty. The accusations received by this bishop were false, and because of it, he no longer accepts them."

QUESTION 2:

"What are you asking of Fathers Ivica Vego and Ivan Prusina for the solution of their problems?"
Response conveyed by Ivan:
"Have both of them pray. In these circumstances, they must be patient."

QUESTION 3:

"What do you expect of us here: priests and people for the solution of this problem?"
Response conveyed by Jakov:
"The Gospa says that one must persist in prayer and in penance."

QUESTION 4:

"The bishop thinks that you are not the true Gospa because you protect the two Friars. Help the bishop so that he may understand. Explain to him your intention."
Answer transmitted by Maria:
"When I read that to the Gospa, she said, pray. Pray for the bishop."

Answers conveyed by Jelena:

"On January 17, 1984, I addressed the following questions to Our Lady through Jelena Vasilj, the intermediary. She formulated spontaneously the questions and said, (into a microphone), what Our Lady dictated to her from the bottom of her heart." (T. Vlasic).

QUESTION 1:

"Dear Gospa, we ask you once again, forgive us for repeating to you so many times the same thing. Explain to us the reasons which have led you to tell Ivica Vego and Ivan Prusina to stay at Mostar, even when the authority of the Church asks them to leave the Franciscan Order. That presents to our bishop, and to other bishops, many problems for the understanding of your apparitions. That is why we are asking you as our Mother, to explain to us, why you did in such a way, and to tell us what we must do so that the understanding and comprehension be re-established."
Jelena's Response:
"Our Lady told me:
It is necessary for you to pray for your priests and for your bishop. Pray so that God's spirit may enlighten all of them, so that they can understand what they must do. I wanted [the two vicars] to stay, so that peace

may be reestablished because [in its absence] they would keep rancor against the bishop all their life and wish him evil. Have them stay then, because there are not many priests in the world. I need priests who are ready to do my will. Pray for all that, because if they stop being priests, things could get even worse."

QUESTION 2:

"The bishop is not in the habit of saying: Our Lady protects rebel Franciscans and does not listen to the Church. Can Our Lady tell us what she wishes to accomplish by such behavior? Could she explain to the bishop that she is on his side and on the side of the Church?"

Jelena's Response:

"Our Lady told me:

I want to guard the Church and all of those who are responsible. I want to protect all priests, the good and the bad, because Jesus said: 'It is not those who are in good health who are in need of a physician!' But that does not mean that I do not protect the bad priests. Understand that well. They could not be good without my protection! Understand well: I want to protect and put on the right path, all priests, because it is necessary that they do my will."

QUESTION 3:

"What do you recommend to our bishop, and to other bishops in order to resolve this problem? How can they resolve it? What must they do to arrive at an understanding and a reconciliation?"

Jelena's Response:

"Our Lady said:

It is necessary to pray very much. They must pray. Let them know that without my help they can do nothing because I am your Mother. Let them ask for my help, because I want to save all of them. They can be saved only by making peace among them, and by renouncing all forms of jealousy. That is the only way to find a solution."

QUESTION 4:

"It has been a long time since the bishop formed a commission. We do not know if he has formed another one. But it is certain that he wants to form it [the bishop was in the process of forming the expanded commission, which will hold its first meeting on the 24th and 25th of the following March]. What does Our Lady recommend to the members of the commission, which is going to examine the events at Medjugorje?"

Jelena's Response:

"Our Lady said:

Have them pray in order to be enlightened by the Spirit of God. He will help them to discover the presence."

QUESTION 5:

"What do you recommend to Fathers Ivica Vego and Ivan Prusina so that they may be able to approach the bishop and establish a dialogue with him?"

Jelena's Response:

"Our Lady told me:

Let them pray for him, and let every misunderstanding be forgotten as if nothing existed. Let them love the bishop and let them pray very much for him. It is in this manner that the problems will be able to be resolved."

QUESTION 6:

"What does our lady recommend still?"

Jelena's Response:

"She did not tell me anything special. However, the Gospa repeated: Have them pray so that the Spirit of God enlightens the bishop."

17. JANUARY 20, 1984:

QUESTION 5 (asked by Maria)

"What do you ask of the bishop so that he can acknowledge you, and that the question of Hercegovina be resolved?"

Response conveyed by Maria:

"I addressed the bishop many messages, but he has not accepted them. Then I sent you [to him], but he still did not receive the Queen of Peace because he is tormented by anxiety. He has taken upon himself all the problems of the diocese instead of confiding them to my Son for a solution. Pray, my dear children, so that he will accept me. From my side, I will ask Almighty God for the grace to be able to comfort the bishop."

CONCLUSION

Since we have discussed these documents at great length, it was indeed necessary to produce them again, and in some order, so as to permit each one to judge them through analysis and discernment.

It deals with texts which have been written from memory by the seers, or second-hand, not without some waverings which sometimes make the understanding of them difficult. Often, one incorrectly perceives the borderline between what Vicka says and what she reports of the Blessed Virgin. The limits of these documents are only too evident.

Astonishing is the polarization formed by asking, again and again indefinitely, this same question of the Gospa: Sixteen times in 25 months. She, herself, observes with a certain humor ("You are only thinking of those two.") this polarization; and one is surprised that she did not answer here as in other times: "Do not ask me such questions." Perhaps she said it without anyone reporting it.

This polarization is explained through the sympathetic friendship of Vicka for the troubled friars. The bishop contributed to it by diseminating widely to the public, the abrupt answers of Vicka which intensified the problem and its urgency. What was he to think of all that? What was he to do? The answers always testified to respect for the bishop. They are often restrained: "Do not fear for Ivan and Ivica. Let them be modest, discreet, patient," etc.

The most constant source of light are the invitations to peace and especially to prayer for the bishop. The seers took this invitation seriously, without acromony. They prayed. They fasted. They sacrificed themselves for the bishop, and for this reconciliation.

All of these positive concerns are very apparent in the last two series of questions asked on January 17 and 20, 1984, which indicated affection for the bishop. That remedies the difficult side of responses from Vicka, where her fiery temperament, whether right or wrong, leads to decisive but non-acromonious expressions.

What is surprising in these last questions, is that Father Tomislav Vlasic starts from the principle presented by the bishop:

"The problem of the Friars of Mostar (the young Franciscans) is the essential point for the understanding and acceptance of the apparitions at Medjugorje."

But this particular point—that this artificial interference was finally considered by both sides as the "essential point"—shows the optical illusion created by a painful conflict.

And that is also felt in the questions which were asked. The first starts from apparent evidence:

"Our Lady, why did you tell Friars Ivica Vego and Ivan Prusina to stay in Mostar?"

This interrogation leads into the response. An inquiry less conditioned would have begun by asking the question:

"Did you really tell the friars to stay? And if so, do you support it?"

It is clear that Vicka's implication, her compassion, and her passion for justice, have affected her intentions. Tomislav and the Blessed Virgin made her see that.

In a word, many factors contribute to make this file of limited value.

First of all, private revelations are not infallible and do not have an absolute value. Benedict XIV and spiritual writers stressed in a classic manner that oracles of the saints, including those canonized, are influenced by surrounding controversies, and are sometimes erroneous in similar conditions. In the great schism of the three Popes, Catherine of Sienna favored the person in Rome, and St. Colette de Corbie favored the one in Avignon.

What of an oracle from Catherine of Sienna against the Immaculate Conception. But if the taking of the position by Catherine of Sienna, Doctor of the Church, against the Immaculate Conception, was witnessed by Saint Antonin of Florence, a Dominican, it is only a second-handed witnessing and it does not seem to be of any consequence. One sees how difficult it is to discern any oracles which have risen in a passionate climate.

Secondly, the messages of Medjugorje are neither leaves of books written in Heaven, nor even a dictation (like certain theologians formerly would have wanted for the Bible, and as the Moslems wanted for the Koran). These private revelations are of a more subtle and more complex nature. Apart from the fact that Heaven adapts itself to the seers, the seers themselves receive the message in their own way (ad modum recipientis), and there is in them, a surging of developments difficult to unravel. It was then inevitable that passions inherent in this conflict, as well as the friendship and compassion of the seers for the two troubled friars (especially Vicka, more sensitive and more ardent), exerted an incalculable influence over the oracles.

The part of the Divine and the human can only be unraveled in an approximate manner.

The repercussions over the seers is all the more evident because the response from the Gospa to the same question asked the same day, at the same time by several seers, presents variants. Vicka, alone, has some cutting remarks on the responsibilities, indeed the culpability of the bishop. And the latter, who widely disseminated his messages in support of his warnings, was not without hardening them, notably those of December 19, 1981, which he cites under this form: "For all the disorder, the most guilty one is Bishop Zanic." He stated it was a sentence referred to in Vicka's diary, (where one does not find this notation). But these matters were known only by the more moderate narratives of Ivan and Ivica, as well as that of Tomislav Vlasic (as seen earlier).

Thirdly, finally, these responses of these seers on a question which did not concern them, take place in the first months at Medjugorje. The seers had hardly left their childhood. They were naively experiencing their first extraordinary communications, and at the same time, were very familiar with the Gospa. They communicated to Our Lady all kinds of questions without sorting them, and they acted toward her as a child who chatters with his mother. The Gospa often talked to them about it. She took several months to make them understand that she was not an employee of the wicket of Heaven, appointed to satisfy every curiosity.

The functions of the apparitions are something else, and the message taking place is at an entirely different level. When the seers understood, and through them, other inquisitive persons, these questions ceased. This episode then shows evidence of a teaching transition which must be taken in all its relativity. The seers no longer question her on it after January 1984.

But finally, one will say, who is right?

It is not appropriate for us to judge them, since Holy See requests, themselves, are confusing. The appeal of the two friars expelled by the sanction (through an interpretation of a request from the Pope to quickly resolve this matter), was refused for a long time, but it had been admitted by the Tribunal of the Apostolic Signature at the beginning of 1986. This supreme tribunal, Court of Appeals of the Church, had concluded its judgment toward the end of this same year, 1986. But since such a judgment involved so many repercussions, including among them certain Roman authorities, the latter succeeded in getting the apostolic signature to suspend this judgment, "sine die."

From the perspective of civil law, some persons will be scandalized that a supreme tribunal does not have sufficient independence to pass judgment, made by those in power and the consequences it could have on them in an inextricable situation. But in what country are the supreme tribunals, even independent ones, exempt from every discreet and defective pressure from the powers in control?

This delay is perhaps simply a sign which is not sufficient to settle a conflict, so complex, in a church where everything rests on charity, and where the right can only mitigate, where charity is absent.[1] In order for a judgment to be able to have all its effects and bear its fruits, it would be necessary, first of all, to have a very deep renewal of hearts, and an inspiration of reciprocal charity, so that a judgment can be made; and not in the spirit of revenge or trauma, of triumph or bitterness, but of conciliation and reconciliation.

The message of Medjugorje has worked well with reconciliations in the village and in the country, and the world, we have seen. So that it may be truly credible and find its proof, it would be necessary that reconciliation return also at the ecclesiastical level. Is it really more difficult to reconcile the clergy than the laity? That is the question pending on this message of Medjugorje.

One thing is clear. The conflict of Hercegovina is marginal. It is an annoying interference in the generous and clear contour of the apparitions. It calls for prayer, patience and initiatives inspired by reconciliatory love, which founded the Church, and which remains its very essence.

---

1. That which seems the most disturbing in these questionable oracles is that there was "precipitation in the matter," and that, not only on the part of the bishop. Pope John Paul II, presided over the session of December 9, 1981, which convened the General of the Franciscans and Bishop Zanic (as the Novissima Admonitio of December 29, 1981 takes into account). It concluded with a request to "resolve the problem as soon as possible" (quam primum: Declaratio dismissionis of April 29, 1982). This judicious concern for a quick solution required, step by step, through different persons of responsibility (the Curia, the Franciscan Order), the choice of hasty solutions which honor their zeal, but not necessarily the judicial regularity for which the Pope was equally anxious. It is thus that the publication of the conclusions, examined in Rome, eliminated any higher appeal. The Apostolic Signature was suspended because of the persons who were responsible for these hasty procedures.

APPENDIX 2

Objections On Ecumenism

A HERESY?

A second problem against the exemplary message of Medjugorje concerns ecumenism. For the Diocesan Commission, today dissolved, it was one of the principal objections, and Rome received it with the gravest attention.

The substance of the crime is the response of the ˚Gospa to a written question given to the seers October 1, 1981 (at a time when they were daily asking all kinds of questions).

Question: "Are all religions good [in Croatian: dobre]?"

Answer: "All religions are equal [iste] before God." (Parish Chronicle, p. 11).

If this answer attributed to all religions the same truth or the same value, the apparition would be disqualified according to the criterion of St. Paul: "Even if an angel from Heaven announces to you another Gospel, let him be anathema." That would not be able to be an angel of God.

A FAITH WITHOUT FLAW

But this disqualifying interpretation would be false, and contrary to the faith of the seers, and the message of Medjugorje. One cannot understand a language, without placing it within its vital, cultural, and linguistic milieu.

The primary evidence is that the seers are strangers to all relativism. Some would rather reproach them for a very candid faith, a "fundamentalism," which takes the Bible literally, the catechism, and the whole teaching of the Church. Their religion is an unconditional love of Christ and of Our Lady, a stranger to every syncretism or contamination.

Did they report literally the answer of the Gospa? It is not evident, because they relate the messages globally, from memory after a rather variable delay, which leaves room for simplifications, approximations, or transpositions. There, restructuring allows for some nuances to escape. From this point of view there is a probability (through textual analysis, as well as for its integrity) that Our Lady responded, in greater substance.

Yes, religions are good (dobre), in the sense in which Vatican II discerned what was good in the great religions: the bond with God and a

344

partial knowledge of God and of Christ. And the substitution of the word "like" for "good" seems a slip of the seers, according to the grade of the language of the environment, so strong that the pen of T. Vlasic has permitted this slip to pass, a fault in perceiving how much it was disagreeable in every other language.

RELIGION EQUALS NATIONALITY IN CROATIAN CULTURE

The Croatian language as it relates to religions has some very special characteristics. In any case, the ambiguity of the response transmitted is understood, only in the concrete situation very well known to the seers, a situation of conflict where religions and nationality are increasingly confused.

On January 10, 1983, Mirjana, questioned on this same point, answers Father Tomislav Vlasic:

> "The Gospa has often said that believers, especially in the villages, for example here in Medjugorje, are in opposition very much to the Orthodox believers and to the Muslims. It is not good. She thus stated that there is only one God, and that men have become separated. You are not Christians if you do not respect other religions, Muslim and Serbian." (Interview of Mirjana by T. Vlasic, in R. Faricy, *Medjugorje,* French Edition, p. 68, Italian Edition, p. 60).

The confusion is evident. To be Serbian is a nationality, not a religion, and if the predominant religion of the Serbians is orthodoxy, the Serbians who exercise power at Belgrade are no longer Orthodox, but atheistic: without religion.

The improper word is the doing of Mirjana who reported, according to everyday language, a remark from the Gospa of several weeks earlier.

This ambiguity is significant of the local milieu. It structures not only the language, but also the institutions. The pegging between religion and nationality is constant there. It is written in the very constitution of the Yugoslav Federation. The Communist government has given the Croats, who have become Muslims, the Muslim nationality, so that they are no longer Croats. Officially, they do not have any nationality other than their religion, a paradoxical situation in an atheistic regime, even though this kind of pegging is currently in existence.[1]

Within this perspective, religion designates people: ("men of religion," as one says in eastern countries), not the doctrines, confessions, or religious institutions. What immediately follows the remark of Mirjana confirms it:

"You are not Christians if you do not respect them."

Often people make fun of others. Not to respect "the other religions," is to make fun of people who practice them. It deals with people and not religions, nor the truth.

---

1. I still remember the answer of a taxi driver from Quebec, who was in disagreement with his archbishop at the time of the Council:

   "And if he continues, I will become an anglo protestant." (A sentence perfectly clear to him, perfectly incomprehensible in the theological domain.)

Fra Stanko Vasilj places historically this wavering of vocabularly between religion—nation—person.

Here in Hercegovina, the Turkish occupation lasted 400 years. During this time, a part of the Croatian population defected to Islam. The Croatian national sentiment was uprooted for it. It is religion which made the difference. Here, only the Catholics were called Krscani (Christians), the Serbes were called Riscani, and the occupying powers, Muslimani (Muslims). Religion defined thus the category to which the people belonged. The word "religion" hardly applied to the doctrine, but to these concrete and complex divisions. For Vicka, the religions, equal before God, means that all men are equal before God. Her grandmother, nearly 100 years old, still thinks according to these categories.

To that may be added the importance which the respect of persons has taken in this Balkan situation. It is a condition of life and of national peace. Catholics, encouraged in it by the Council, honor that very highly. And their remarks on the matter avoid only one ambiguity: That which would despise or humiliate other people. That can explain certain errors of transmission of the texts, in this environment.

These ambiguities existed in my entire interview of June 24, 1987 with Vicka. (Daria Klanac, a competent and sensitive interpreter, expressed to me her embarrassment several times.)

R. Laurentin: "Who asked you the question: Are all religions good [dobre]?"

Vicka: "Someone asked me to ask this question, but I do not remember who."

R.L.: "Theologians see, in the response, a grave error. Is Jesus Christ equal or like Mohammad or Buddha? And do these religions give salvation which is in Jesus Christ?"

Vicka (for whom the references to Mohammad or Buddha are from the Hebrew) answers beyond this haze:

"If someone had asked for the explanation immediately, that would have been clearer. After several years, I do not dare to interpret it myself. I will leave that to the theologians. I will pray so that they will have the light. The Blessed Virgin told me that 'All religions are equal before God.' That is to say, that all men are equal before God, and that it is not God who has made divisions but man."

I insisted upon her to clarify, and she added:

"We are all equal before God, without taking into account the religion or nation to which we belong. Let us respect one another!"

In other words, religion and nation (which severely divide the Yugoslav Federation), must not hinder the respect of persons. A good answer. Nevertheless, I insisted:

R.L.: "But for you, is Jesus equal to Mohammad or Buddha?"

"She does not understand these words, Daria Klanac (who translated her response as follows) told me."

Vicka: "Jesus is true God and true man. Men make divisions. All men are equal. Love is true mercy. The Blessed Virgin is great. She is our Mother. She cannot be compared to any other person."

In this conversation, constantly, Vicka's faith formed by Our lady, led her to a commentary which went beyond the vocabulary of her environment and the ambiguous transmission. The questionable phrase means very much for her: "All men, equal before God, must be respected to whatever religion they belong."

This point is very important culturally in this country, and the achievement of Medjugorje has made this respect of persons progress here and there beyond ancestral or ideological passions.

A LIGHT MOTIF

Several converging messages bear on this point.

On August 18, 1982 (CP.77), Mirjana transmitted a question to the Gospa on the subject of a young girl, undoubtedly Catholic, who married an Orthodox. The response began with an analogous ambiguity:

In my eyes and in the eyes of God, everything is equal.

No more than the Church, the Blessed Virgin did not forbid mixed marriages, and she invited one to respect the equality of persons, but also the goodness of the true faith. The end of the response confirmed it. Finally, the Blessed Virgin advised against this marriage, for concrete reasons and the rightness of the faith.

It is better if she does not marry this man, because she will suffer and her children, also. She will only live and follow with difficulty the path of her faith.

The Gospa's response to Maria on the matter of the cure of an Orthodox Hungarian gypsy (cited earlier, page 306) clearly stated the meaning of the message:

The Muslims and the Orthodox, like the Catholics, are equal before God and before me because you are all my children.

The theologian will say: "Not all in the same degree." But the humility of the seers does not take advantage of the privileged filial relationship which they live. How fortunate! Maria reports well the essence: All men are entrusted to Mary as her children, and she loves them with the same love, without discrimination, and without forcing them previously to all forms of reciprocity.

The other episode (cited ib.) where a young Muslim sees the light, then benefits from an apparition, is in the same vein. The equality of persons belonging to different religions, not only values the rights of man and the respect for persons, but also the fact that God loves them, and that His grace calls them with this sort of predilection of which the Gospel is testimony. According to the most classical theology, the Catholic Church has the fullness of means for salvation, but grace is not restricted to the frontiers of the Church.

In the interview of January 10, 1983, T. Vlasic insisted:

"If the Muslim religion is good, what is the role of Jesus Christ?"
Mirjana answers prudently:
"I did not speak with the Gospa about that. She only explained to me what I have just said." Then she added: "That occurs especially in the villages, that is, this division [scornful] provoked by religions. One must respect the religion of each one, but preserve your own for yourselves and for your children."

JESUS CHRIST, SOLE MEDIATOR

In Fr. Faricy's book, he reported this other message (undated):

> *In God, there are no divisions and no religions. It is you in the world who have created divisions. The sole mediator is Jesus Christ. The fact that you belong to such or such religion is not without importance. The Spirit is not the same in each Church.*

On October 7, 1981 (a little after the troubling response of October 1st), a priest had asked this question:

"Are there other mediators between God and man, other than Jesus Christ, and what is their role?"

That was a trap question, since the Apostle Paul declares (in *1 Tim.* 2:5), that "there is only one mediator between God and man." Vicka and Jakov, who conveyed the question, do not fall into the trap. They thus transmitted the response from the Gospa:

There is only one mediator between God and man. It is Jesus Christ.

Kraljevic reports a convergent answer of the apparition in response to a question:

"Do there exist any differences among those who belong to different churches, or to different communities?"

Answer: *That does not amount to the same thing as praying; it doesn't matter in which community. The presence of the Holy Spirit is not as strong in every church, and the power of the Holy Spirit acting on priests who lead the communities, is not the same. All believers do not pray in the same way. The sole mediator of salvation is Jesus Christ.*

If the vocabulary of the environment is ambiguous, the faith of the seers is not. There, commitment to Christ and to Mary is unconditional, and absolute.

The heart of the problem lies in the point of the message itself: "It deals with promoting ecumenism through love, in reference to persons," beyond ideologies (and I do not confuse ideologies with dogma!). The seers have perfectly understood that. Their entire lives show it. They are so engaged in this love without boundaries that they would be wrong in trying to place what they do not know: the proper value of each religion evaluated by the Council (Declaration Nostra Aetate), and the questions relative to truth. It is not a scorn of the truth. It seems to them, on the contrary, all too evident, so that they feel the need to clarify the absoluteness of their commitment to the one true God, to Christ the sole Mediator and sole Saviour. They live on this side of the problems and temptations, which would make such an affirmation useful.

The theologians at the Sorbonne had intelligently succeeded in condemning Joan of Arc. Her peasant faith fell victim to the "wisdom of the learned." Today's theologians would likewise be inclined to condemn the seers of Medjugorje, but such condemnations show particularly, the lack of cultural understanding which often deals between theological abstraction and the ingenuous faith of Christians, that is their expression, with conditions. It took seven centuries to admit that Joan of Arc was right against her wise judges. May our century not repeat their errors of judgment and save on such a lengthy venture. The heresy which some impute to the seers, and to her who is appearing to them, is evidently foreign to them, and the ambiguities are to be interpreted according to their culture.

The message of Medjugorje, such as it has been given, by bits and pieces, at the risk of questions, and especially, such as it is lived without ambiguity by exemplary believers, holds this:

Love everyone without discrimination as God loves them first, freely before all men and with a paradoxical predilection for sinners. (*Mt.* 18:12-13). It is the central point of the message of Christ. Contrary to the theories of faith without religion, and according to the statement of the Council Nostra Aetate, religion as a bond with God, is good. This bond, where it exists, comes from God and goes to God.

The divisions are not the work of God, but of sinful men who have strayed from revelation. Let us then love the scattered sheep without ill feelings or a superiority complex, because we are all sinners, and it can happen that the publicans and the prostitutes will precede us into the Kingdom of God if one day they receive the grace. You, who are witnesses of this grace, give them first and foremost the testimony of love, which will draw them to the whole truth.

APPENDIX 3

The Luminous Phenomena

Since the beginning, luminous phenomena have been observed at Medjugorje. One can classify them according to their nature and the places where they appeared. We will present them according to the date when the phenomenon first appeared.

1. DIVERSE LIGHTS

Some lights appeared on the hill of the apparitions on June 26th, 1981, and it is one of the reasons that attracted, from that day on, a crowd of more than 1,000 people. Later accounts have been more rare, and inaccurately certified.

2. MYSTERIOUS FIRE ON THE HILL

On October 28, 1981, several hundred people saw, on the hill of the first apparition, a fire which burned without consuming anything. In the evening, the Blessed Virgin told the seers:
It is a forerunner of the great sign. (K58).

3. PHENOMENA AROUND THE CROSS AT KRIZEVAC

Beginning October 21st, 1981, and at six other times that month (from the 22nd to the 27th), then more rarely (especially from the 17th to the 22nd of March), the arms of the cross, then the entire cross, disappeared. In its place, there appeared a luminous column, or rather a brilliant silhouette, mounted on a globe which recalled the Virgin of the Miraculous Medal. I have collected three video cassettes which have filmed this phenomenon on two different days (two on the same day, and at the same time).

4. SIGNS OF THE SUN

Numerous witnesses have observed at Medjugorje, signs similar to the miracle of the sun which took place at Fatima on October 13, 1917: 32 cases after June 24, 1984. We have likewise collected, in addition to numerous photos, some video cassettes, more or less reliable, because some alternations of flashes and shadows could be due to feedback from the photo-electric cell exposed to the sun's radiance. The rainbow-colored bubbles which these pictures and video cassettes often present, can be the normal effect of back lighting.

In a certain number of cases, the center of the sun, whose brilliance harms the eyes, becomes white, or flat gray. Witnesses compare it to a shining host because the periphery of the sun, which remains luminous, forms a brilliant and flashing ring. When the phenomenon is reduced to that, it seems capable of being explained naturally. Someone made me experience this phenomenon at a sunset in Brittany, independently of all religious context.

But this explanation does not in any way restrict all the phenomena. It is astonishing that some important groups have been able to look at the sun at a time when it is very high in the sky "without being inconvenienced," in any way. It would be necessary, also, to explain why the sun seems to spin as it did in Fatima, and why its rays pulsate themselves toward the earth.

5. STELLAR PHENOMENA

Some pilgrims have seen, and even filmed, phenomena which seemed to them, particular to the stars. They have sent me a video cassette of one of these very rare, yet less significant phenomena.

6. INSCRIPTIONS

The word MIR (Peace) was written in the sky August 24th and many people saw it. "MIR LJUDIMA" (Peace to the people) was written in light on a wall during the apparition on December 29, 1981.

Given the idea of the frequency; 35 phenomena of this kind have been noted in the parish Chronicle, from October 14, 1981 to October 3, 1983. After that, someone had sent me approximately fifty written testimonies, photos and videos.

The language of the signs, especially of the light, is a biblical and even evangelical language: "There will be signs in the heavens" announced Jesus in Lk. 21:11. The signs of Medjugorje have been stimulating and fruitful for many witnesses. They remind them of the power and the presence of God, whom they had forgotten.

To what extent are these signs natural or supernatural? We will try to shed light, or at least, to limit this question more in a monograph, the study of which is in progress. This excuses us from expanding on this appendix, necessary to place the facts in a proper context, and to permit a reading which is better documented, than the present volume.

APPENDIX 4

Prayer Intentions
Given By The Gospa At Medjugorje

We group these intentions according to the principal focus of interest: God, His plan, His word, the pastors, prayer and fasting, Medjugorje, peace, and resurrection.

LET US PRAY

GOD

For the triumph of Jesus (Sept. 9, 1984).
For the glorification of God through us (Jan. 16, 1986).
For a knowledge of the glory of the Lord (Nov. 28, 1985).
For the experience of joy, caused by a meeting with Jesus (Dec. 11, 1986).
For God's blessing (Nov. 6, 1986).
For the outpouring of the Holy Spirit (Mar. - Apr., 1983; May 9, 1985).
For the coming of the Spirit of Truth (June 9, 1984).
For parish renewal by the Holy Spirit (Mar. 30, 1984).
For obtaining the gifts of the Holy Spirit (Apr. 17, 1986).

HIS PLAN

For the realization of God's plan (Oct. 24, 1984).
For the knowledge of our role in God's plan (Jan. 25, 1987).
For the accomplishment of all the plans which God wants to realize through us (Jan. 30, 1986).
For the conversion of Satan's trials, to the glory of God (Feb. 7, 1985).

HIS WORD

For anchoring the word of God in our hearts, through daily meditation of Holy Scriptures (Apr. 19, 1984).
For learning to pray and to read the Bible in the family (Feb. 14, 1985).

PASTORS OF THE CHURCH

For the Pope (Nov. 1981).
For the Bishop (May 25, 1983, a frequent intention.).
For the authorities of the Church (Mar. - Apr., 1983).

352

PRAYER AND FASTING

For learning to pray with love (Nov. 29, 1984).

To pray without ceasing (Nov. 13, 1983).

For our prayer to become a channel for others (Nov. 17, 1984).

For learning in prayer, the path of joy. (Feb. 25, 1987).

For prayer to lead us to humility (Feb. 10, 1984).

For the world's understanding that prayer is the only road to peace (Oct. 29, 1983).

For our learning to fast through love and not only through habit (Sept. 20, 1984).

For the avoidance of wars and catastrophies, through our prayer and our fasting (July 27, 1982).

CONVERSION AND RECONCILIATION

For the conversion and reconciliation of the world (October 15, 1983).

For the conversion of sinners (Aug. 2, 1984).

For the world to become aware of sin, in which it is floundering (Feb. 17, 1984).

For the conversion of all mankind (Apr. 4, 1984).

For world understanding of the last call of Mary to conversion (May 2, 1982).

For receiving, each month, the Sacrament of Reconciliation (Transfiguration 1982).

For the reconciliation of mankind with God, and with one another (June 26, 1981).

PURGATORY

For the souls in Purgatory, our future intercessors (Nov. 6, 1985).

For concerned souls, who are in Purgatory (July 21, 1982).

For the souls of Purgatory who do not receive prayers of intercession (July 21, 1982).

MEDJUGORJE

For the realization of all of Mary's plans at Medjugorje (Sept. 27, 1984).

For the continuation of Mary's presence at Medjugorje (Jan. 2, 1985).

For the understanding of all that Mary gives us at Medjugorje (Apr. 25, 1987).

For defeating Satan's objectives in the parish (Aug. 1, 1985).

The Church recognition of the supernatural character of Medjugorje (June 3, 1983).

LOVE AND PEACE

For obtaining the gift of love (May 28, 1985).

For our understanding of the love-sacrifice, by loving those who harm us (Oct. 7, 1985).

For our conversion into good, through love, that which Satan seeks to destroy and have for himself (July 31, 1986).

For our understanding of Mary's love for us (Mar. 1, 1982).

For the peace granted to those who pray to God (Oct. 23, 1986).

For peace and humility of heart (Feb. 11, 1984).

For the growth of a great peace and a great love in us (Sept. 29, 1983).

ABBREVIATIONS

Ba   Barbaric, Slavko: (Account of the inner locutions of Jelena Vasilj and Marijana Vasilj.)

Bl   Blasis, Yves-Maria: (Apparitions of Medjugorje, 500 Messages to Live) Montreal, Queen of Peace, 1986

BN   (Boa Nova), Sameiro, 4700 Braga, Portugal.

Bo   Botta, M. and Frigerio: (The Apparitions of Medjugorje), Pessano, 1984.

Bu   Bubalo, Janko: (A Thousand Encounters With the Blessed Virgin), Paris, O.E.I.L. 1984.

C   Castella, Andre, and Ljubic: (Medjugorje, Invitation for Prayer and Conversion), Hauteville, Paris, 1986. Reference to book of Ljubic Lj.

CP   (Parish Chronicle), from Fr. Tomislav Vlasic, 1981.

D   Dugandzic, Ivan: (Chronological Study of the Apparitions).

DN   (Is the Virgin Mary Appearing at Medjugorje?) and supplemental updates by Fr. Rene Laurentin, December 1984 through July 1987.[1]

DV   Diaries of Vicka: July 1981 through March, 1982. (DV #1, #2, #3.)

EM   (Medical and Scientific Studies of the Apparitions of Medjugorje), H. Joyeux and R. Laurentin, O.E.I.L. Paris, 1985)

F1   Faricy, Robt. and Rooney, Lucy: (Medjugorje, Mary the Queen of Peace) Tequi, Paris, 1984.

F2   Faricy, R. (The Heart of Medjugorje; Mary speaks to the World). Preface by R. Laurentin, Fayard, 1986.

Fr   Fr. Frigerio: (Scientific Study of Medjugorje) Como, Mescat, 1986.

G   (Gebetsaktion Medjugorje) Wien. (German text: "Action of Prayer in Medjugorje")

J   Jelena: (Journal), as transmitted to Fr. Tomislav Vlasic.

K   Kraljevic, Svetozar: (The Apparitions of Medjugorje) Fayard, 1984.

L1   Laurentin, Rene: (Is the Virgin Mary Appearing at Medjugorje?) 1984

L2   Laurentin, Rene: (Medjugorje, The Story and Messages of the Apparitions) O.E.I.L. Paris, 1986

L3   (Medjugorje) presented by R. Laurentin, DDB, Paris, 1987.

Lj   Ljubic, Marija: (The Virgin Appears in Yugoslavia), Hauteville, Parvis, January, 1985.

M   Miravalle, Mark: (The Message of Medjugorje), Doctorate Thesis, University Press of America, 1986.

MG   (Messages of Thursday), Lecco, Ruscomviaggi, 1987. (In Italian)

MM   (Messages of Mary) 15 rue du Champ du Pardon, 76000 Rouen, France.

T   Totto, George: (Medjugorje, Our Lady's Parish) Medjugorje Information Service, St. Leonard's on the Sea, England, 1985.

VB   Vlasic, Tomislav and Barbaric, Slavko: Four volumes of meditations on Our Lady's messages, 1984 through 1987. (In the United States, the first two volumes are known as the Grey Book and Blue Book). Friends of Medjugorje, West, Texas.

---

1. In the United States, these supplemental updates include: "The Apparitions at Medjugorje Prolonged" and, "Latest News of Medjugorje" published by The Riehle Foundation.

Publisher's note: The above list of texts comprise material primarily available to the author, (Fr. R. Laurentin), in Europe, and through his studies in Medjugorje. Not all of these texts are available in the United States, or even translated into English. They are shown here, principally as a point of reference.

MEDJUGORJE
BY FATHER RENÉ LAURENTIN

The following works of Father Laurentin have been translated into English, and are currently available.

Is The Virgin Mary Appearing at Medjugorje?
   By Word Among Us Press
The first book of the author on Medjugorje and a complete unfolding of the events through 1984.

Scientific and Medical Studies
   By Veritas Co., Dublin, Ireland
Two years of the complete studies on the seers.

The Apparitions at Medjugorje Prolonged
   By The Riehle Foundation
Update book through June, 1986.

Latest News—Sixth Anniversary
   By The Riehle Foundation
Update book through June, 1987.

Messages and Teachings of Mary at Medjugorje
   By The Riehle Foundation
700 messages and the application of the theology involved, to Scripture and to Catholic Doctrine. Includes extensive study of the teachings of Mary at Medjugorje.

Learning From Medjugorje
   By Word Among Us Press
Update book including an overview of the most important elements.

Seven Years of Apparitions
   By The Riehle Foundation
Update book current through Fall, 1988.

If you wish to receive copies, please write to:

THE RIEHLE FOUNDATION
P.O. Box 7
Milford, OH 45150

All contributions are used for the publishing and/or distribution costs of providing spiritual material to a world desperately in need of learning more about and living in God's peace and love.